IMAGES
of America

OPELOUSAS

I0805818

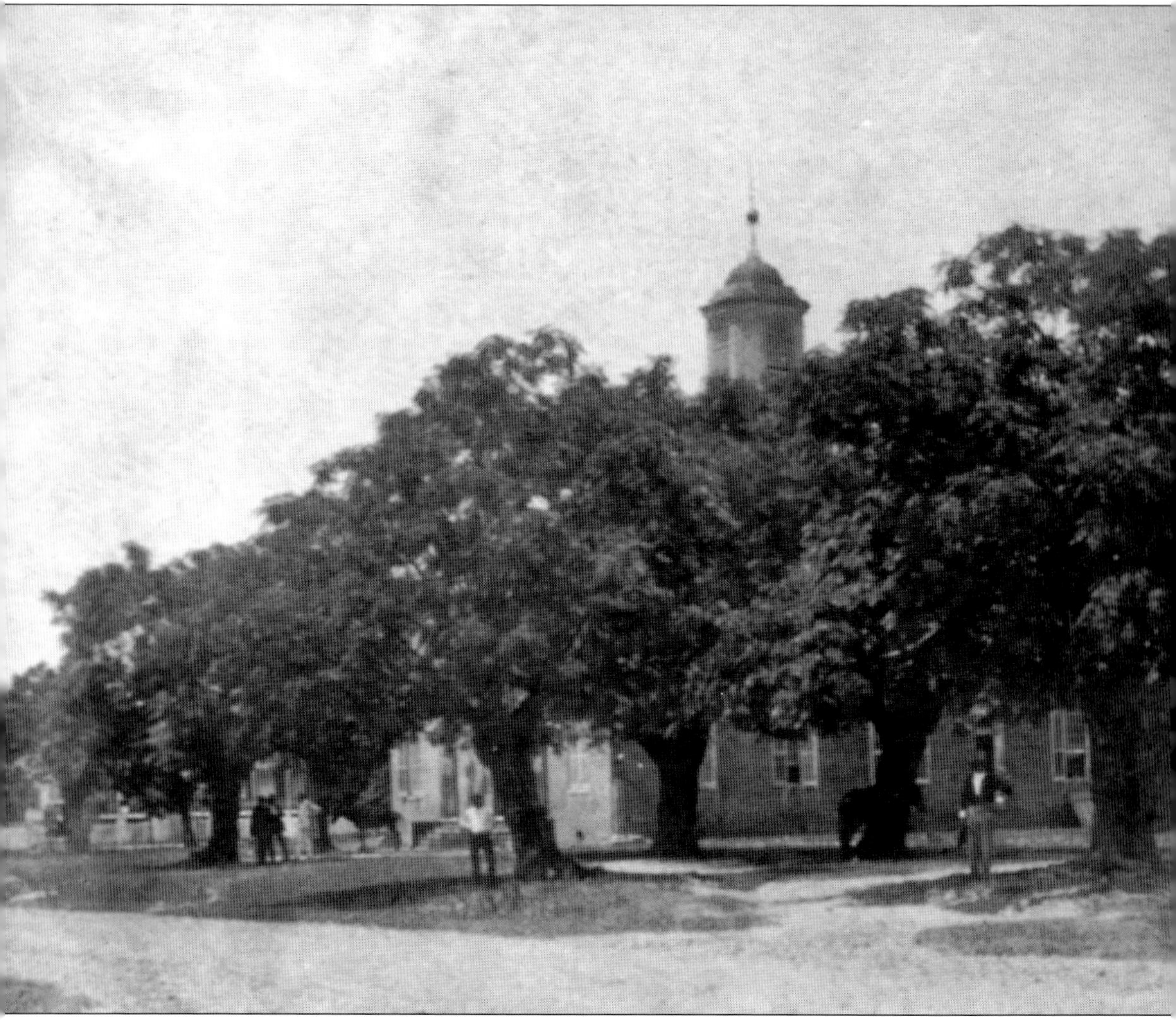

This photograph, taken in the early 1880s, shows the St. Landry Parish Courthouse, constructed around 1847, that was destroyed in an awful 1886 fire. Although it was determined that the fire was deliberately set, no one was ever charged for the crime. For a few months, the parish was involved in a fight over the location of the new courthouse. In the end, Opelousas won out and continued as the seat of St. Landry Parish. Later that year, a new courthouse was constructed on the square in downtown Opelousas, the fourth building to sit on that square since the first one in 1806. (Courtesy of Scott Longon.)

On the Cover: The Elk Restaurant, owned and operated by Charles Adrien "Didee" Lastrapes, is pictured on Bellevue Street in the early 20th century. Lastrapes, pictured at right, made Opelousas baked duck and many of the other tasty dishes he created famous around the state and the nation. Besides the Elk Restaurant, Lastrapes later opened Didee's Restaurant that operated on Market Street in downtown Opelousas for over five decades. (Courtesy of Dorothy Dunbar.)

IMAGES
of America

OPELOUSAS

Carola Lillie Hartley

ARCADIA
PUBLISHING

ISBN 978-1-4671-0807-2

Published by Arcadia Publishing
Charleston, South Carolina

Printed in the United States of America

Library of Congress Control Number: 2021951105

For all general information, please contact Arcadia Publishing:
Telephone 843-853-2070
Fax 843-853-0044
E-mail sales@arcadiapublishing.com
For customer service and orders:
Toll-Free 1-888-313-2665

Visit us on the Internet at www.arcadiapublishing.com

Dedicated to the memory of Dorothy Myrtle "Dot" Dunbar (1923–1998), a respected Opelousas woman and entrepreneur who devoted her life to the community she loved; to my aunt and godmother Edna Lafleur Delery (1907–1992), who taught me to love history; to my wonderful son, André Andrepont; and to my loving husband, Tim Hartley.

CONTENTS

Acknowledgments

For over 50 years, I have collected photographs and historic documents related to Opelousas, the place where I was born, the place I have lived most of my life, and the place that holds my heart. My son, André Andrepont, suggested in 2002 that I share my photograph collection in a book. My husband, Tim Hartley, cheered me on, seconding my son's suggestion. After almost two decades of thinking about it and writing several other Opelousas books and four years of writing stories about historic Opelousas for the *Daily World* newspaper, I finally decided this year to share my collection in this book for all who love Opelousas to enjoy.

Thank you to my family members who have encouraged me to continue to share my knowledge and collection, especially my husband, Tim Hartley; my parents, Charles and Antonia Lafleur Lillie; my siblings, Charles W. Lillie, Rose Lillie Taylor, Bernardine Lillie Anderson, Joseph V. Lillie, Robert J. Lillie, and Thomas H. Lillie; my son and daughter-in-law, André and Angelic Lafleur Andrepont; and my stepdaughters, Heather Parke and Danielle Hartley. Thank you to my longtime friends who have remained loyal to me, especially Roseanne Mitchell, Sherl Picchioni, Judith Estorge, Sherri Landry, Wanda Juneau, Vern Nagy, Bruce Morgan, Louella Guidry Blanchard, Margaret Dupuis Sweeney, Butch and Priscilla Mellott, Bill and Claudia Spence, and Estelle Perrault. And thank you to others who supported my efforts, including Thom and Madeline R. Daly, John Ed Bradley, Melanie Lee Lebouef, Robbie Sebastien, Jonathan Sebastien, John Christ, Charles Ross, Cam Leach, Paul Scott, Wilbert Guillory, Rebecca Henry, Johnny Wright, Huey Bourque, Mayor John Joseph, Judith and Irv Mellman, Flavia Alaya, Maria Perez, Deborah Boykin-Greenberg, Linda Koch, Sharon Alexander Bond, Allison Rawls Bullock, Mollie McClure, Brenda McCauley, Tommy Lafleur, Judy Vondracek, Mary Doucet, Bobby Dupre, Etha Simien Amling, Freddie Herpin, Bobby Ardoin, Mayor Mike Thibodeaux, David Vidrine, Karen L. Cox, Alex Da'Paul Lee, Neal Bertrand, Rebecca Manouvrier, Hadley Castille, Harold H. Comeau, W.A. Welch, Elizabeth Fontenot Ritter, and Carolyn Fontenot. Also, thank you to Andrepont Printing Inc. for helping to scan a few of the photographs.

Thank you to the members of my Facebook groups who like the history I share about Opelousas and Southwest Louisiana. A special thank-you to all who have contributed photographs to use in this book, including Scott Longon, Alex Da'Paul Thomas, Donald Cropper, Savoie Sausage, Dorothy Dunbar, "Chubby" Haynes, Vernon and Joyce Haynes, Madelyn and Thom Daly, Jeremy K. Semien, David Parnell, John Ed Bradley, Jonathan Sebastien, Emile Ventre IV, Chris Ventre, Robbie Sebastien, the Malcolm Miller family, the Martin Roy family, Bodemuller the Printer Inc., Andrepont Printing Inc., Angela Marie Roberson, Bob Bienvenu, Marty Cosgrove, and Nia Henry.

Unless otherwise noted, all photographs in this book are from my collection. Please enjoy them as much as I do.

INTRODUCTION

The plaintive call of the mastodon echoed across the terrain as the native people of Louisiana's prehistoric cultures roamed the land. According to archeologists and anthropologists who study the area, that was over 12,000 years ago, long before Opelousas became a town. When the first French explorers arrived at the end of the 17th century, the people they encountered were members of the historic Attakapas and Opelousas tribes. The town takes its name from the Opelousas tribe who wandered the vast area today known as Southwest Louisiana.

During the 18th century, the French took control of the territory, with trappers and traders, known as *coureurs de bois* (runners of the woods), appearing on the scene to trade with the native people. Among the earliest to arrive were Joseph Le Kintrek and his partner Joseph Blanpain. Assisting the partners was a man named Ihersome Dupont, who arrived with his wife, Marie Elizabeth Dupont, the first known woman settler in the area. Le Kintrek and Blanpain brought three Africans with them, the first enslaved people to arrive in Opelousas. By the 1740s, others settled in the region, including Jacques Courtableau, the son-in-law of Le Kintrek, who became one of the largest landowners and the leader of the area settlers.

New people arrived, and in 1763 the Poste du Opelousas was officially established with Louis Gerard Pellerin named as its commander. During that same year, Spain took control of Louisiana, and Spanish soldiers arrived on the scene a short time later. By the end of that decade, to the displeasure of the French inhabitants, the Opelousas Poste was ruled by Spain. Land grants were offered to entice others to the area. The Opelousas population quickly increased with the arrival of free people of color from the New Orleans area and free Blacks and Acadians who were ousted from Canada and fled to Louisiana with about 10 families settling in Opelousas.

Religion played an important part in the earliest history of Opelousas. Louisiana church records show that on May 16, 1756, a Catholic priest from the Natchitoches Post came to the home of Jacques and Marguerite Le Kintrek Courtableau in Opelousas to baptize Jacques André Desbordes, the grandson of Joseph Le Kintrek.

According to early civil records, around 1765 or 1766 a Catholic church building was erected on the banks of the Opelousas River, now called Bayou Courtableau. This church was called the Church of the Immaculate Conception, constructed in the area the settlers named Church's Landing, located near the present town of Washington, Louisiana. Some historians claim that a larger church was constructed on that same site in 1774. However, since the earliest records of the church archives state the church was constructed in 1776, the Diocese of Lafayette uses 1776 as the founding of the Opelousas church.

In 1796, Michel Prudhomme and Madam Tesson, two early Opelousas inhabitants, donated land near Prudhomme's plantation, and a new church building was erected on that site. The name of the church parish was changed to St. Landry Catholic Church, in honor of the saint-bishop who served Paris from 650 to 661 AD.

The Spanish ruled Opelousas until the beginning of the 19th century when it was ceded back to France in 1802. On November 27, 1803, Fr. Louis Buhot, pastor of the St. Landry Catholic

Church, wrote in the church records, "Here ends what belongs to the Spanish Government." He later wrote, "Here begins the French Government which by taking possession of this post on this 18th day of December 1803, filled with joy all true Frenchmen, who form the majority of all the inhabitants of Opelousas."

A short time later, the priest and all Opelousas inhabitants discovered France sold Louisiana to the United States, and they were part of that new country. On April 10, 1805, Opelousas was named the seat of the County of Opelousas, part of the Territory of Orleans. In 1807, the territory was reorganized into parishes with Opelousas designated the seat of St. Landry Parish, a title it holds to this day. A courthouse was built on land in what would become the center of the present city. Businesses opened around the courthouse, and the Opelousas commercial district was born.

Although much has been written about the role men played in the development of the Opelousas commercial district around the courthouse, it is important to understand the role of women in the town's economic history. Since Louisiana was governed by French Civil Law (sometime called the Napoleonic Code) at that time, women of early Opelousas, even those of mixed race, had rights that women of other areas did not have. They could and did own property and possess assets as single women or file lawsuits and act as successful and respected business owners as married women independent of their husbands. Some of the early Opelousas women who owned property and businesses included Marie Françoise Venus, Marie-Jeanne Lemelle, Manon Baldwin, Mrs. Frederic Pigeon, Rose Thierry, Rachael Fergerson Gradenigo, Dorothy Laas, and several others during the later years.

Soon people from other areas of the United States began to arrive in the territory and eventually made their way to Opelousas. Those new citizens were people of different ethnic groups and cultures with different religious beliefs. One of those men was Elisha Bowman, who came to Opelousas in 1806 and organized a Methodist society. The first year he accepted 17 members into the new church, the first Methodist church founded west of the Mississippi River. That church today is known as the Louisiana Memorial United Methodist Church. Other religious groups arrived, and over the years that followed, Opelousas had members of other protestant faiths and the Jewish faith among their citizens.

On April 30, 1812, Louisiana became a state. At that time, the community was known as Opelousas Church. It continued to grow and prosper with more people from other countries as well as those from northern areas of the United States moving into the town. Soon Opelousas had a population that represented people not just of French, Spanish, African, and Acadian heritage, but those from Germany, Ireland, England, Italy, and other areas. During the next century, immigrants from Eastern Europe, Asia, and South American countries joined the population, making the town a sort of cultural gumbo.

The New Orleans *Louisiana Gazette* of November 12, 1817, describes Opelousas as follows: "The only town in Opelousas is what is called Opelousas Church. It is handsomely situated upon the east side of a point of woods jutting into the prairie. It began to flourish before the war, but during its existence, it went to decay. Since peace has been established, it looks up again and there can be no doubt but in a few years it will rapidly increase. Its buildings are a Roman Catholic Church, an academy, a courthouse and public jail. There are four taverns, five stores, one saddlers' shop, one tanner's shop, one tailor's shop, two boot and shoemaker's shops, one silver smith's shop, about 25 dwelling houses plus out houses."

On February 14, 1821, Opelousas was officially incorporated as a Louisiana town. As the town continued to grow, in 1827 a new brick St. Landry Catholic Church was built. According to the August 3, 1827, edition of the *United State Gazette* newspaper of Philadelphia, the church was opened on July 10 that year, with 1,000 people in attendance for Mass. The article states the church served about 1,000 to 2,000 people at that time.

By 1830, Opelousas was a flourishing community with two hotels, the *Opelousas Gazette* newspaper, multiple businesses and professionals, coffee houses, restaurants, saloons, a town market, a fire department, and an opera house. During that decade, the College of Franklin was established in Opelousas on land near the northwest section of the town. That college operated for about a decade and later was used as a private high school. Also in the 1830s, Opelousas had a state bank. Later in the 1840s, the town had another newspaper called the *St. Landry Whig*.

During the decade that followed, two newspapers opened for business—the *Opelousas Courier* and the *Opelousas Patriot*, which replaced the *St. Landry Whig*. During the 1850s, the town continued to grow and prosper with more and more businesses opening. The Catholic Church organized two schools in Opelousas—St. Mary's Academy for boys in 1855 and the Academy of the Immaculate Conception for girls in 1856. At that time, there were other private schools for both boys and girls in and around Opelousas.

The start of the Civil War in 1861 greatly affected Opelousas. Several of its young male citizens left town to join the fight, and many of those did not return. In 1862, when Federal troops took control of Baton Rouge, the state capital was moved to Opelousas where it remained for several months. At that time, the home of former lieutenant governor Homere Mouton on Liberty Street was used as the governor's mansion to house Gov. Thomas Moore for his stay in the town. Opelousas came under attack by the Union army on October 21, 1863, and the town was occupied for several weeks.

A few years after the war, the Opelousas African Baptist Church was organized by Rev. J.P. Davenport in a blacksmith shop on June 29, 1867. It eventually became Little Zion Baptist Church, the first Baptist church in Opelousas.

Opelousas struggled through Reconstruction late in that decade with political bickering that eventually led to violence on September 28, 1868. On that day, members of the Democratic Party attacked members of the Republican Party. It ended with multiple deaths. Some historians called that incident the Opelousas Massacre, while others refer to it as the Opelousas Riot.

Opelousas continued to struggle as the 1870s began, but good times arrived when the period of Reconstruction ended in Louisiana in 1877. Opelousas citizens celebrated what it called Thanksgiving Day on May 10, 1877, with events in town and throughout St. Landry Parish. In 1874, the St. Joseph School was opened by the Catholic Church to serve the African American population. During the 1870s, the Opelousas Female Institute was opened on South Street. By the end of that decade, Opelousas was gradually returning to its golden days.

The coming of the railroad in 1881 led to population growth and economic development for Opelousas. Rail travel opened the town to the rest of the state and the country. Merchandise and goods could now be shipped out of and brought into town, which led to more business and industry for the community. In the 1890s, the town had a new opera house, two newspapers, several hotels and boardinghouses, many social halls, and two banks. In 1893, the St. Landry High School, a public school, was opened in a new building on North Market Street. In 1897, The 7th District School for Blacks was founded by Mount Olive Baptist Church and operated until 1918. Bicycles came to town during the 1890s, as did the game of baseball. By the end of the 19th century, Opelousas had electricity, a water plant, and telephones.

In 1898, the town changed its political form of government to the Lawrason Act, which provided a more uniform type of government. Instead of a board of police with a president, Opelousas now had an elected mayor and board of aldermen. Additional civic clubs and groups were organized for social and business purposes, including the Opelousas Progressive League, formed to promote economic development.

By the turn of the 20th century, Opelousas was called one of the most progressive towns in Louisiana. As the 1910s began, the town had several banks, public and private schools, a business school for adults, two newspapers, hotels, several drugstores, a beautiful opera house, a motion picture theater, automobiles, and so much more. In 1919, the Opelousas Progressive League became the Opelousas Chamber of Commerce, which continues to serve the business community today.

Education for young people improved at the start of the 20th century. There were more public and private schools for the town's population. In 1908, a new Academy of the Immaculate Conception (AIC) Catholic school was built at the corner of Main and Church Streets. In 1911, the St. Joseph Industrial College opened in Opelousas with Leonard Dwight "L.D." Lang, a graduate of St. Joseph College at Montgomery, Alabama, and a close associate of the noted educator Booker T.

Washington, as its director. In 1914, the town helped the school board with constructing a new brick building for the St. Landry High School on South Street. In 1918, the town assisted with the moving of the old school building to the corner of Vine and Academy Streets where it was remodeled and used as a new public school for African American students, called the St. Landry Training School. In 1919, the Diocese of Lafayette established a new church parish in Opelousas dedicated to the African American population. The new church was named Holy Ghost Catholic Church with Fr. James Hyland as pastor. Father Hyland immediately combined St. Joseph School with the church, and in 1921, Holy Ghost School was opened.

Education opportunities continued to improve during the 20th century. St. Landry High School became Opelousas High School in the early 1920s. It eventually moved to a new building on South Market Street, with the old South Street structure becoming the elementary school. In the 1960s, it moved to the new building on Judson Walsh Drive in the south part of town. The St. Landry Training School existed until 1953 when a new building was constructed on East Leo Street. The new school was renamed J.S. Clark High School in honor of Joseph Samuel Clark, the first president of Southern University and A&M College in Baton Rouge. In 1969, J.S. Clark High School and Opelousas High School were merged for the purpose of integration, and that Opelousas High School is still in operation today. In 1970, the Academy of the Immaculate Conception and Holy Ghost School merged and became Opelousas Catholic, which continues to operate today on Prudhomme Lane.

Journalism history was made in Opelousas On Christmas Eve of 1939 when John Thistlethwaite and Ducote Andrepont published the first offset printed newspaper, called the *Daily World*. In 1986, Opelousas made political history when John W. Joseph was elected as the first African American mayor of Opelousas. Mayor Joseph won the election for a second term, serving the community until 1994 when he retired from office.

Throughout its long history, Opelousas has been known for its hospitality. Its fairs and festivals through the ages were great successes in the community, attracting many tourists to the town. Some of those festivals included the Cotton Carnival of the 1920s and the Louisiana Yambilee Festival that was started in 1946 and continued until 2012. The town is also known for its culinary culture with great restaurants and eating establishments. It is the hometown of a variety of well-known chefs such as internationally known chef Paul Prudhomme and his sister Enola Prudhomme. Other prominent chefs include Tony Chachere, who created a special seasoning and opened Tony Chachere's Creole Foods in Opelousas, and Eula Savoie, who made Savoie's Cajun sausage and roux famous. Another chef, known for his Opelousas baked duck, was Charles "Didee" Lastrapes, who owned and operated the Elk Restaurant and later Didee's Restaurant in Opelousas for many years. Gene Paillet, Marie Lemelle, Shirley Lemelle, and Amos Daniels were others known for their cooking skills.

Opelousas is the "Zydeco Capital of the World." Clifton Chenier, the king of zydeco, and brother Cleveland Chenier were from Opelousas. Other musicians include internationally known Cajun fiddler Hadley J. Castille; singer Lil' Bob; and Rod Bernard, nationally known for the swamp pop music of south Louisiana.

Citizens who have brought other honors to the town include Jim Bowie, hero of the Alamo; Charles Edmund Nash, Louisiana's first African American congressman; Fr. Joseph Verbis Lafleur, designated a Servant of God and a World War II hero who gave his life for his country; Rodney Milburn, won the gold medal in the 110-meter hurdles in the 1972 Summer Olympics; and novelist John Ed Bradley.

The many photographs presented in this book showcase over a century of Opelousas history. Those images illustrate the ups and downs of the community and its road towards a better future as it entered the 21st century. Since each picture is worth a thousand words, the story of the town comes alive for all who view this book. Enjoy!

One

Opelousas, The Place

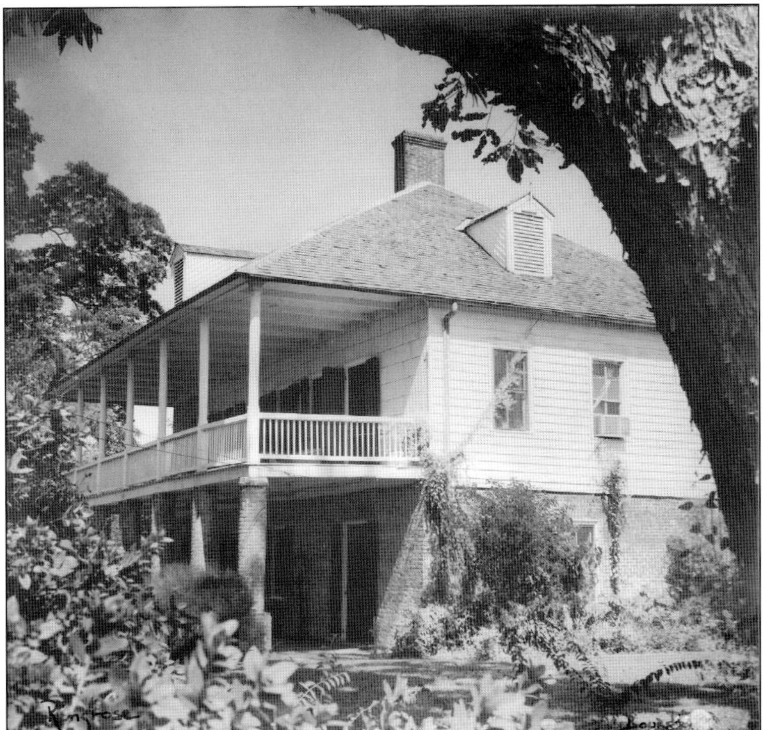

One of the oldest buildings in Opelousas, the Ringrose Plantation home, is pictured here in the 1960s when it was owned by the L. Austin Fontenot family. Built by Michel Prudhomme in the late 1700s, it became the home of the Michael Ringrose family in the 1890s. Today, it is known as the Michel Prudhomme Home. (Photograph by Bourdier Photography.)

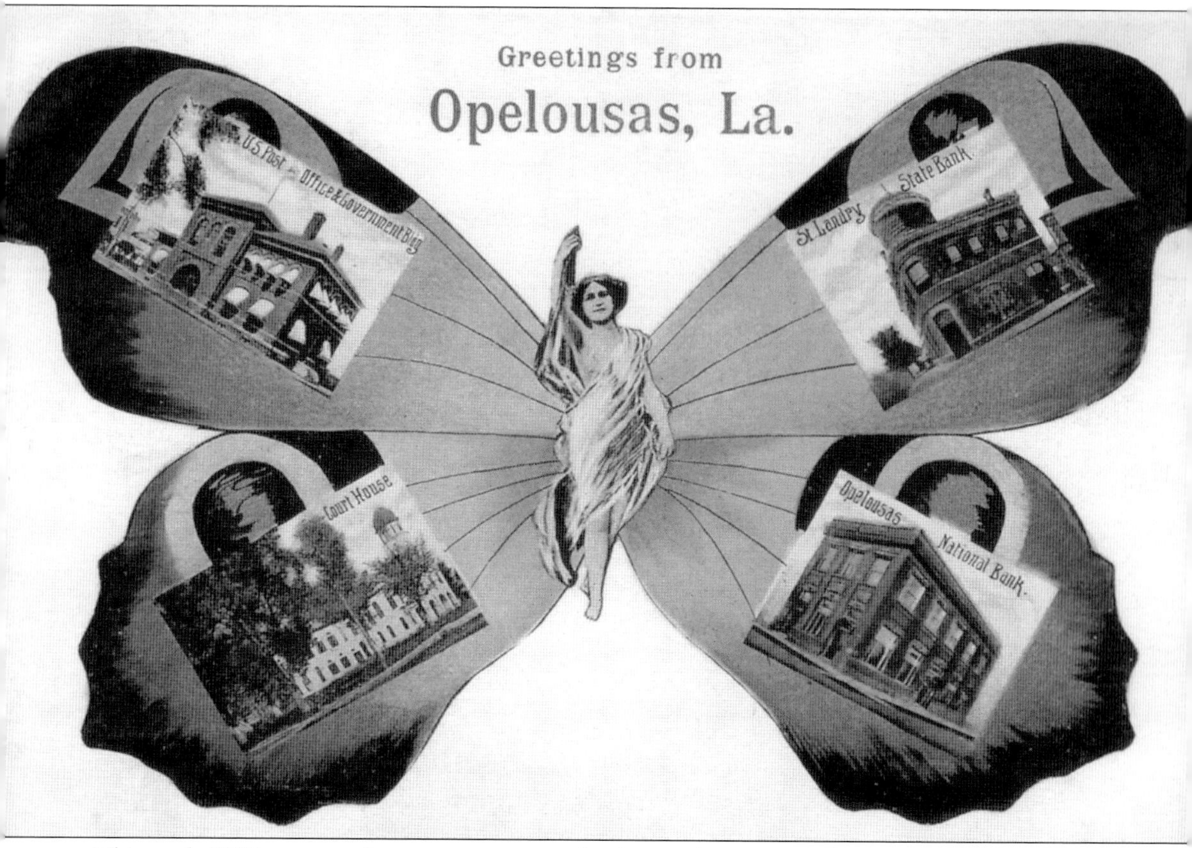

This early-1900s postcard greets visitors to Opelousas, Louisiana, the city that takes its name from the Indians who lived on the land when the first European explorers arrived during the end of the 17th century. Poste du Opelousas was settled by the French and Spanish in the mid-18th century. It became the seat of St. Landry Parish in 1807 and was officially incorporated as a town on February 14, 1821. Pictured on the postcard are, from left to right and top to bottom, the federal building and post office, St. Landry State Bank, St. Landry Parish Courthouse, and the Opelousas National Bank.

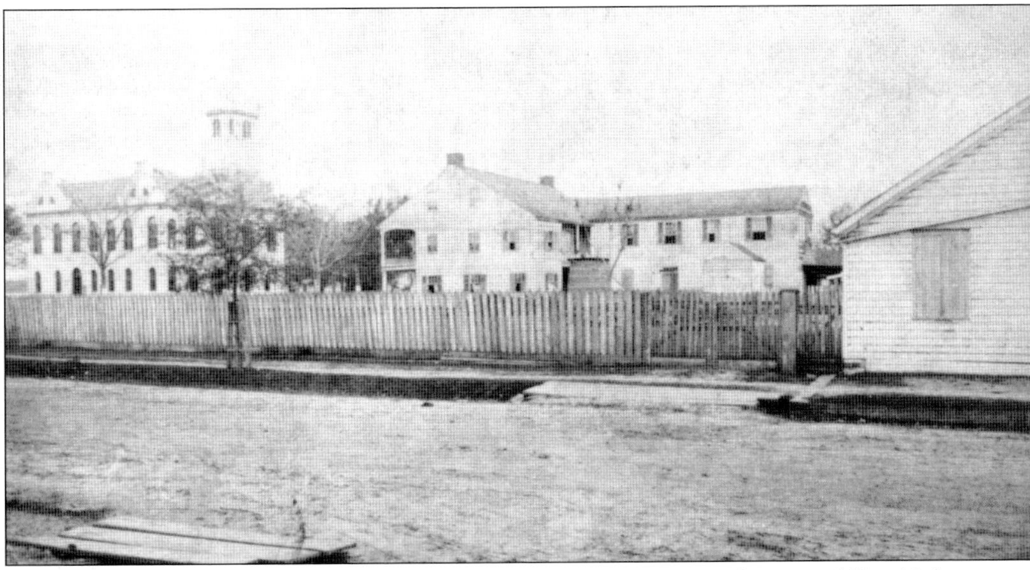

This photograph, taken in 1887 by George O. Elms, presents a glimpse of late-19th-century Opelousas. The St. Landry Parish Courthouse, constructed in 1886 to replace the one destroyed by fire that year, is pictured across Court Street from the Eureka Hotel. The old hotel dates to the beginning of the 19th century when it was called the Eagle Hotel. Later in that century, Manon Baldwin, a free Black woman, owned the building until her death in 1857. Following that it was called the St. Landry Hotel, and some historians claim was used by the state legislature in 1862 when Opelousas served as the capital of Louisiana during the American Civil War. After the war, it became the Eureka Hotel and later the Lacombe Hotel.

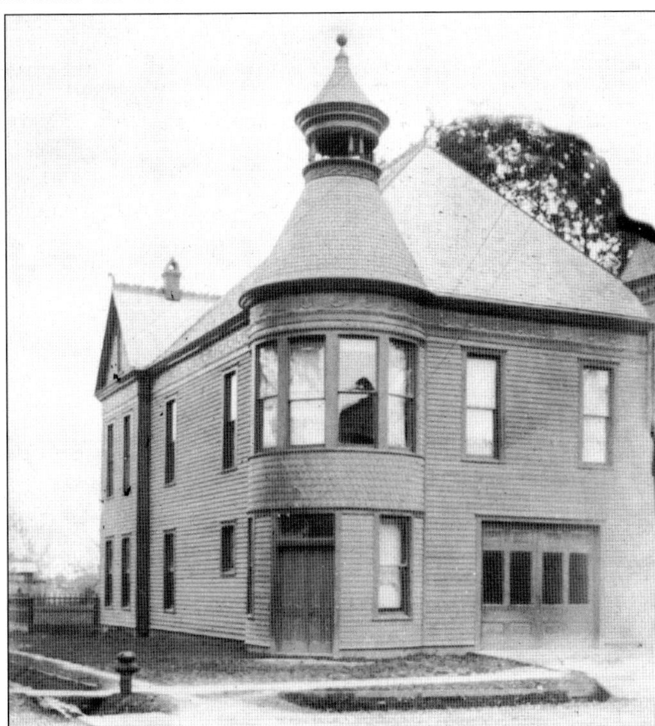

Opelousas had a fire department soon after the town was incorporated and had a fire truck by 1828. Over the years, that truck was housed in different buildings. During the latter part of the 19th century, Opelousas had a beautiful new fire station and hall located on the southeast corner of Union and Bellevue Streets. This photograph from the late 1890s shows the building where the town's fire engine was housed at that time. (Courtesy of Emile Ventre IV, Chris Ventre, and Jonathan Sebastien.)

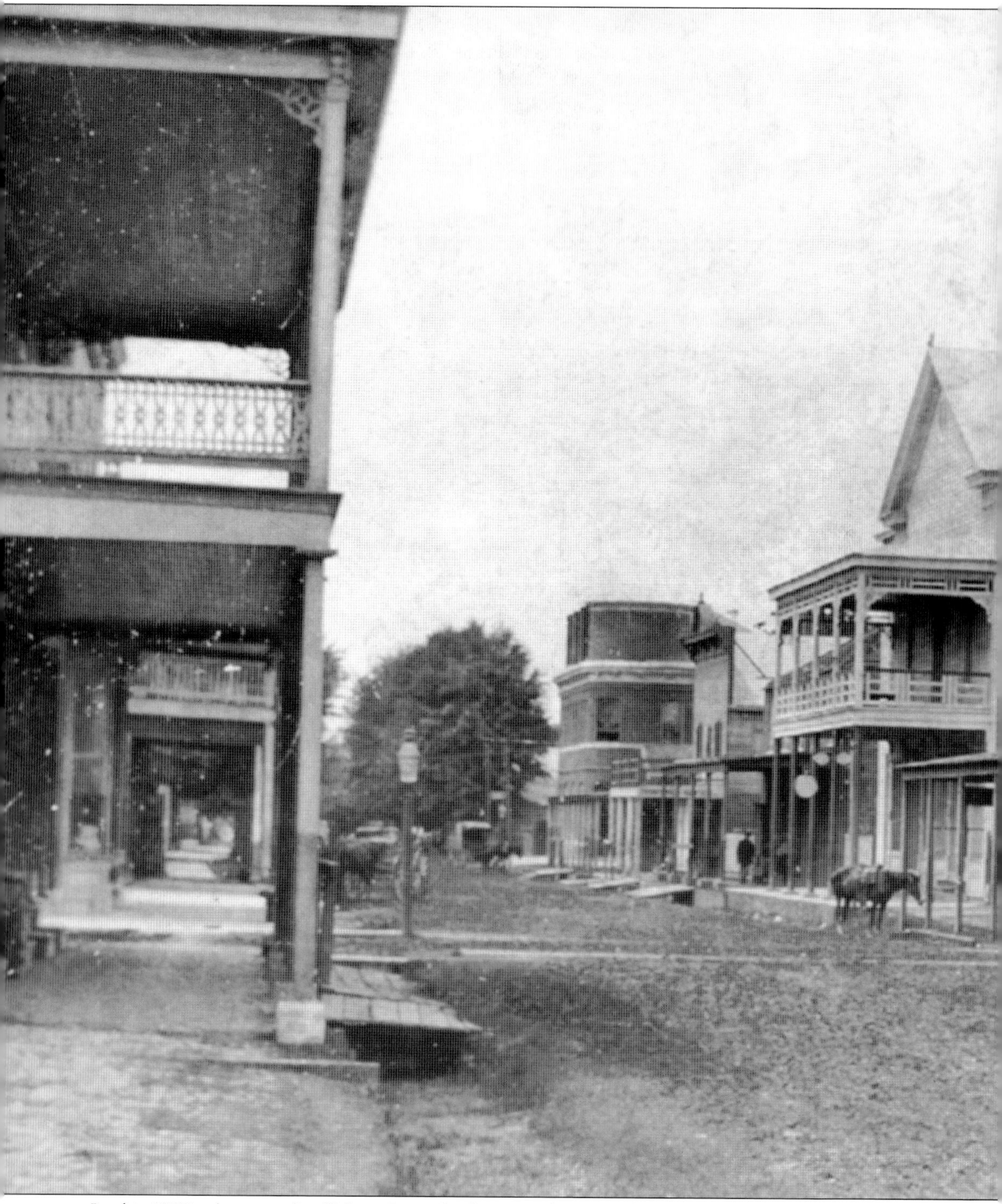

In this 1890s photograph of Main Street looking south in Opelousas are some of the most successful businesses of that time, many owned by the town's Jewish population. Traveling south on Main Street to the left is the store of Solomon Jacobs on the northeast corner. Across Bellevue Street on the southeast corner is the store of David Roos and Son. To the right, on the northwest corner of

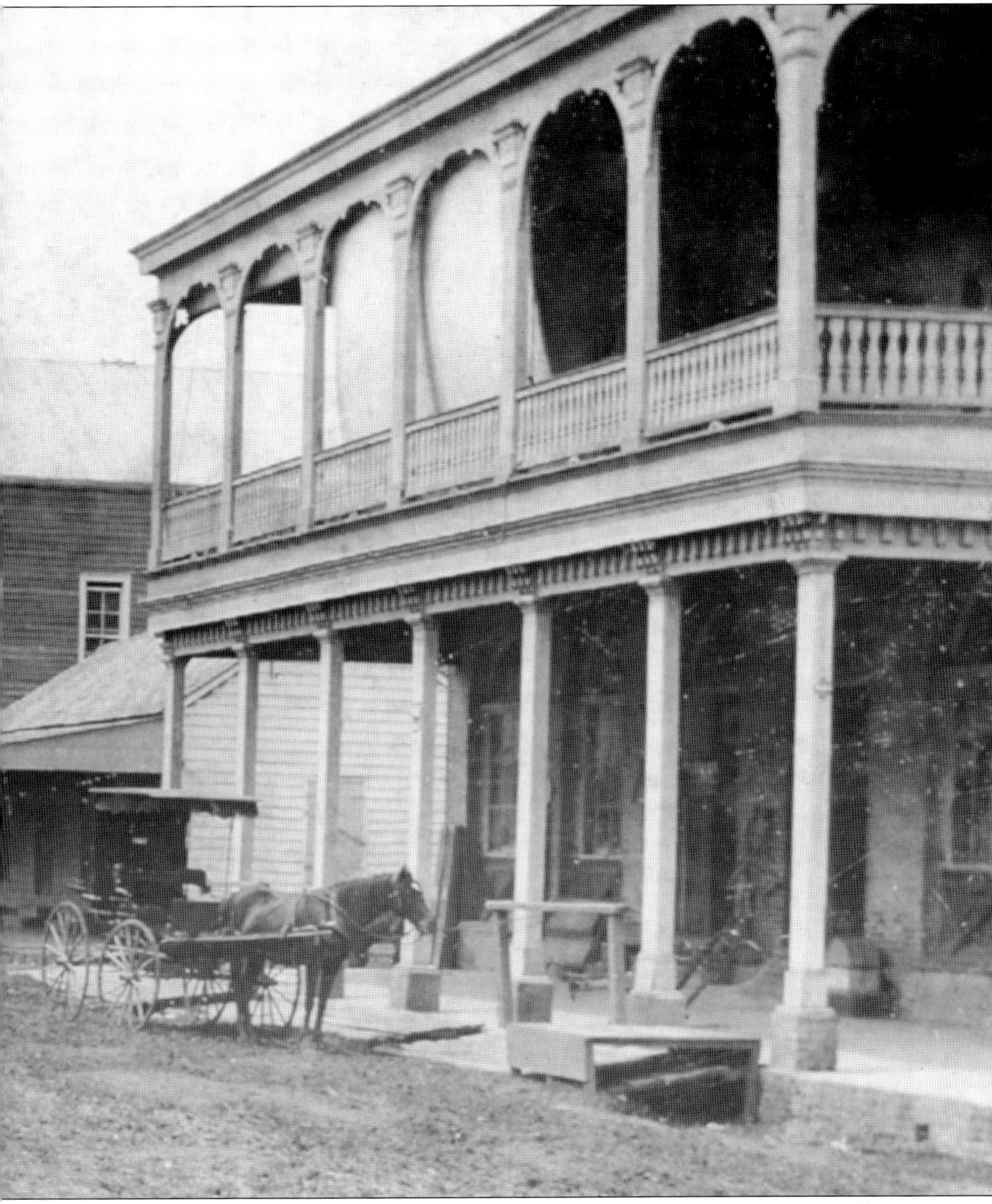

Bellevue and Main Streets, known as Bloch Corner, is the store of Joseph Bloch. Across Bellevue Street heading south is the Bijoux Coffee House, and next door is the Sandoz Opera House. To the far right on the northwest corner of Main and Landry Streets is the business of Charles Ealer, and on the southwest corner is the St. Landry State Bank.

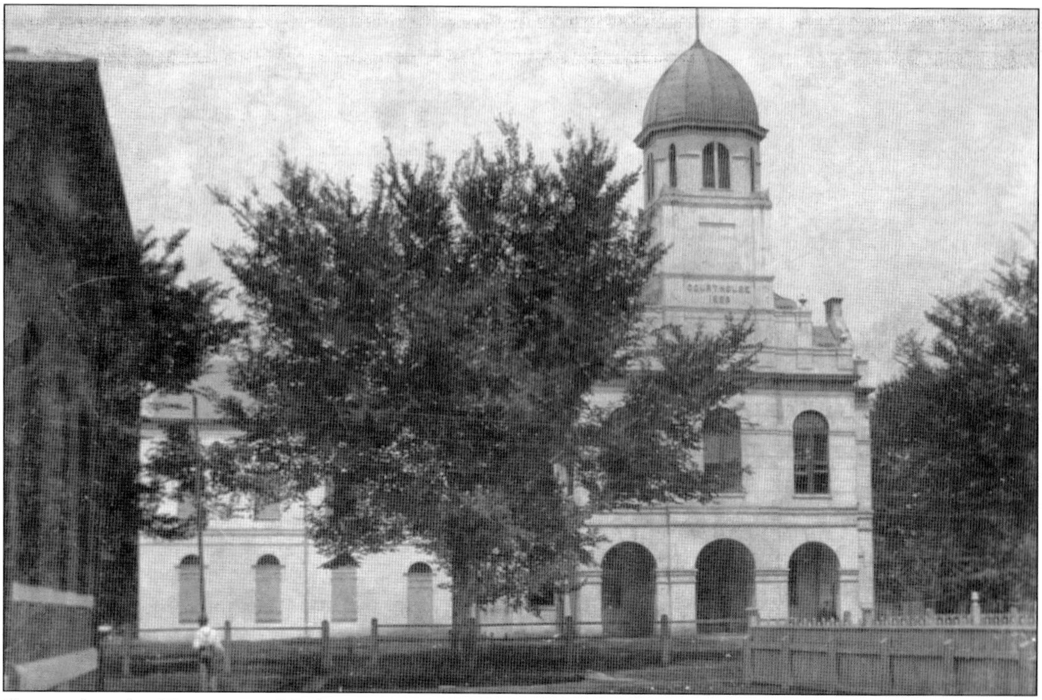

Soon after the Territory of Orleans was organized into parishes in 1807, Opelousas was named the seat of St. Landry Parish, a title it holds to this day. Since the local Catholic church was named St. Landry, the new political parish also became St. Landry, in honor of the saint-bishop who served Paris from 650 to 661 AD. The first parish courthouse was constructed on property that soon became the center of the new town. The building pictured in this 1890s photograph is the fourth courthouse constructed on that property, the heart of the Opelousas community today.

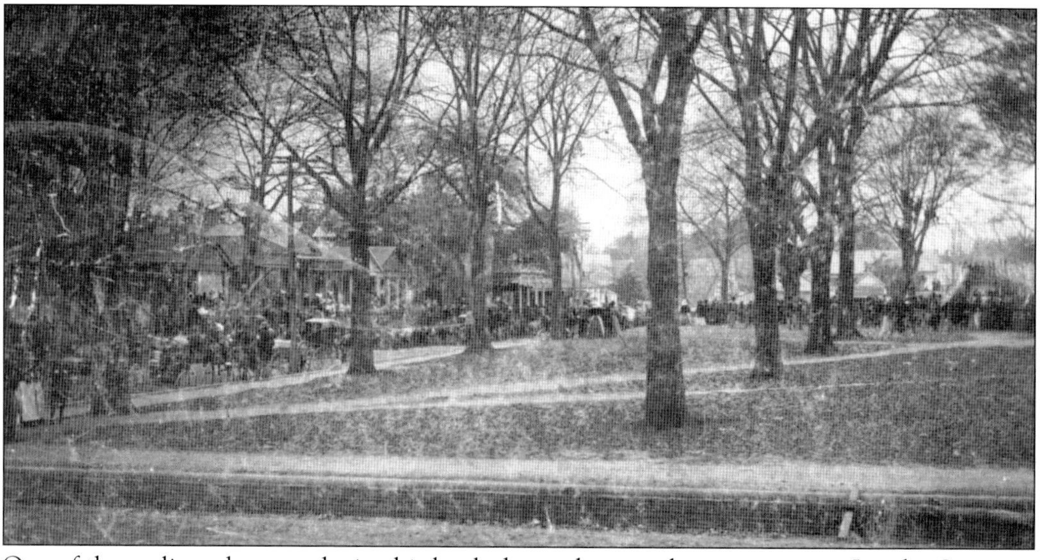

One of the earliest photographs in this book shows the courthouse square on Landry Street in downtown Opelousas. For over two centuries, the courthouse square was the gathering place for most of the town's activities. This 19th-century photograph shows a group of citizens coming together on the square, facing Landry Street, for a special Opelousas event.

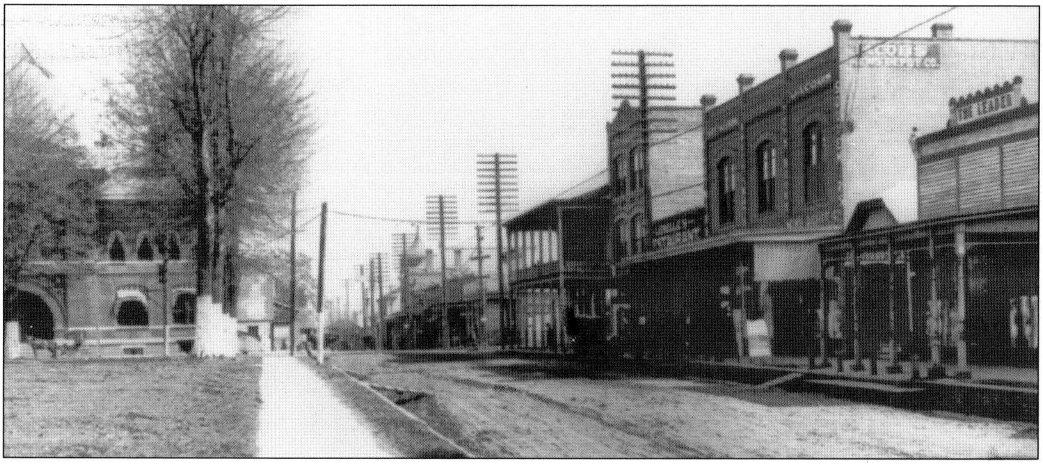

The Opelousas commercial district is one of the oldest in the area, going back to the early 1800s. Shown in this photograph are some of the successful businesses that were located in the district during the early part of the 20th century. To the left in the middle of the block is the *Jacobs News Depot*. On the southwest corner that intersects with Court Street is the Robert Chachere Store, which operated there for several decades. On the northeast corner is the Opelousas Post Office and Federal Building, constructed in 1891.

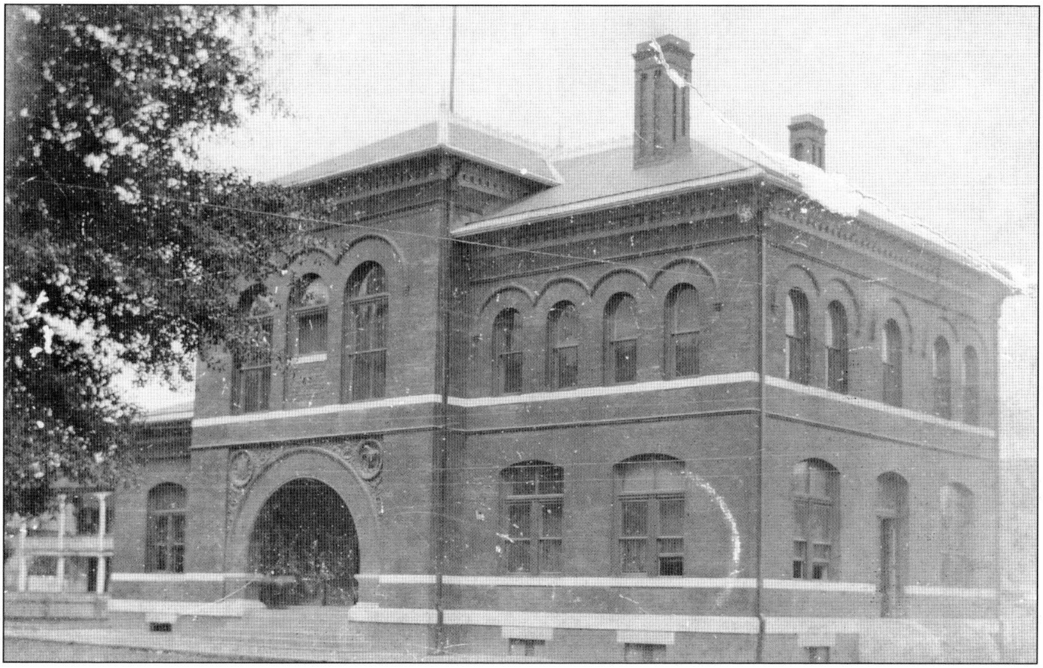

On February 20, 1792, the US Postal Service Act established the US Post Office Department. After the Louisiana Purchase, the United States provided postal service to the areas that were part of that purchase, including Opelousas. By 1807, Opelousas had its first postmaster. Over the years, the post office was housed in several different locations. In 1891, the town had a permanent post office building when the one pictured here was constructed on the corner of Court and Landry Streets in downtown. Although two other structures erected in later years replaced this post office, the building pictured here is listed in the National Register of Historic Places and remains in downtown Opelousas today.

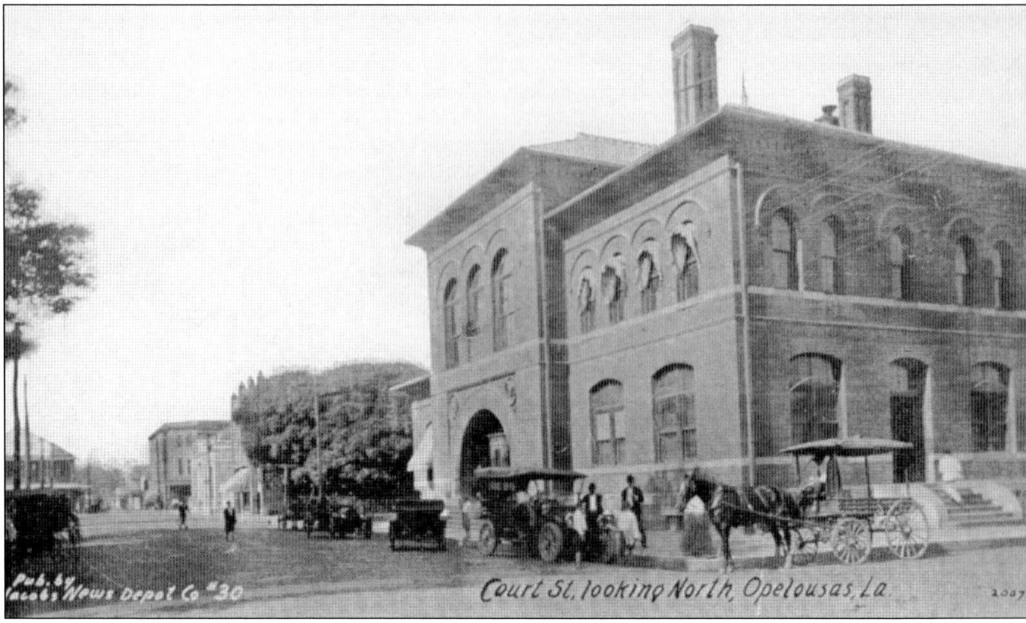

A view down Court Street, looking north from Landry Street, is pictured in this c. 1915 postcard produced by *Jacobs News Depot* in Opelousas. On the right is the Opelousas Post Office and Federal Building, and on the far right on the northeast corner is the Union Bank and Trust Company, constructed in 1911. Across Bellevue Street on the northeast corner of Court Street is the new Lacombe Hotel, and across the street on the northwest corner is the Budd Building, which hosted several businesses, including a saloon and the Elk Restaurant during that time.

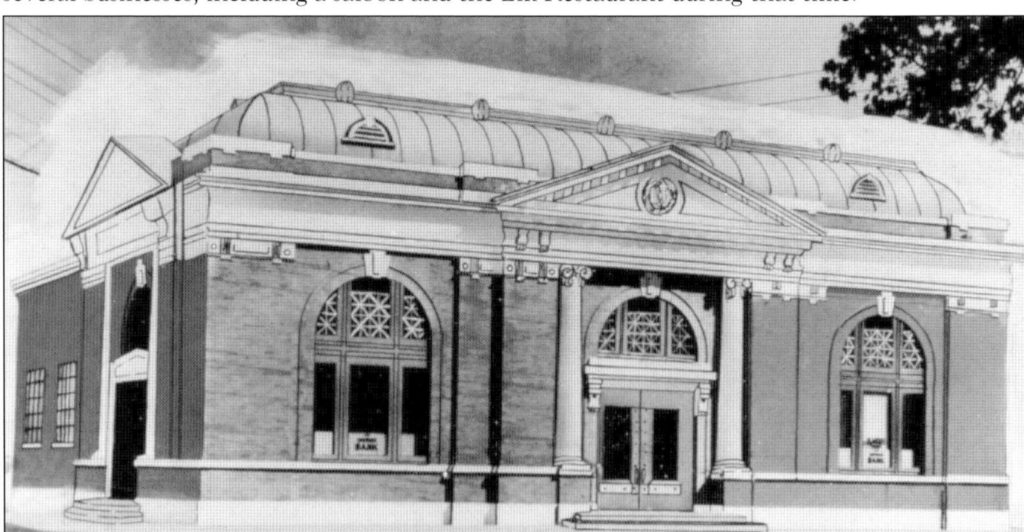

The Union Bank and Trust Company, shown in this photograph on the corner of Court and Bellevue Streets, opened for business in Opelousas in 1911. Soon after it was opened, this building was constructed to house the bank. Later, the bank merged with Planter's Bank and became Planters Trust and Savings Bank, which operated in the building until the 1950s when a new structure was constructed on the northeast corner of Bellevue Street. The Union Bank building still stands on Bellevue and Court Streets in downtown Opelousas.

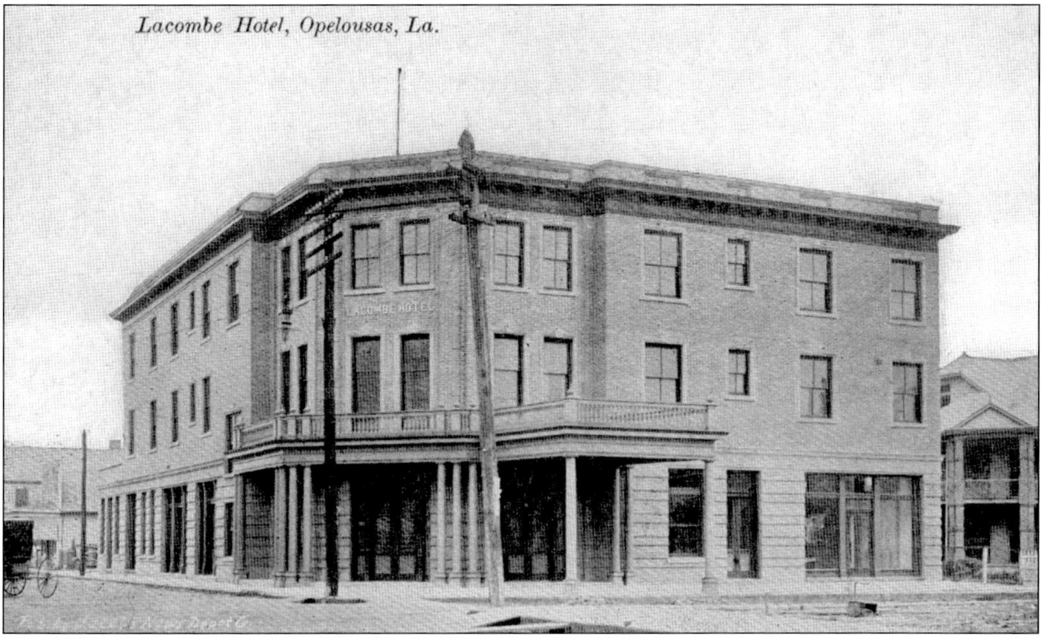

After five years of planning and raising the necessary funds, the new Lacombe Hotel, pictured above, was constructed on the northeast corner of Court and Bellevue Streets in Opelousas in 1909. In the 1920s, the hotel was sold, and the name changed to the James Hotel, after the deceased young grandson of Adam Budd, the new owner. The James Hotel operated in Opelousas until the 1950s when it was demolished so that the new Planters Bank could be constructed on that corner. To the right of the hotel is the Littell home, also demolished in the 1950s so the property could be used for Planters Bank parking. The photograph below shows the office of the new Lacombe Hotel on October 27, 1915. Pictured at the hotel desk is manager G.B. Cretin on the right and clerk Eddie Durio on the left. The new hotel was just a few doors down from the old Lacombe Hotel, which stood on Court Street for over a century.

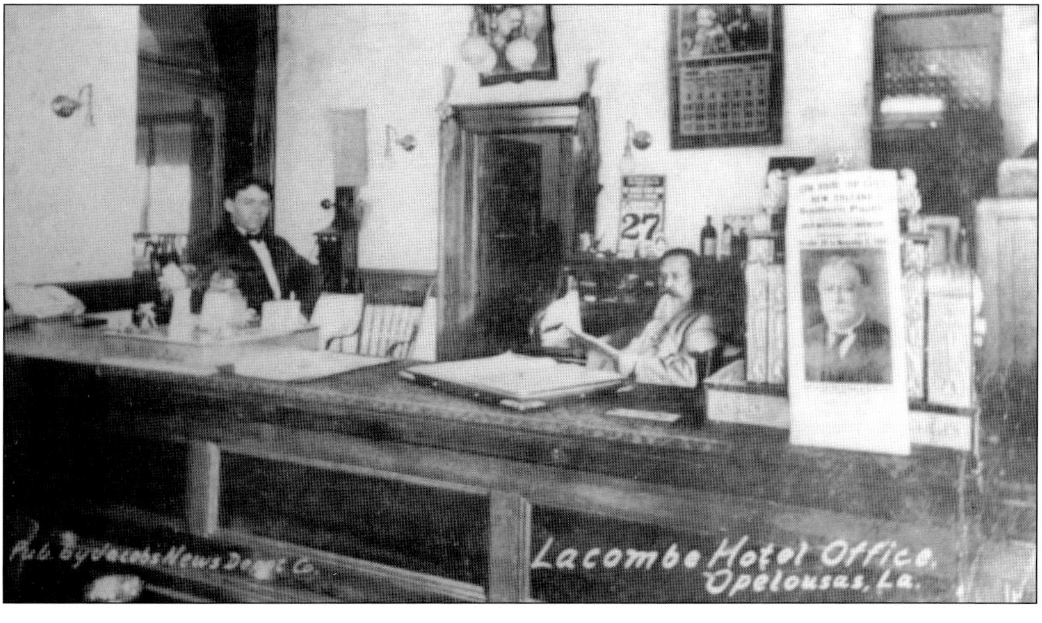

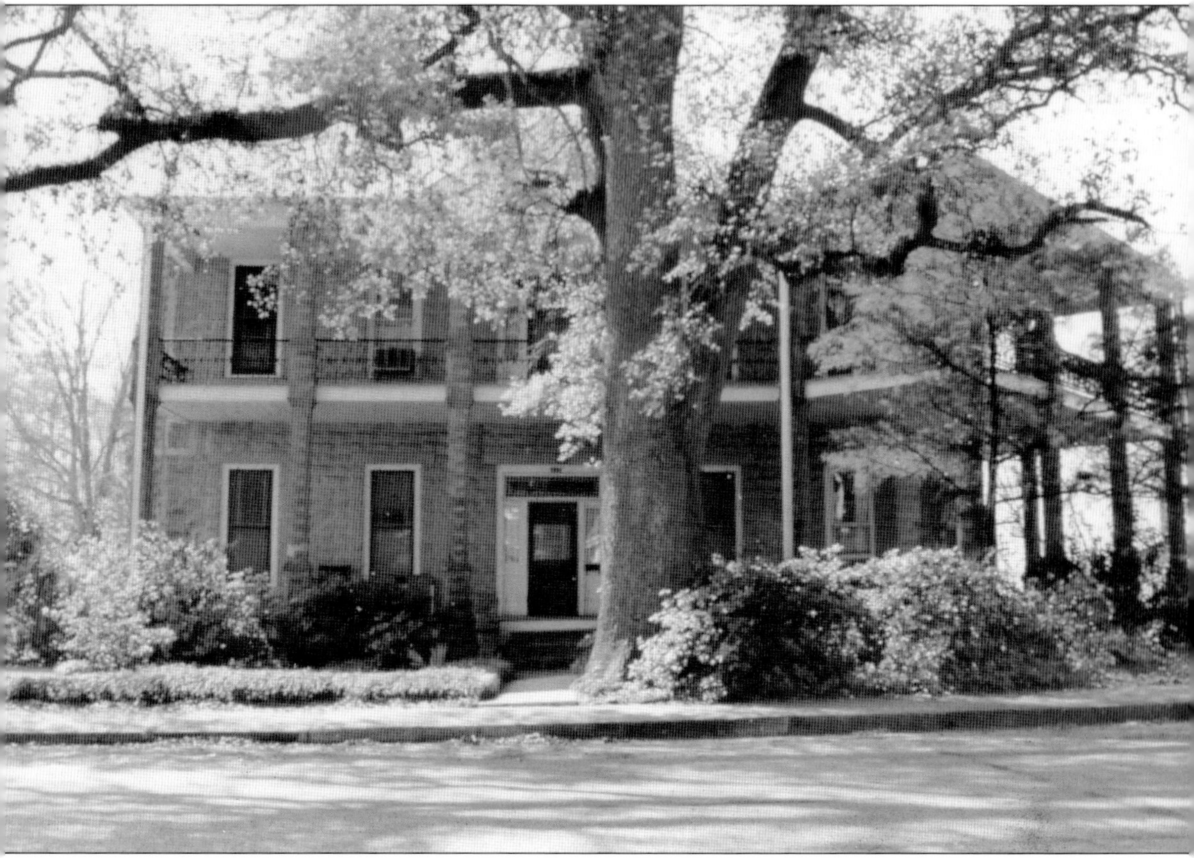

Located on the corner of Vine and Liberty Streets is one of Opelousas's most historic homes, pictured here in 1989. Built in 1908, it was the family home of Marion Lewis Swords (1857–1916), who served as sheriff of St. Landry Parish for 16 years. Although a controversial political figure of the early 20th century, Sheriff Swords played an important role in Opelousas history. He was killed by outlaw Hilaire Carriere in a shootout on July 17, 1916. When this home was constructed, it was called one of the most beautiful homes in Southwest Louisiana.

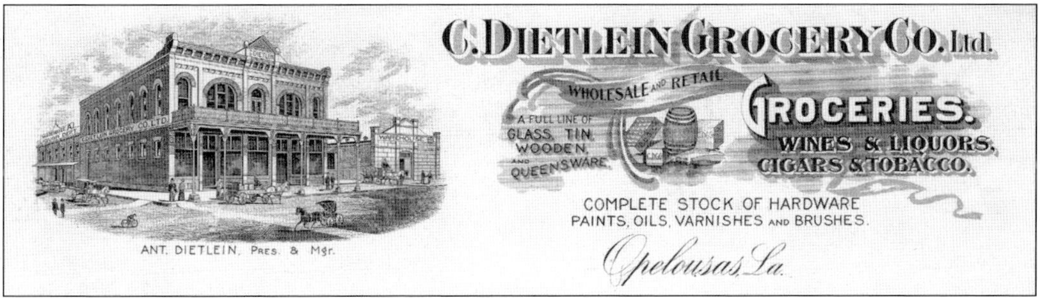

The top of this invoice shows a drawing of the building that housed the C. Dietlein Grocery Co. Inc. on the southeast corner of Main and North Streets in Opelousas for over two decades. It was later owned and operated as Blackshear's store until 1916 when it was sold to Martin Bordelon, who moved his motor car business into the building.

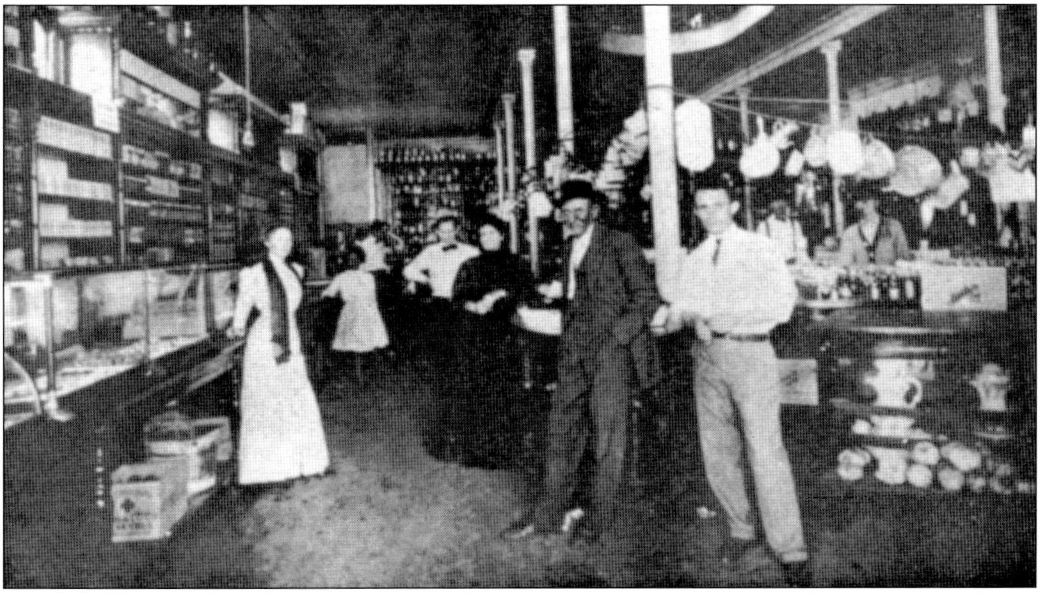

The interior of the P.T. Blackshear and Sons store that operated in the Dietlein Building on the corner of Main and North Streets is shown in this c. 1910 photograph. P.T. Blackshear, with help from his family, ran the general merchandise store in Opelousas from 1902 until it closed sometime prior to 1916. In 1916, the building was sold to Martin Bordelon, who relocated his automobile business there where it remained for almost a century.

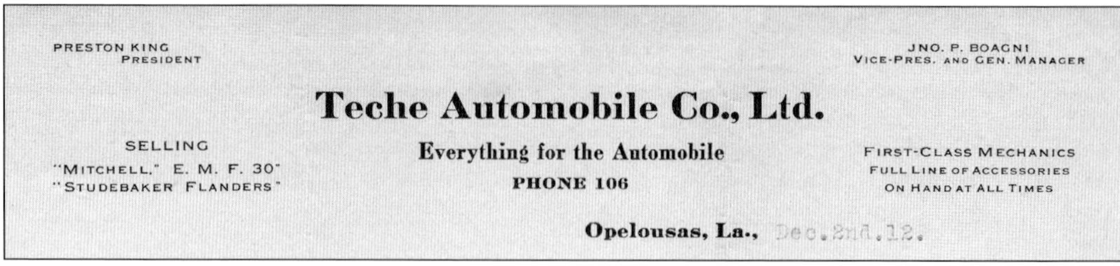
PRESTON KING
PRESIDENT

JNO. P. BOAGNI
VICE-PRES. AND GEN. MANAGER

Teche Automobile Co., Ltd.

SELLING
"MITCHELL," E. M. F. 30"
"STUDEBAKER FLANDERS"

Everything for the Automobile
PHONE 106

FIRST-CLASS MECHANICS
FULL LINE OF ACCESSORIES
ON HAND AT ALL TIMES

Opelousas, La., Dec. 2nd. 12.

The first automobile dealership in Opelousas was the Teche Automobile Co., opened on Main Street in Opelousas in 1911. Preston King was the president of the company, and J.P. Boagni was vice president and general manager. The company was first opened in New Iberia and moved to Opelousas in 1911, where they handled Michell and Studebaker automobiles.

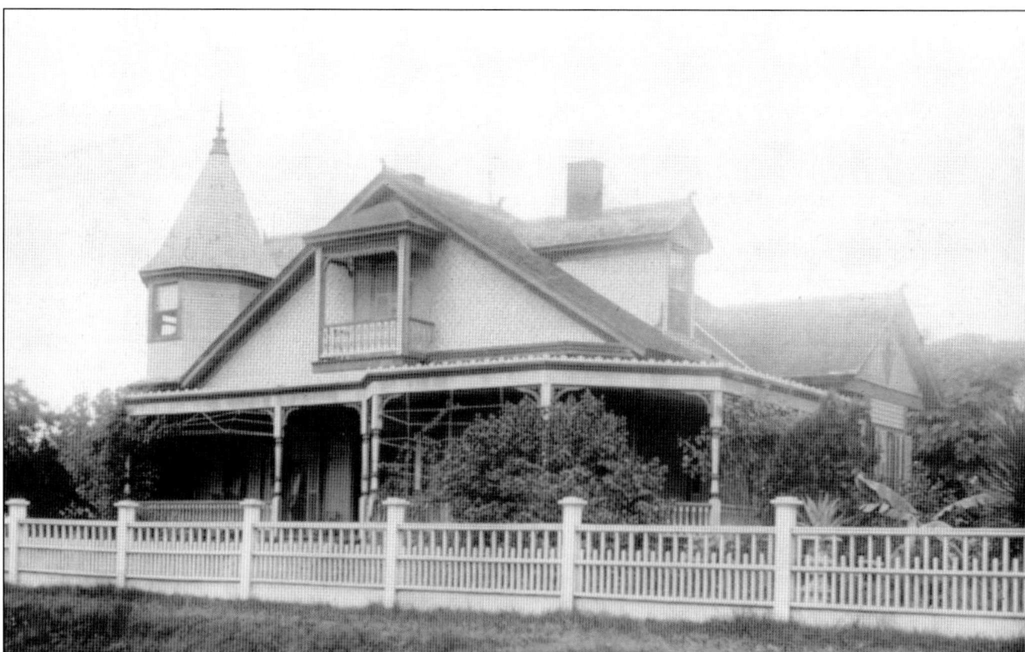

The home of Dr. Lionel Bienvenu and family, which once stood on South Union and Cherry Streets, is pictured here. Dr. Lionel Bienvenu and his brother Dr. Oscar Bienvenu operated the St. Rita Infirmary in Opelousas. He practiced medicine for 24 years until he died on February 7, 1946. The Bienvenu home was eventually sold and moved out of Opelousas. Opelousas had many other doctors during its history, including Dr. Emile Donato Sr. (1871–1937), the town's first accredited African American doctor, who received his medical license in New Orleans on October 7, 1895. (Courtesy of Bob Bienvenu.)

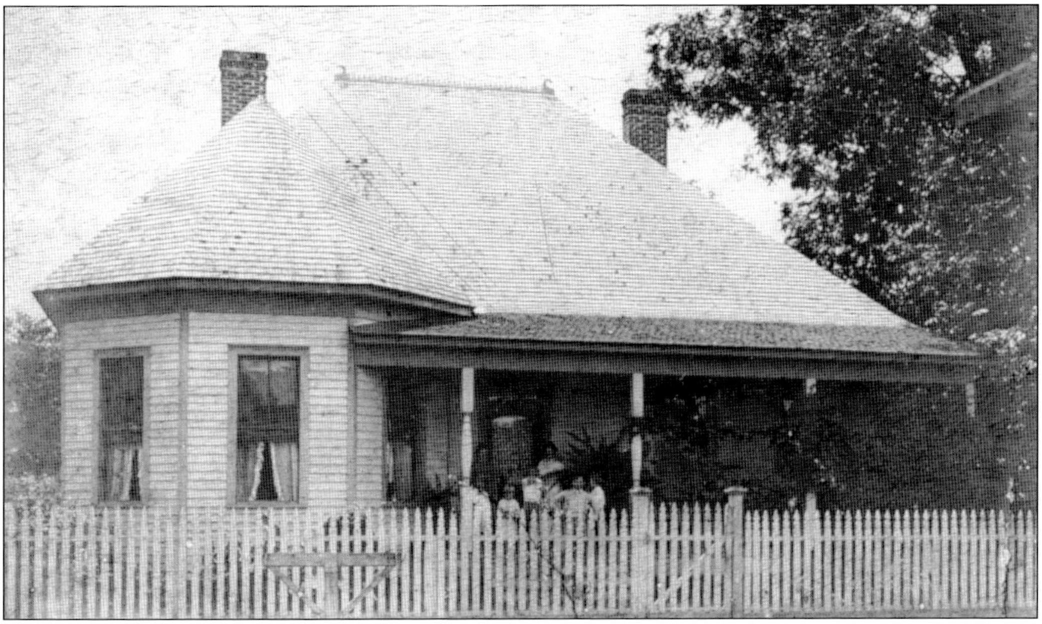

These two photographs show the home of Celestine Chachere Brooks, the widow of Tom Brooks, on East Grolee Street. Following the death of her husband, Celestine built this home in 1900 where she and her children lived for about eight years. The above photograph shows the home soon after it was built. The image below shows the home in 1905 after it was remodeled and a second floor added. When the Brooks family moved to New Orleans around 1909, the home was sold to Vance Miles Sr., who lived there with his wife and children until he died in 1944. His widow, Mathilde Lacombe Miles, continued to live in the home until 1950 when she moved to Alabama. Then the Young family occupied the home until 1974 when the Andrepont family purchased the home, named it Yesterday, and lived there until 1999.

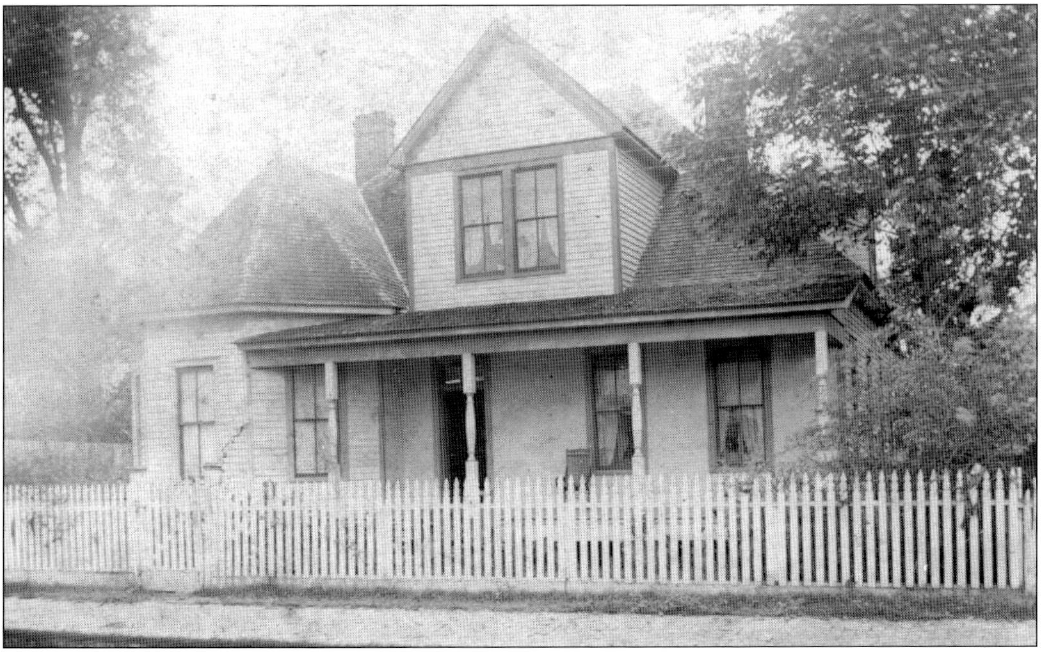

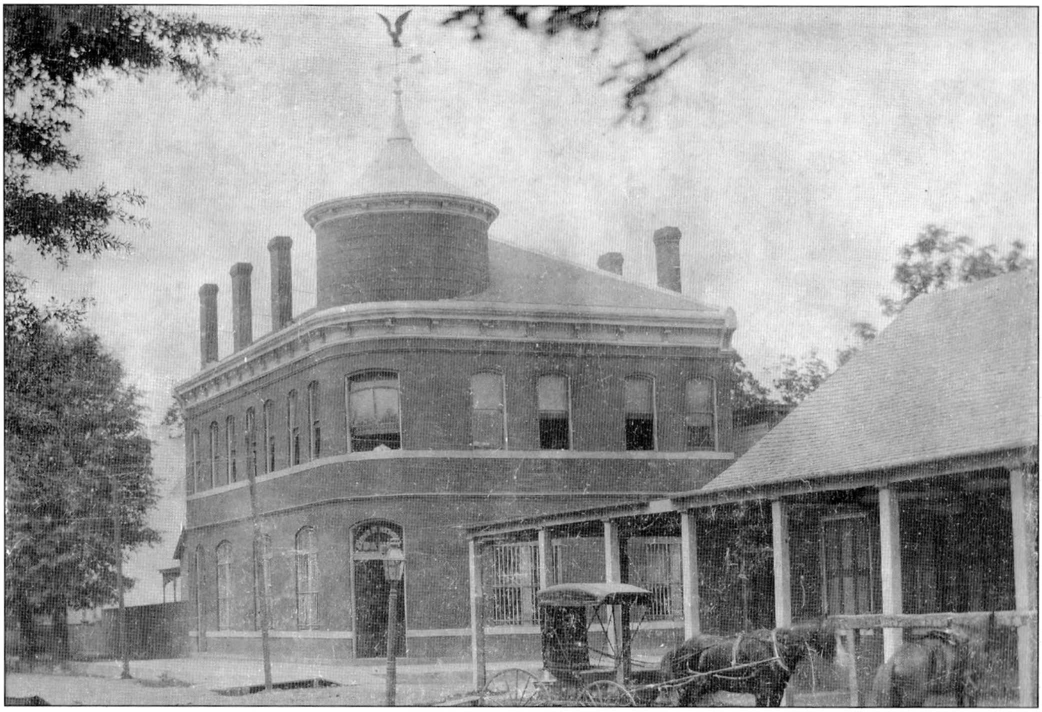

Located on King's Corner, the intersection of Main and Landry Streets, the St. Landry State Bank is pictured here in the late 1890s. The bank was organized in 1888 as the First National Bank of Opelousas. In 1893–1894, it became the St. Landry State Bank. Eventually, it merged with other local banks and became St. Landry Bank and Trust Company, which operates in Opelousas today. Across Main Street on Ealer's Corner is the jewelry store and business office of Charles Ealer, a prosperous businessman and community leader who lived in the 19th century.

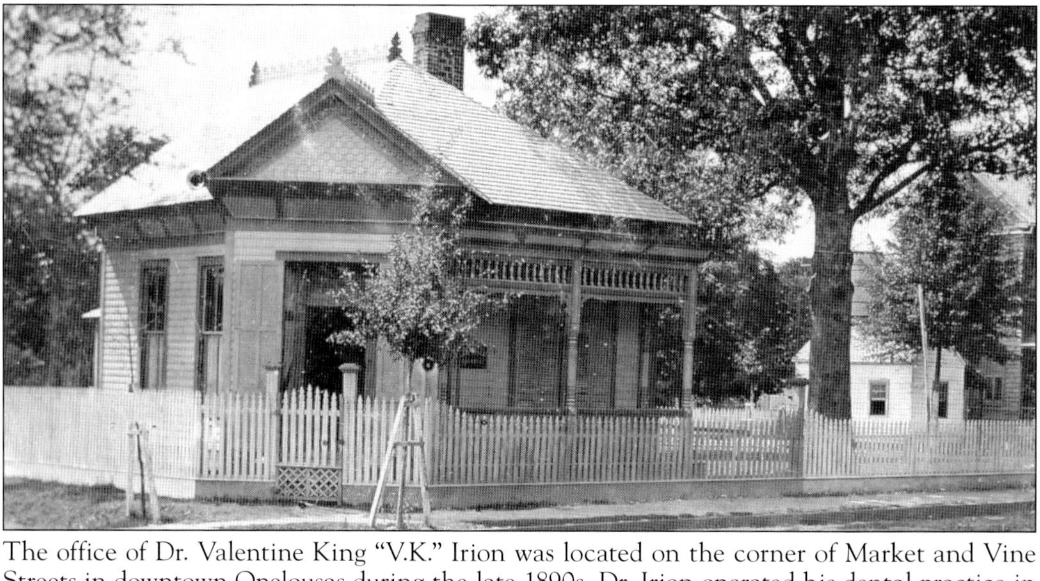

The office of Dr. Valentine King "V.K." Irion was located on the corner of Market and Vine Streets in downtown Opelousas during the late 1890s. Dr. Irion operated his dental practice in Opelousas from 1888 to 1896. He also served for a short time as the first principal of St. Landry High School when it opened on Market Street in January 1894.

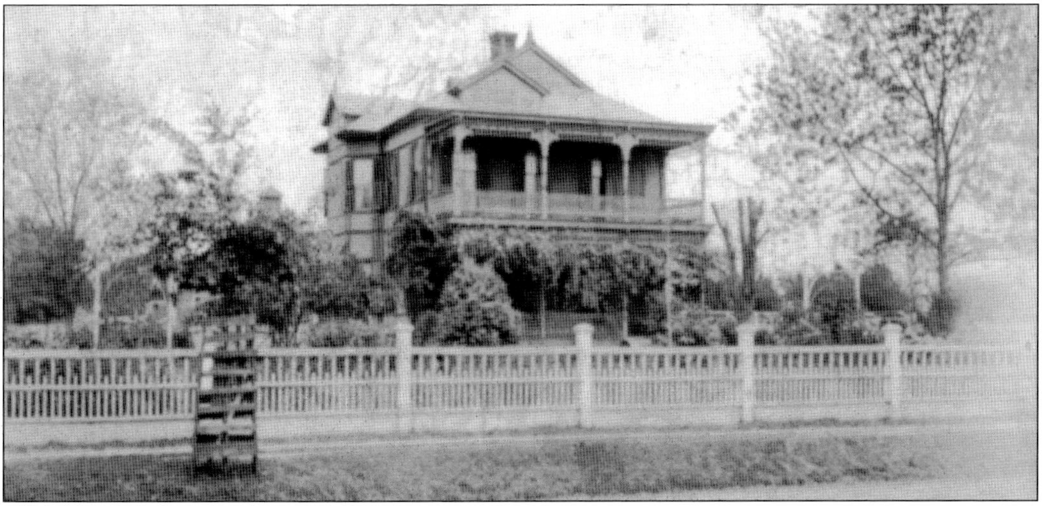

This magnificent house constructed by C.D. Stewart during the 1890s, once stood on Union Street in Opelousas. Stewart constructed many of the buildings in the Opelousas area during that time, where he was known as a master builder. The house in this photograph was offered for sale in the *St. Landry Trade Review*, published by the Courier Newspaper Company in 1896. (Courtesy of Emile Ventre IV, Chris Ventre, and Jonathan Sebastien.)

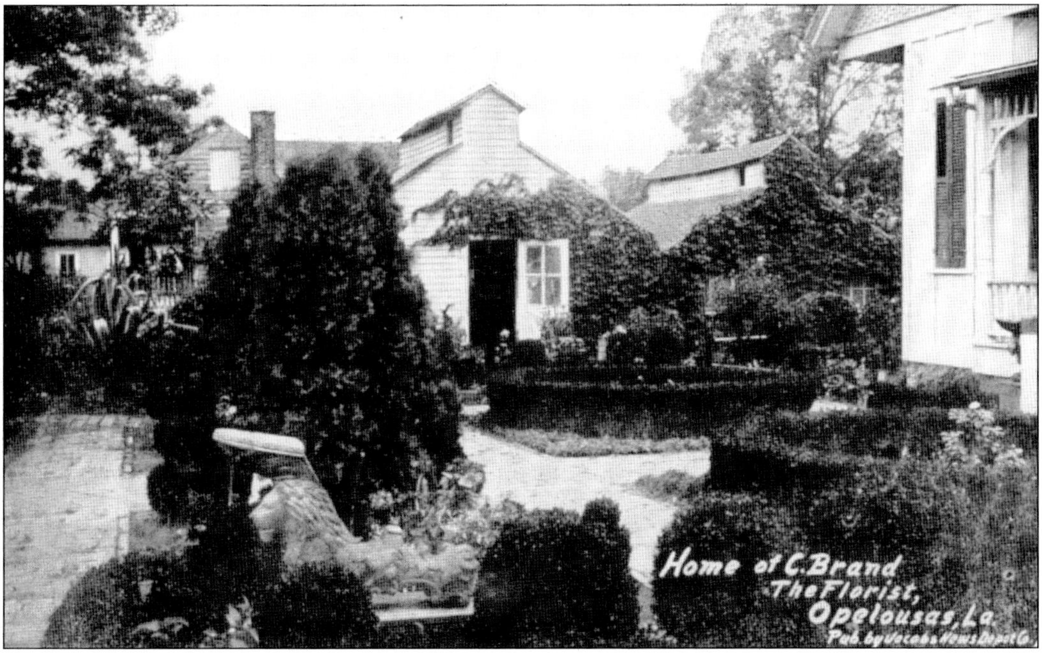

Conrad Brand, known as "Frank, the Baker," was a businessman, a florist, and a baker. He owned businesses in Opelousas following the Civil War until he retired in 1898. He was a community leader involved in many of the local clubs and organizations. Brand died on March 10, 1911, and is buried in Myrtle Grove Cemetery. In 1909, the flower garden at the Conrad Brand home was featured in a publication by the Rock Island-Frisco Passenger Train line called "Everyman's Land—A Description of Louisiana." That garden became so well known that Aaron Jacobs of *Jacobs News Depot* took a photograph and made this postcard that became popular with tourists and citizens alike.

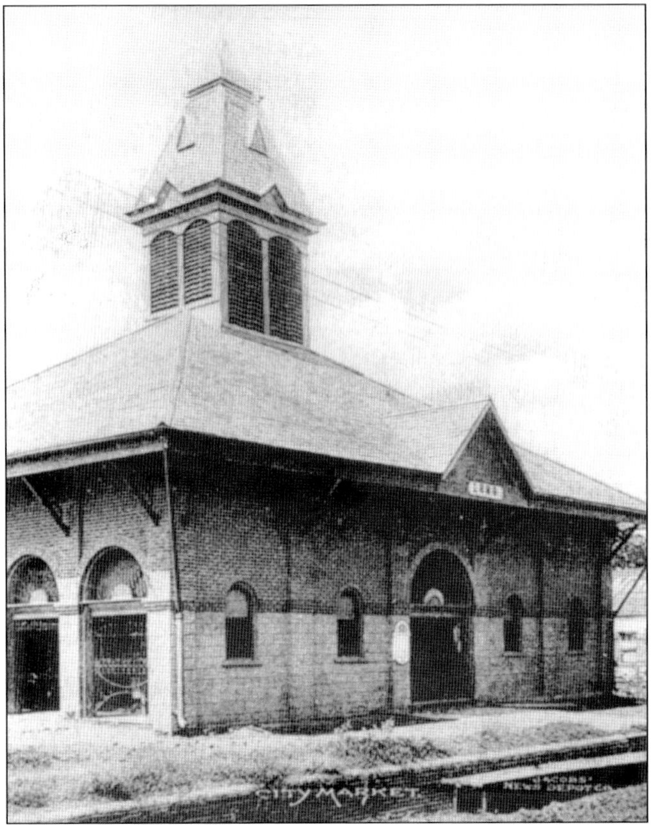

The existence of a town market was noted in records soon after Opelousas was incorporated in 1821. New town market buildings were constructed in 1853 and 1867. In 1888, the town market building (left) was constructed on the corner of Market and Bellevue Streets. That old town market building was remodeled in 1932 and became Opelousas City Hall, shown in the photograph below. Opelousas City Hall remained in that building until 1962, when a new city hall building was constructed on Court and Grolee Streets. The old city hall building is today listed in the National Register of Historic Places.

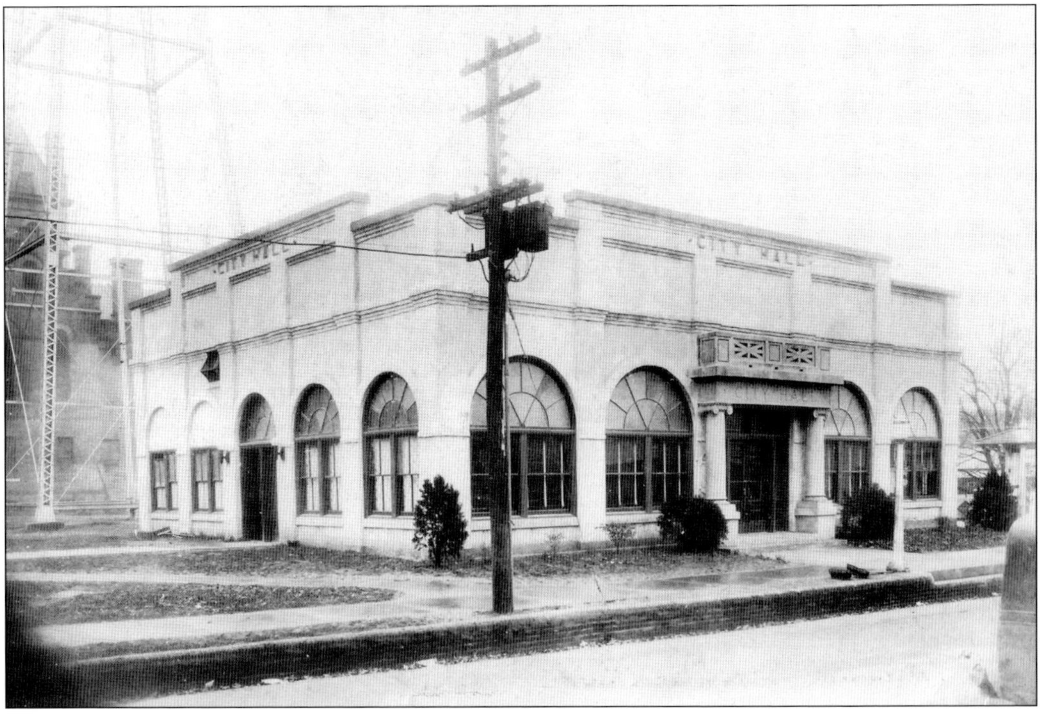

Two

PEOPLE OF OPELOUSAS

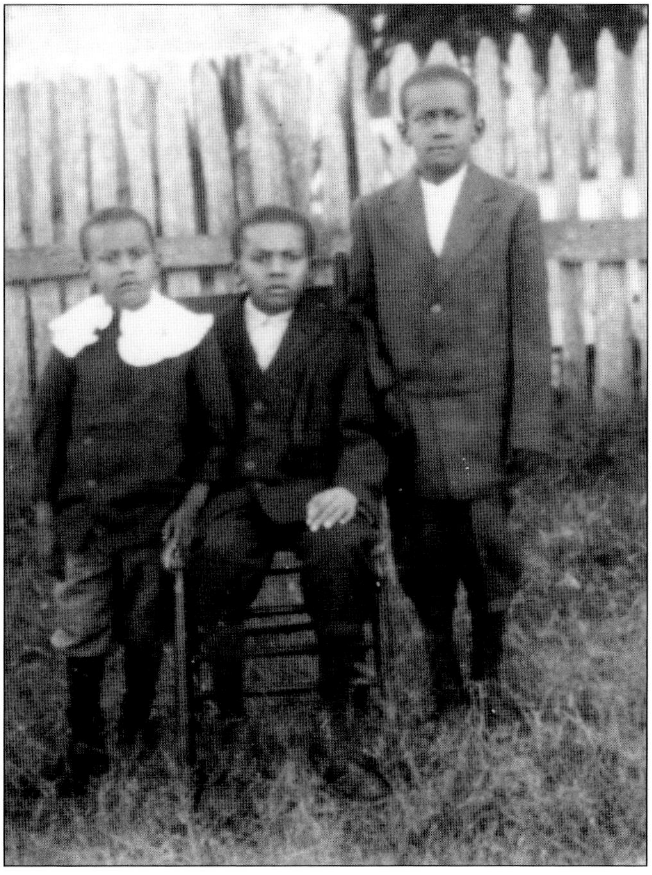

Photography arrived in Opelousas just a few years before the Civil War when traveling photographers came into the area from time to time. Following the war, a few local photographers opened galleries in the area, producing pictures of Opelousas people of that century. This 19th-century tintype photograph shows three young citizens who were part of the Opelousas population at that time.

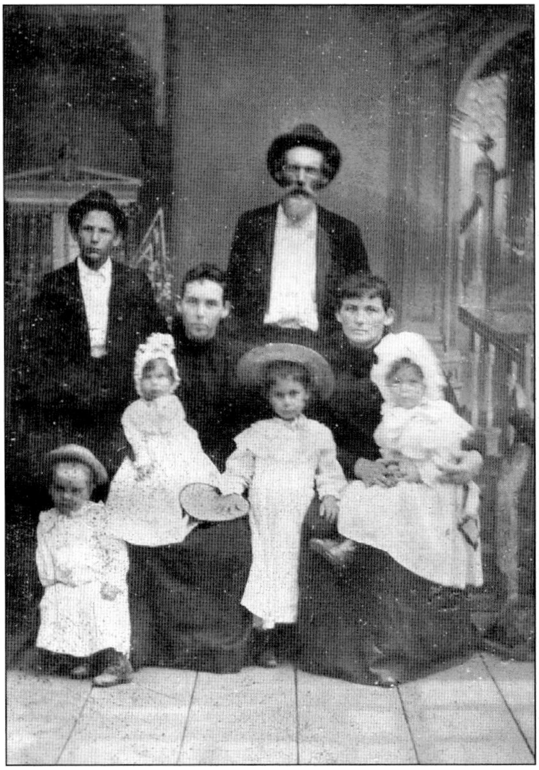

This tintype photograph shows an unidentified Opelousas family in the latter part of the 19th century. The people pictured here lived during an interesting time in Opelousas history. The Civil War was over, the town survived through the Reconstruction period in Louisiana, and by the time this picture was taken, Opelousas was on its way to becoming one of the most progressive towns in the state.

Many Louisiana veterans of the Civil War made a trip to Nashville, Tennessee, to attend a large, well-publicized reunion of Confederate veterans at the Tennessee Centennial and International Exposition, held June 22–24, 1897. Among those who attend were men from Opelousas and St. Landry Parish, including Dr. Ambrose "J.A." Derbanne, a traveling dentist who lived in Washington but also did work in Opelousas. Dr. Derbanne is the man with the long, white beard pictured in the center of this photograph. (Courtesy of Madeline and Thom Daly.)

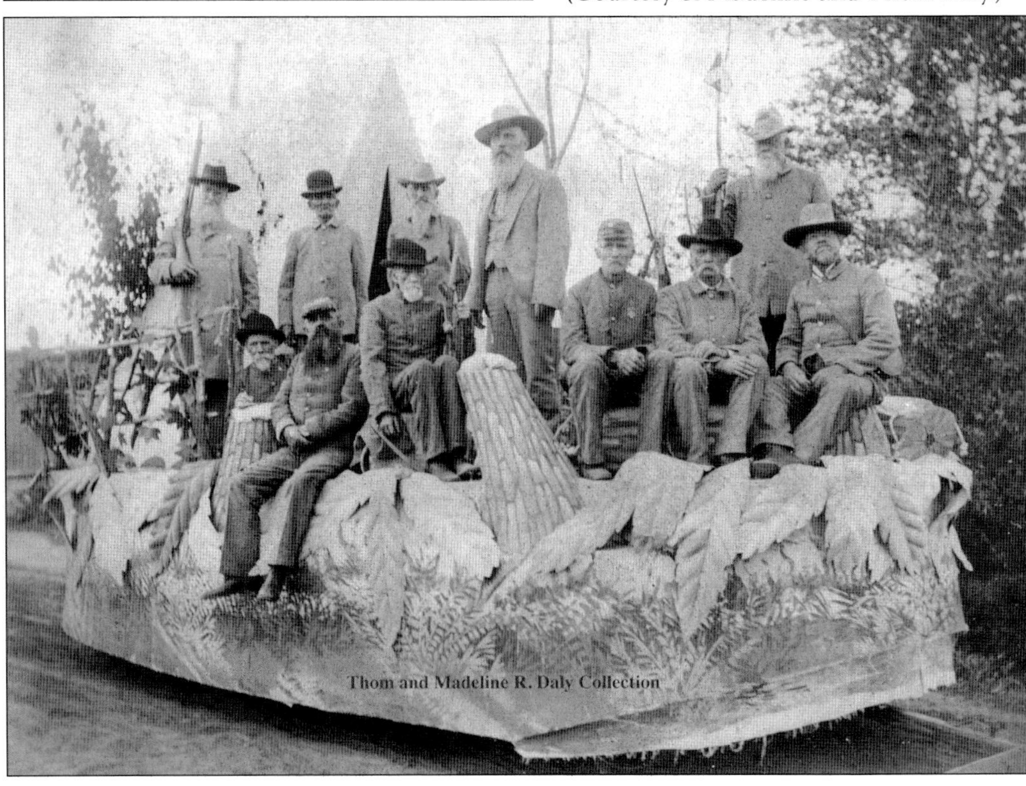

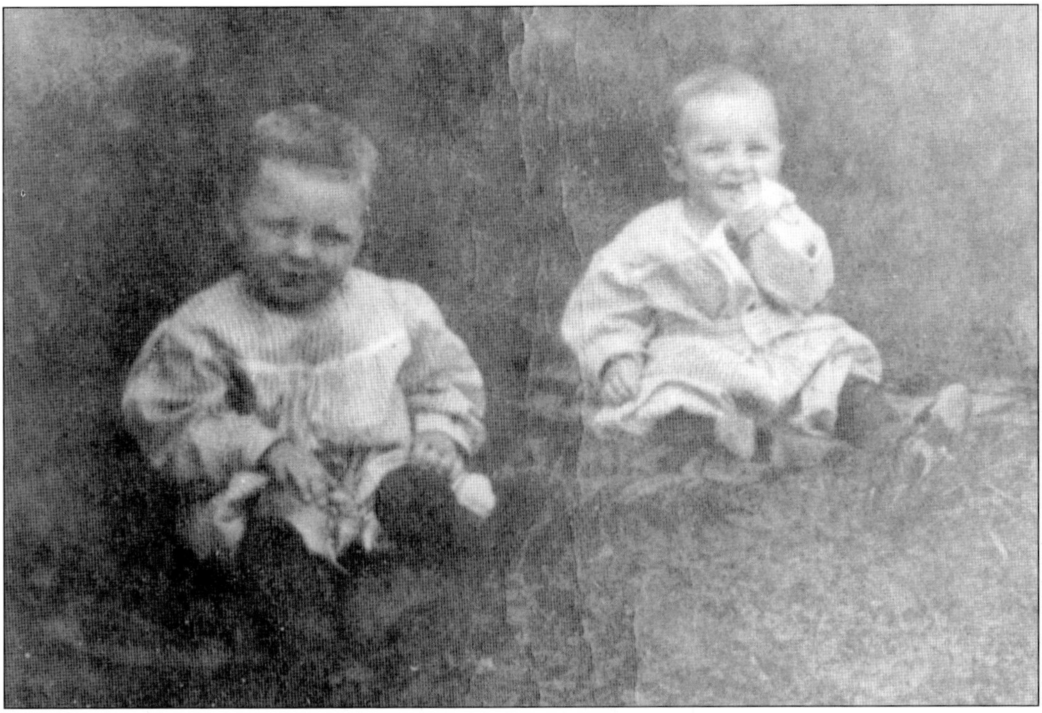

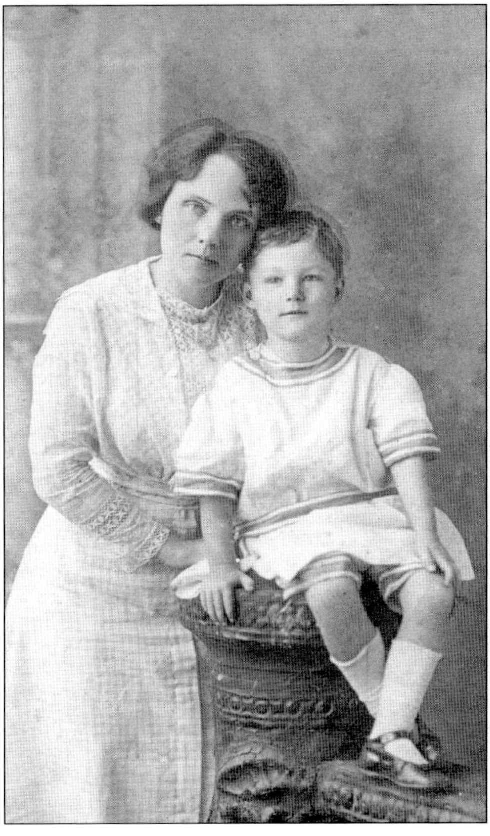

The Dunbar kidnapping took place in Opelousas in 1912 and dominated national news; the case would last until 1915. It involved the disappearance of Robert "Bobby" Dunbar, the four-year-old child of Clarence Percy and Lessie Dunbar. On August 23, 1912, during a family outing at Swayze Lake near Opelousas, Bobby disappeared. After a nationwide search, a young boy resembling the missing child was found in Mississippi. The Dunbars went there and claimed that boy as their child. However, a North Carolina woman argued the child was her son Bruce Anderson. A Louisiana judge decided that he was the Dunbar child. He returned to Opelousas and was raised as Bobby Dunbar. William Walters, the man with the boy in Mississippi, was arrested, charged with kidnapping, and tried in St. Landry Parish. He was found guilty, but the Supreme Court reversed that decision, and Walters went free. A century later, DNA proved the child was not actually Bobby Dunbar; however, that DNA did not prove he was positively Bruce Anderson. The above photograph shows Bobby Dunbar at left with his younger brother Alonzo on the lawn of their home on Main Street in early 1912. The picture at right is Bobby with mother Lessie Dunbar soon after he was returned to Opelousas.

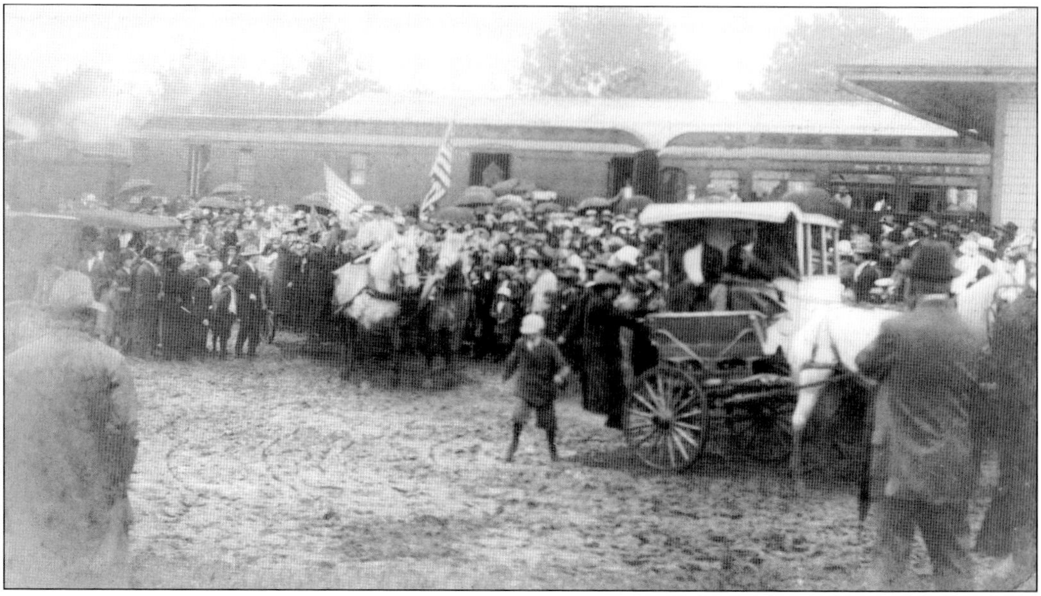

Thousands gathered at the Opelousas depot in 1913 to welcome young Bobby Dunbar back home to Opelousas. He was traveling from Mississippi with his parents, who went there to claim the boy that some thought was their missing son who vanished from Swayze Lake in 1912. The Dunbar family was welcomed with a community celebration when they arrived in Opelousas.

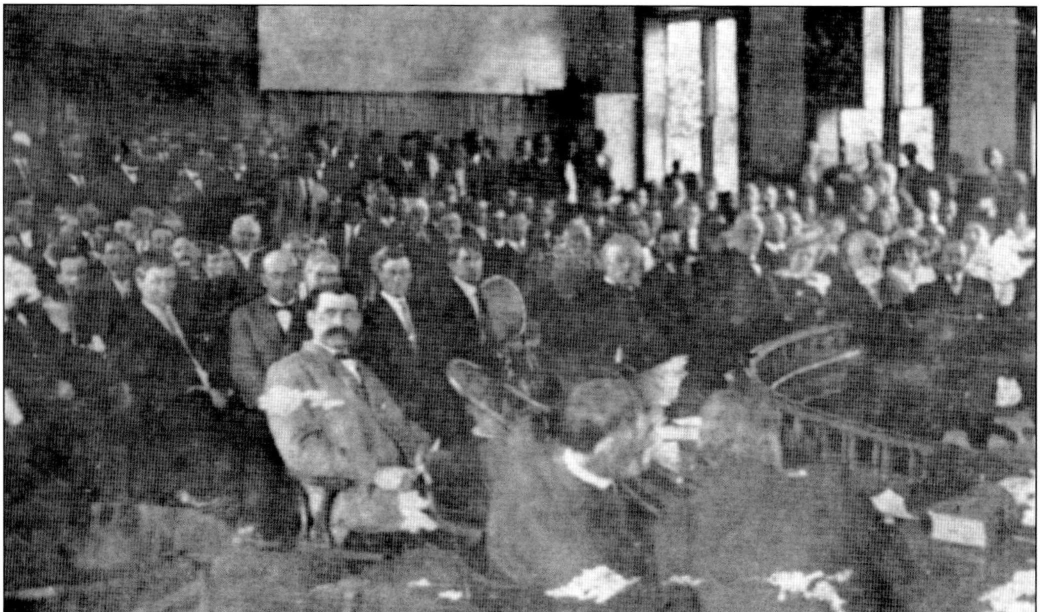

The St. Landry Parish courtroom was filled in April 1914 for the trial of William Walters, accused of kidnapping four-year-old Bobby Dunbar in August 1912. The trial and other areas in and around Opelousas were filmed in a movie later shown at the Princess Theater in Opelousas.

Yves Andrepont, son of Cleophas "Bob" Andrepont and Gondrine Mouille, was born near Opelousas in Plaisance. After several years as a cotton planter and cotton gin owner, he ran and was elected to the state legislature, serving from 1900 to 1904. He won the election for St. Landry Parish clerk of court in 1904, a position he held until 1912. He later became a newspaper publisher and remained an important part of the Opelousas community, where he was known as "Big Daddy." Yves Andrepont died on Monday, April 27, 1942, at the age of 72 at his home on East Grolee Street in Opelousas.

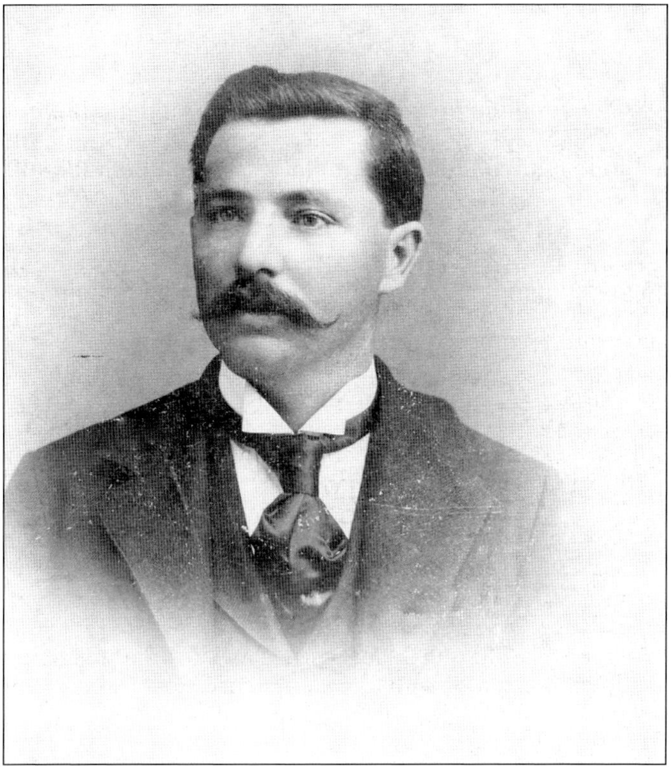

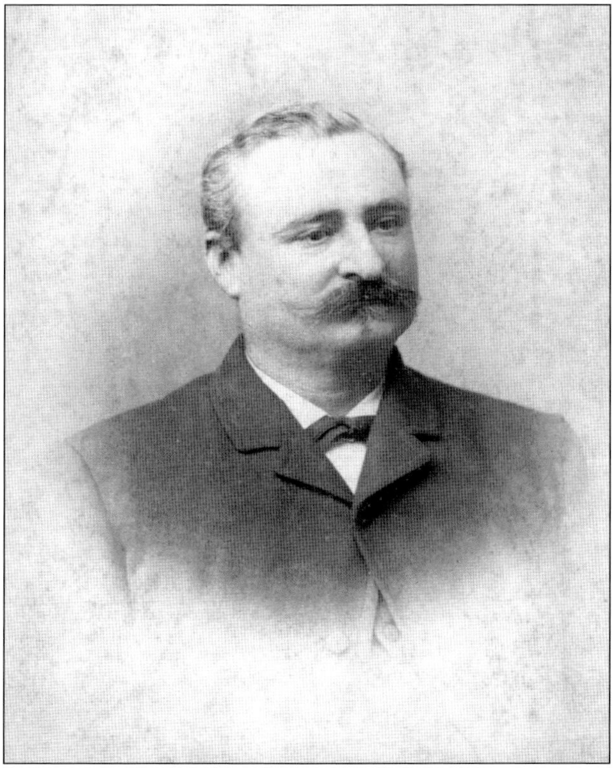

Charles Jackson Thompson (1850–1916), an Opelousas businessman who served as mayor of Opelousas and superintendent of education for St. Landry Parish, is pictured here in the early 1900s. He held the office of mayor from 1894 to 1898 and became superintendent in 1904, a position he held until his death in 1916. (Courtesy of Madeline and Thom Daly.)

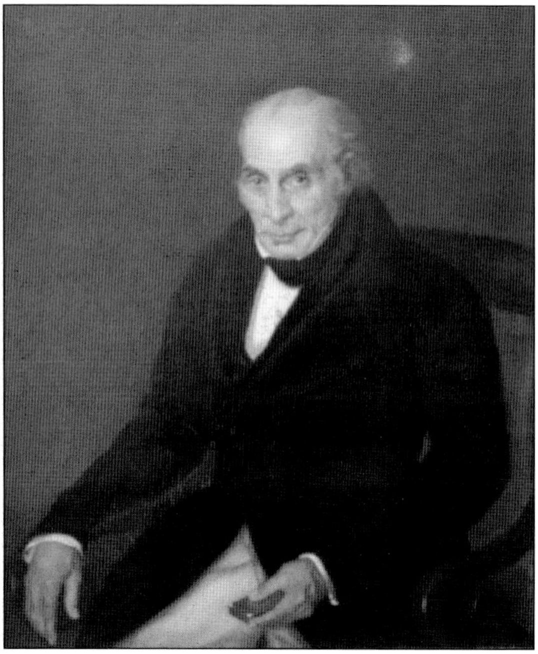

Martin Donato, shown in this portrait, the son of Donato Bello (1740–1787) and Marie Jeanne Tailliefert (1742–1833) was born in New Orleans on October 22, 1760. As a young mixed-race gentleman of African descent, Martin came to Opelousas where he became a large property owner and an independent money lender. He had several children with his wife, Marianne Duschene, and other children with another woman. Many of his descendants live in Opelousas and the St. Landry Parish area today. (Courtesy of Jeremy K. Simein.)

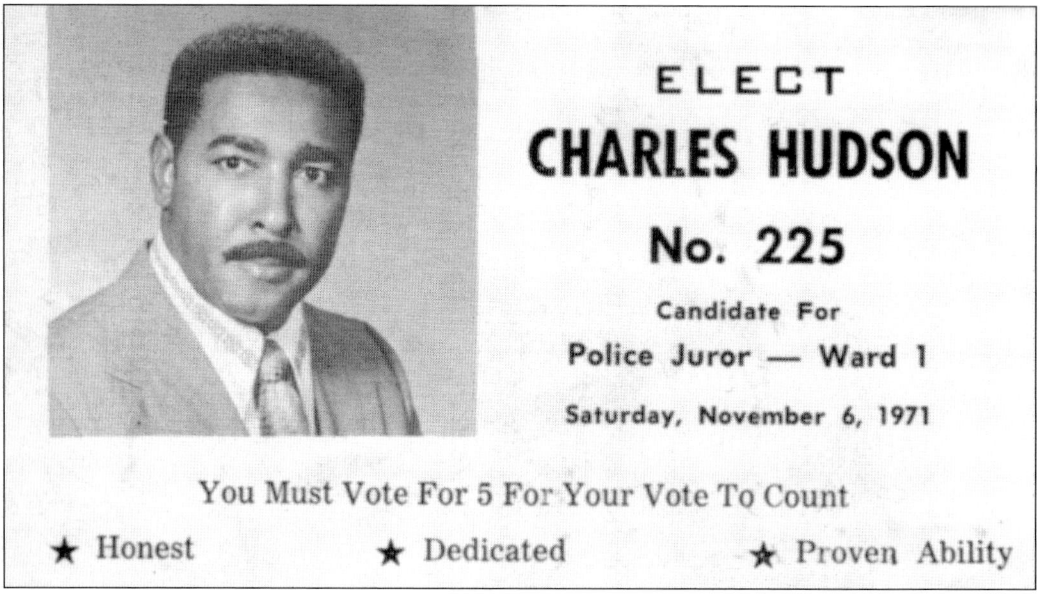

The first African American state representative from Opelousas was Dr. Charles "Doc" Hudson, who was elected in 1991. Doc Hudson was an educator and community leader in St. Landry Parish for nearly 50 years. He demonstrated his commitment to education by serving as a high school mathematics teacher for 10 years and later as the principal of two elementary schools. He was equally committed to public service and served his community as an elected official for nearly 30 years. First elected to the Opelousas City Council in 1974, he served three consecutive four-year terms before becoming deputy secretary for the Louisiana State Department of Transportation and Development from 1984 to 1988. Dr. Hudson was later elected to the Louisiana House of Representatives in 1991, where he served until his death in May 2004. Dr. Hudson is shown on the political card used when he ran for the St. Landry Parish Police Jury in 1971.

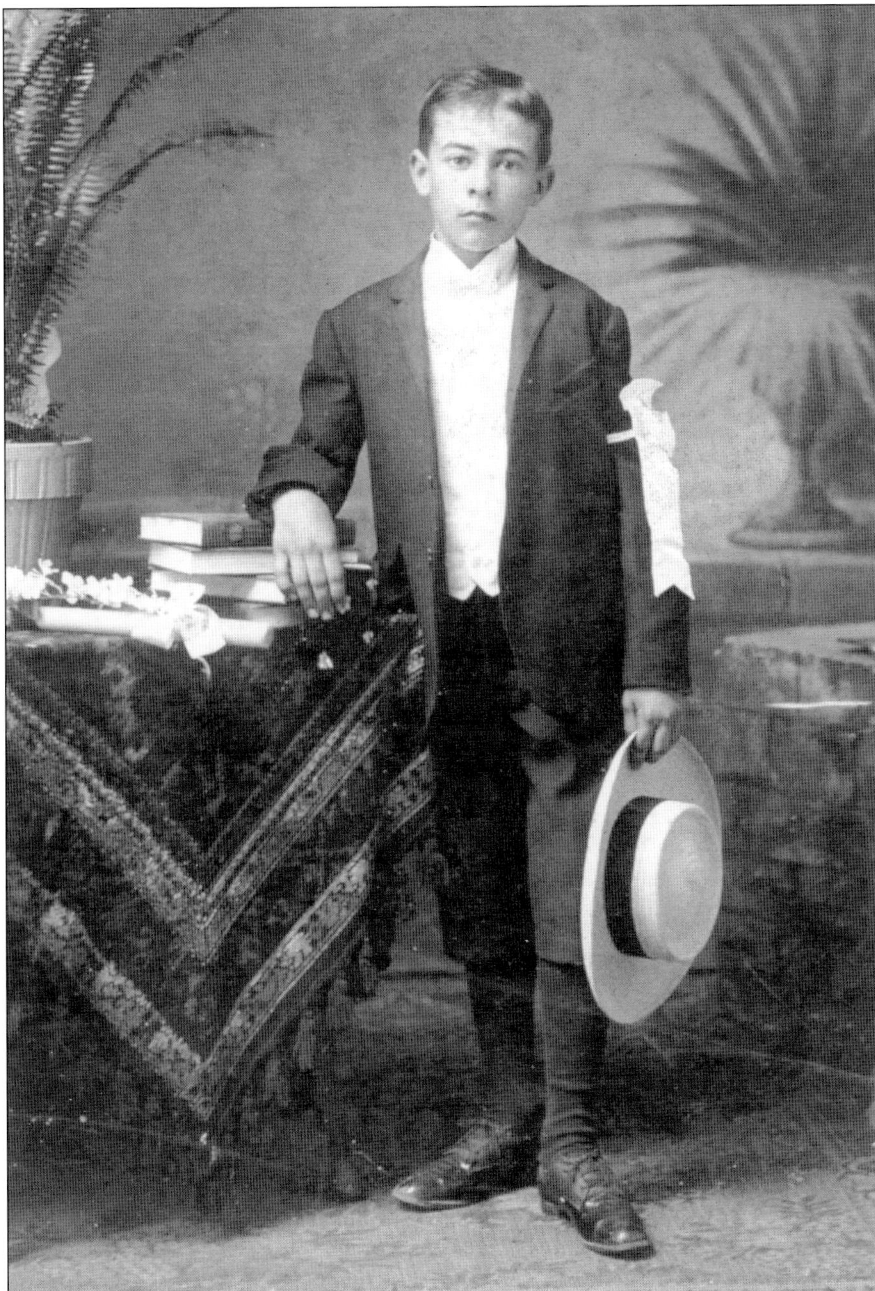

Born on December 22, 1893, Louis Ashton Close was the son of Antoine Close and Alice Lafond Close of Opelousas. A graduate of St. Landry High School, Ashton was a well-liked young man with a bright future working as an automobilist for the Russell Motor Car Company in New Orleans. On Saturday evening, October 18, 1913, he lost his life in an automobile accident in that town. The 19-year-old's body was returned to Opelousas the following day for funeral services held on Monday, October 15, with burial in the St. Landry Catholic Church Cemetery. In the 1940s, his remains were moved to Bellevue Memorial Park Cemetery, where he is buried next to his mother and father.

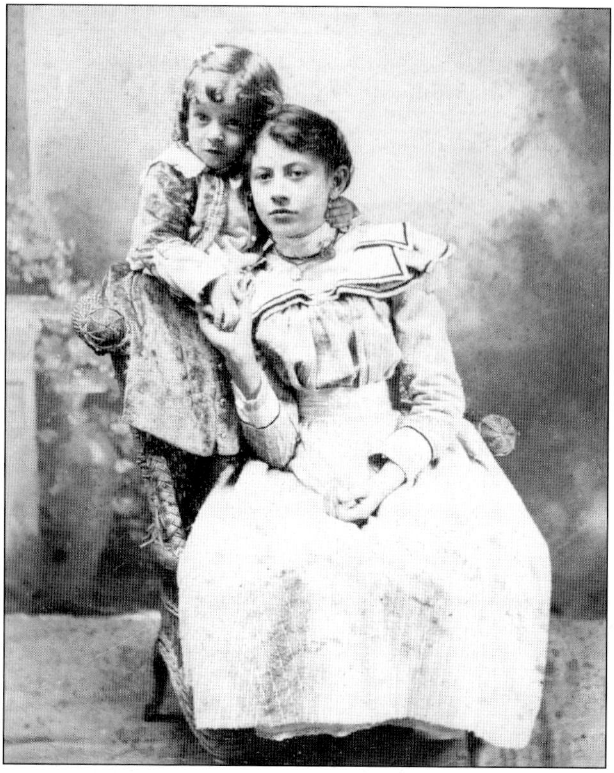

Clothilde Lassalle, the daughter of prominent Canadian-born Opelousas businessman Joseph Lassalle, is shown with a young unidentified child in the photograph at left from the late 1890s. Born on October 4, 1884, Clothilde never married and lived her entire life in Opelousas where she was a postal clerk for 42 years. Below, Clothilde is pictured with an unidentified gentleman at her family home in Opelousas in the early 1900s. She died on July 28, 1967. (Courtesy of Emile Ventre IV, Chris Ventre, and Jonathan Sebastien.)

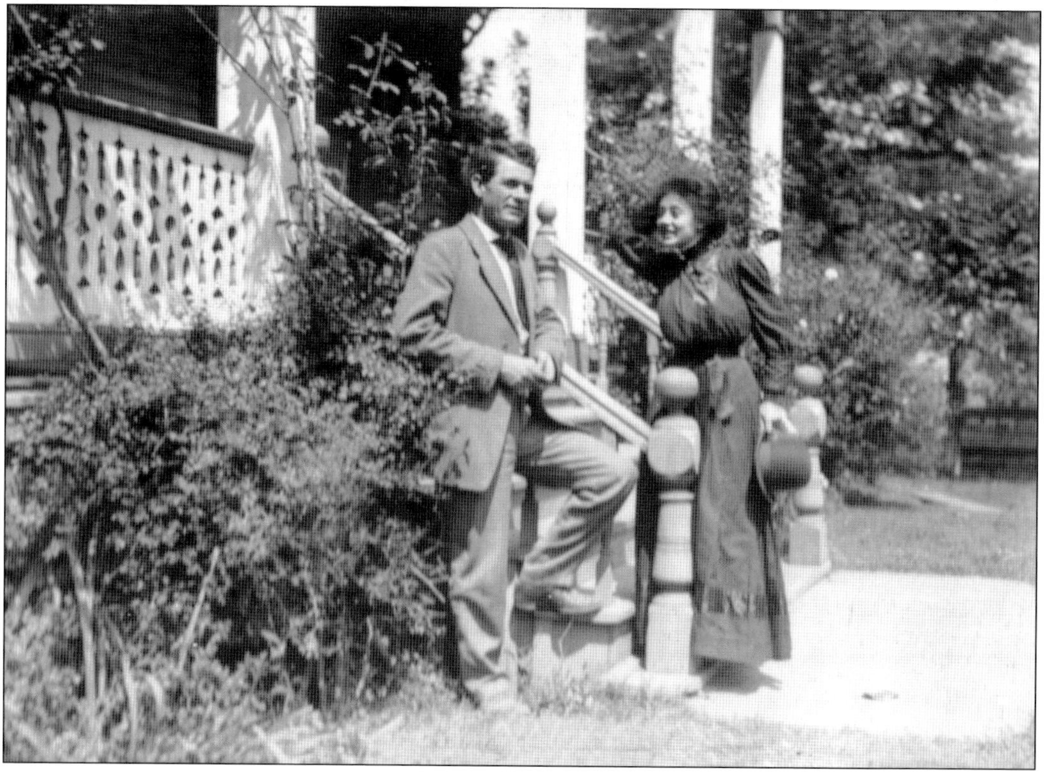

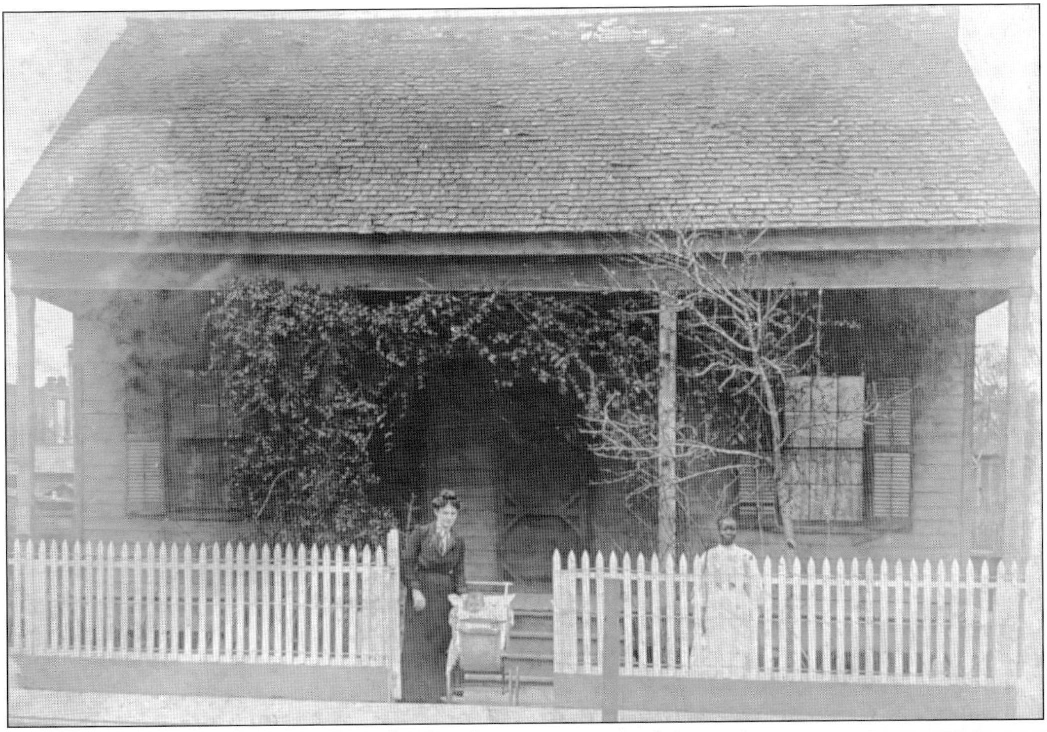

Marie Fannie Christman Bowden, the daughter of Antoine Christman (1830–1919) and Malvina Benguerel (1836–1884), was born in Opelousas on December 24, 1857. She married Thomas P. Bowden on June 15, 1881, at St. Landry Catholic Church. The couple had three children. Fannie lived over a hundred years and had an amazing memory, often telling stories of the Federal occupation of Opelousas during the Civil War. Following the death of her husband in 1900, Fannie lived with her daughter, also named Fannie, until her death on March 3, 1958. The above late-19th-century photograph shows Fannie with her son and an unidentified maid outside her parents' home on East Bellevue Street in Opelousas. (Courtesy of David Parnell.)

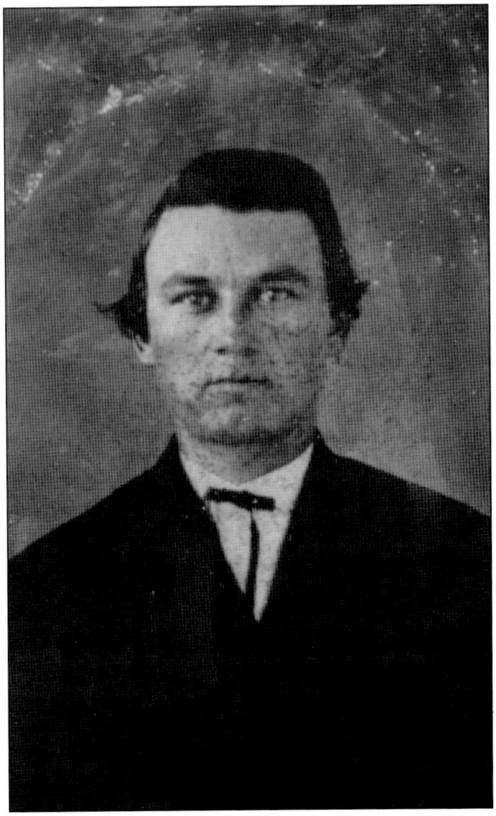

Robert Dunbar Sr., the son of Samuel W. Dunbar and Mary Ann Chandler, is pictured in this early-19th-century tintype. Robert, born in 1848 in East Feliciana, Louisiana, moved to the Opelousas area with his family prior to 1870. On April 23, 1872, he married Madeline King (1852–1930) and settled in the area just north of Opelousas, on the road to Washington, Louisiana. Robert died on January 27, 1932, in St. Landry Parish.

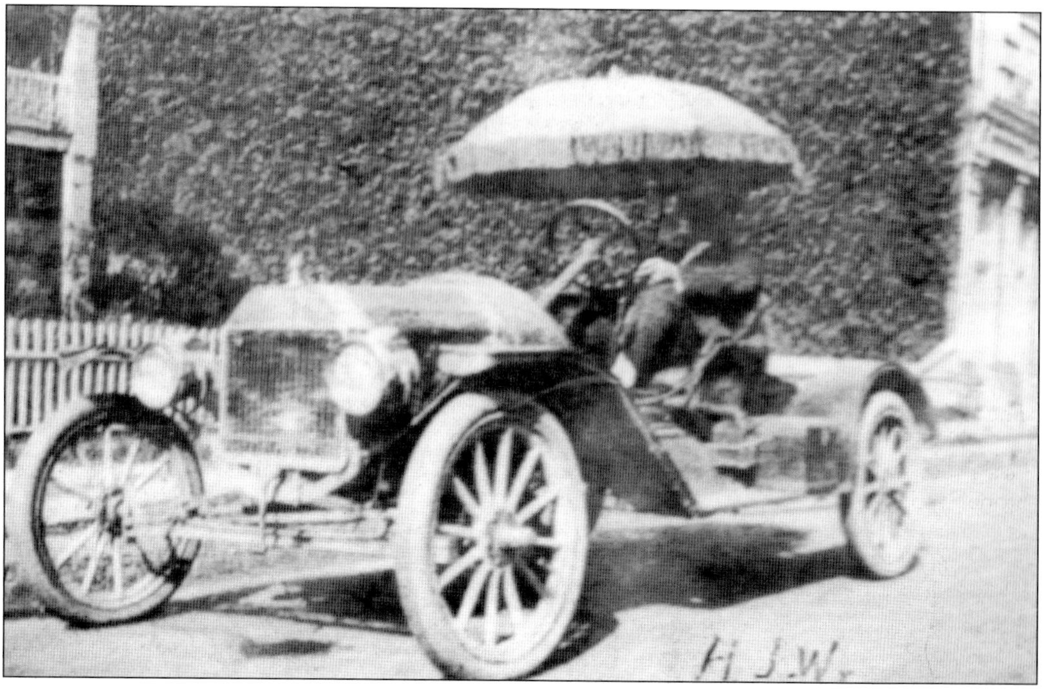

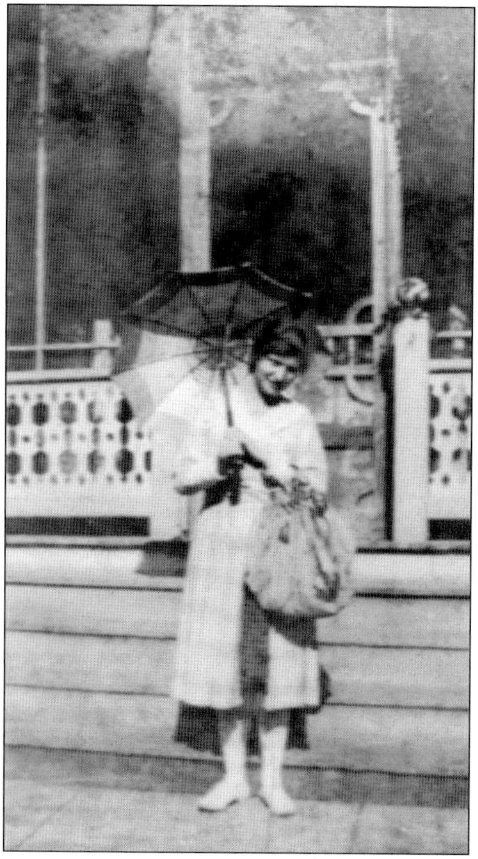

The first horseless carriage arrived in Opelousas at the turn of the 20th century when Allie Burton Pickett arrived from Wisconsin in his automobile to open the Bertha Telephone Company in town. The above photograph, taken over a decade later, shows local Opelousas businessman Harvey J. Wier in his Ford automobile as he rides by the Littell home on Bellevue Street around 1915. Wier, who was involved in the oil industry for many years, owned one of the early automobiles in Opelousas.

Lola Colosha, pictured at left, was well known in the Opelousas community during her lifetime. She stands in front of the home that was built for Leonce E. Littell and his wife, Elizabeth Gibbs Littell, on Bellevue Street in downtown Opelousas in the latter part of the 19th century. Colosha worked for several years as the ticket seller at the Princess Theater and later the Rex Theater on Landry Street. This home became the office for the Littell and Lawler Real Estate Company in 1903. In the 1920s, it was used for a while as the Opelousas Chamber of Commerce office. The Littell home was demolished in the mid-1950s so a drive-through window lane and the parking lot for Planters Trust and Savings Bank could occupy the property.

Located in Bellevue near Opelousas, Stonewood was built in 1900 for Dr. Lawrence H. Daly and his wife, Nourma Juliette Hockaday. The stones used in the construction were shipped directly from England. Pictured in their c. 1911–1912 Pratt-Elkhart touring car are the Dalys and one of their sons. The driver is unidentified. The house was later owned by Hal and Audrey Low Bramlett. Today, Stonewood is owned by the Jim Phillips family. (Courtesy of Madeline and Thom Daly.)

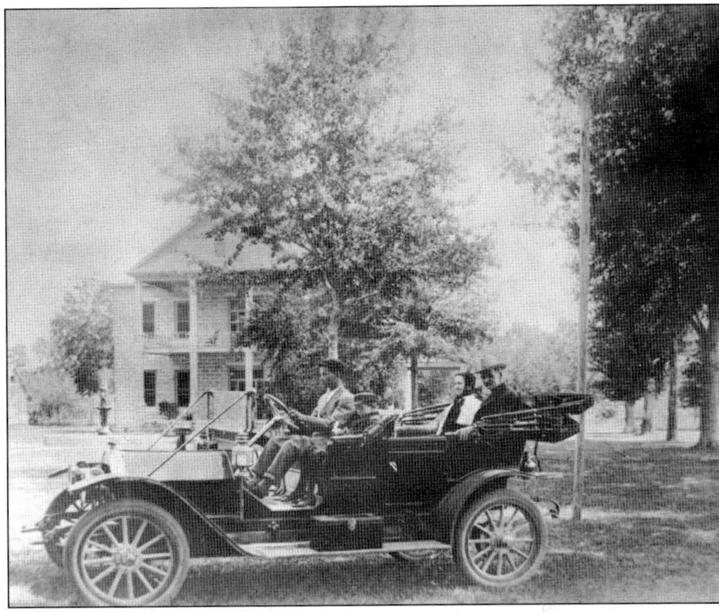

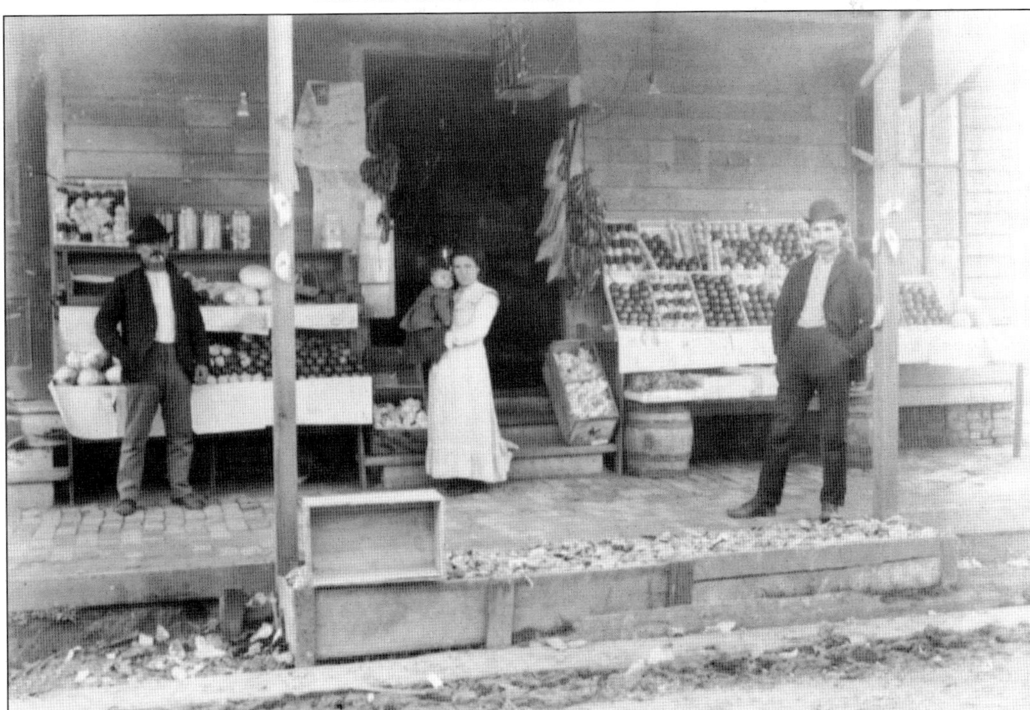

On September 29, 1883, the *St. Landry Democrat* newspaper announced Jacques Alphonse Ventre was building a roomy and substantial store building on the corner of North Court and Grolee Streets in Opelousas. He opened his business shortly after. The business, shown in this late-1800s photograph with unidentified family members, was relocated to another building but remained a family business. Although only food and home products were sold when it first opened, the Ventre store later became a mercantile and, even later, a dry goods and shoe store that operated until the 1950s. (Courtesy of Emile Ventre IV, Chris Ventre, and Jonathan Sebastien.)

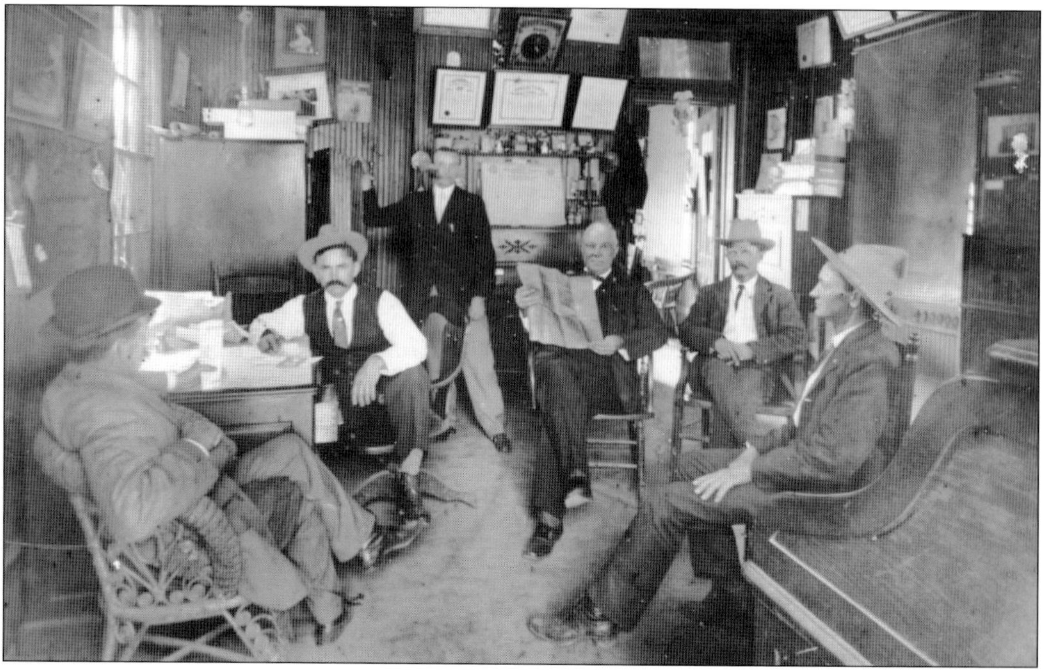

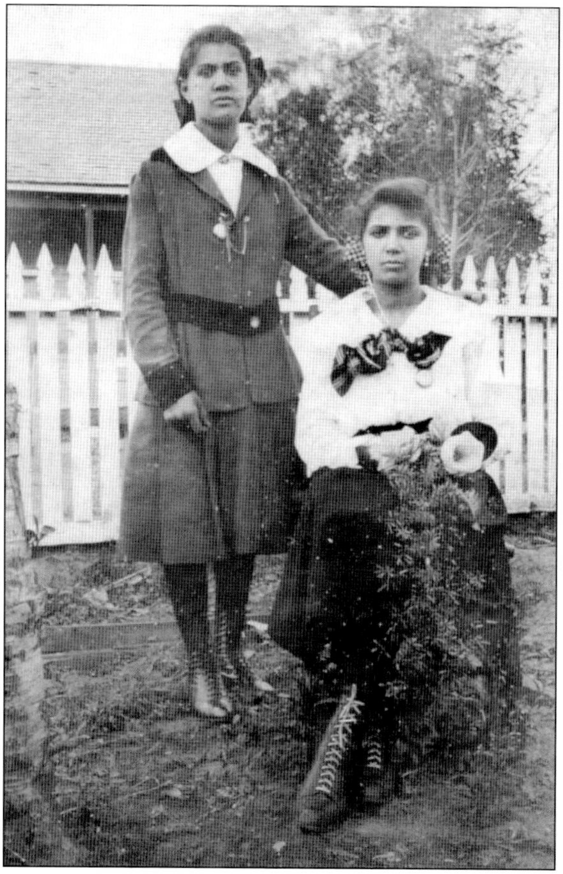

This photograph depicts a 1907 real estate deal being finalized in the office of C.P. Dunbar & Brother Real Estate Agency in Opelousas. At that time, Dr. W.E. Hawkins of Bayou Chicot sold 2,000 acres of pine lands in St. Landry Parish to the Crowell and Spencer Lumber Company of Alexandria, Louisiana, for $50,000. Pictured are, from left to right, Dr. W.E. Hawkins, C.P. Dunbar, Archie Dunbar, Henry "H.E." Estorge, Carl Woods, and Bass Taylor.

Anita and Ferdie Gills [Gales], pictured here, were daughters of Antoine Gales and Octavie Guidry. According to genealogist Alex Da'Paul Lee, Anita married Samuel Coco, and Ferdie married Ernest Loither Chachere Jr. These sisters are descendants of Pierre Guidry of Acadia and Martin Donato Bello, a wealthy free man of color. (Courtesy of Alex Da'Paul Lee.)

Pictured at left in this photograph is Frank Daly, the son of Dr. Lawrence and Nourma Daly, with his fiancée, Ruth Thompson, enjoying an outing around 1916. Ruth was the daughter of Lelia Lott Randall and C.J. "Jack" Thompson, who was a former mayor Opelousas and served as superintendent of St. Landry Parish schools for many years. The popular Opelousas couple were married on September 14, 1916, in Gulf Port, Mississippi. They were the parents of Frank Truman Daly, who owned and operated Daly Motor Company in Opelousas for many years. (Courtesy of Madeline and Thom Daly.)

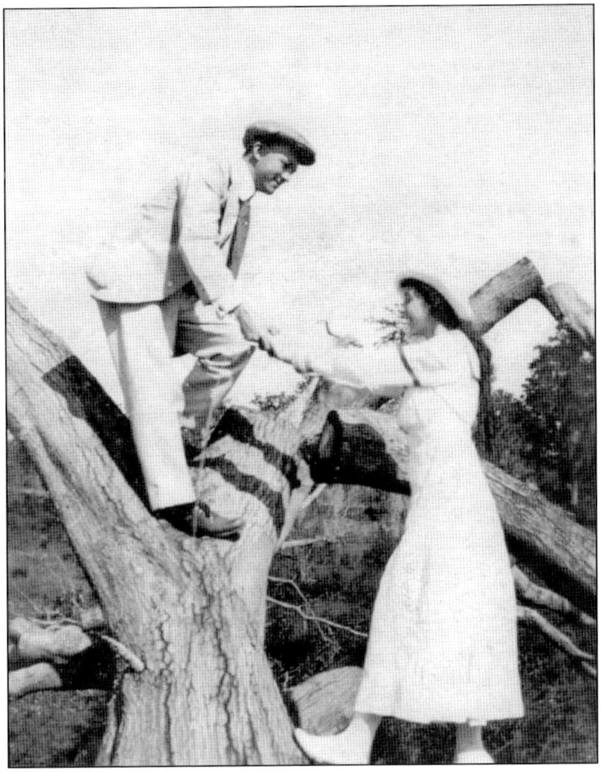

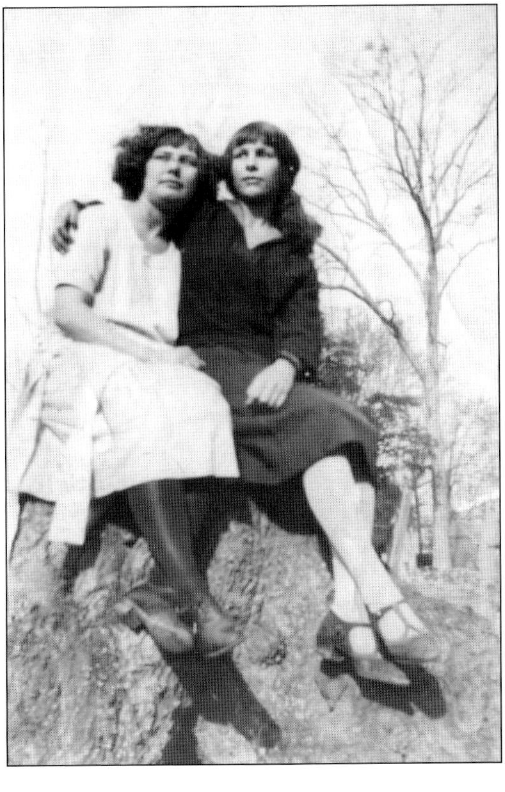

Pearl Prather (left) is shown with her friend Mildred Kingsbury (right) on the grounds of Opelousas High School in 1924. Following her graduation from high school, Mildred Kingsbury was crowned the first Miss Louisiana at the pageant held in New Orleans in 1931. She later married Gantt Nicholson of Washington. She owned the Nicholson House of History in that historic town where she lived until her death in 2001.

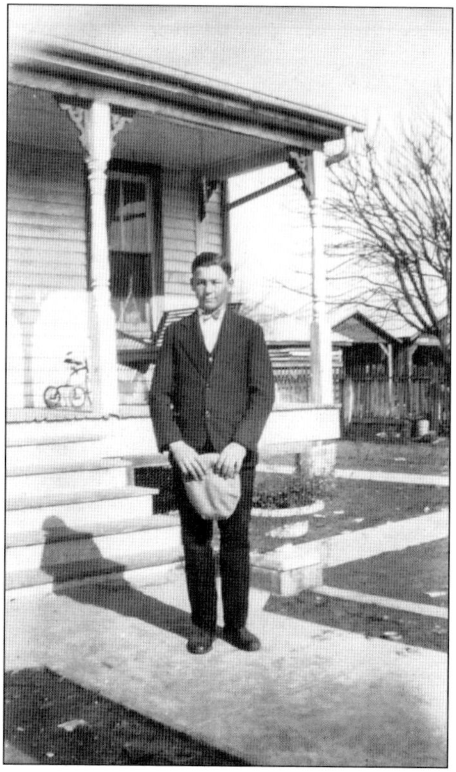

Joseph Verbis Lafleur (1912–1944) is shown in front of his sister's home on West Grolee Street in Opelousas around 1927. The son of Valentine Lafleur and Agatha Dupre Lafleur, young Verbis left Opelousas about that time to begin his studies to become a Catholic priest at St. Joseph's Minor Seminary in St Benedict, Louisiana. He was ordained on April 2, 1938, and celebrated his first mass on April 5 at St. Landry Catholic Church in Opelousas. In 1941, he became a chaplain in the US Army Air Corps, was captured by the Japanese a year later, and held as a prisoner of war until he was killed on September 7, 1944. Father Lafleur, a hero of World War II, was designated a Servant of God in 2021, on the path to possible beatification and canonization.

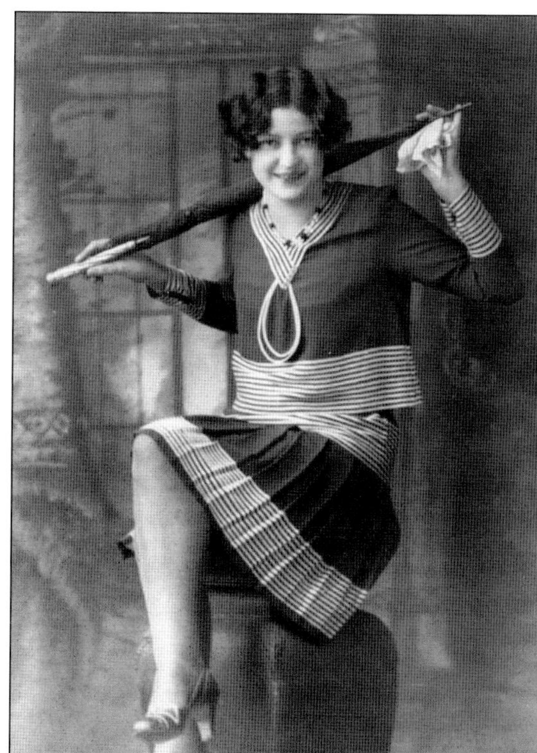

Edna Lafleur, the second child of Agatha Dupre Lafleur and Valentine Lafleur, was born in Ville Platte, Louisiana, on December 10, 1905, and moved with her mother and siblings to Opelousas in 1925–1926. On October 12, 1941, she married Baldwin Hunter Delery. Edna was a registered nurse who served the New Orleans area at Hotel Dieu Hospital for many years. She was well versed in history and genealogy and spent her life studying the history of the Lafleur and Dupre families of Louisiana. She also devoted her life to keeping the memory of her younger brother, Servant of God Rev. Joseph Verbis Lafleur, alive, writing two books about his life. She died on February 21, 1993.

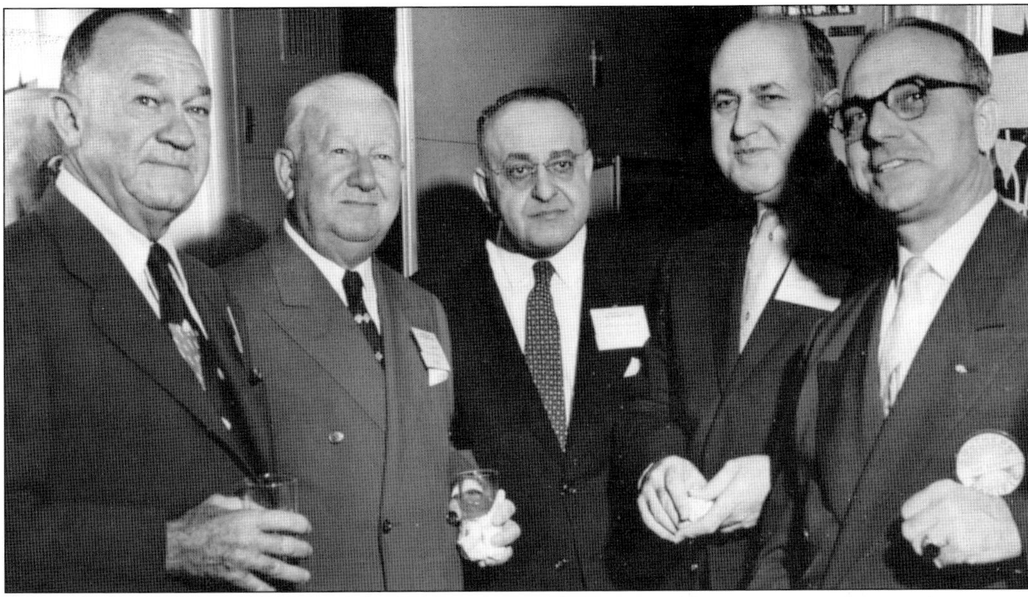

A group of Opelousas business leaders gathered for a social hour at an event in downtown Opelousas was a familiar sight during this period in the history of the town. Pictured enjoying the evening event during the 1950s are, from left to right, Frank Truman Daly, president of Daly Motors; Lawrence J. "Teco" Larcade, president of Planter's Trust and Savings Bank; Anthony "Tony" Abdalla, owner of Abdalla's Department Store; Jake Abdalla, owner of Abdalla Furniture Store; and Sam ? with South Pacific Railroad. (Courtesy of Madeline and Thom Daly.)

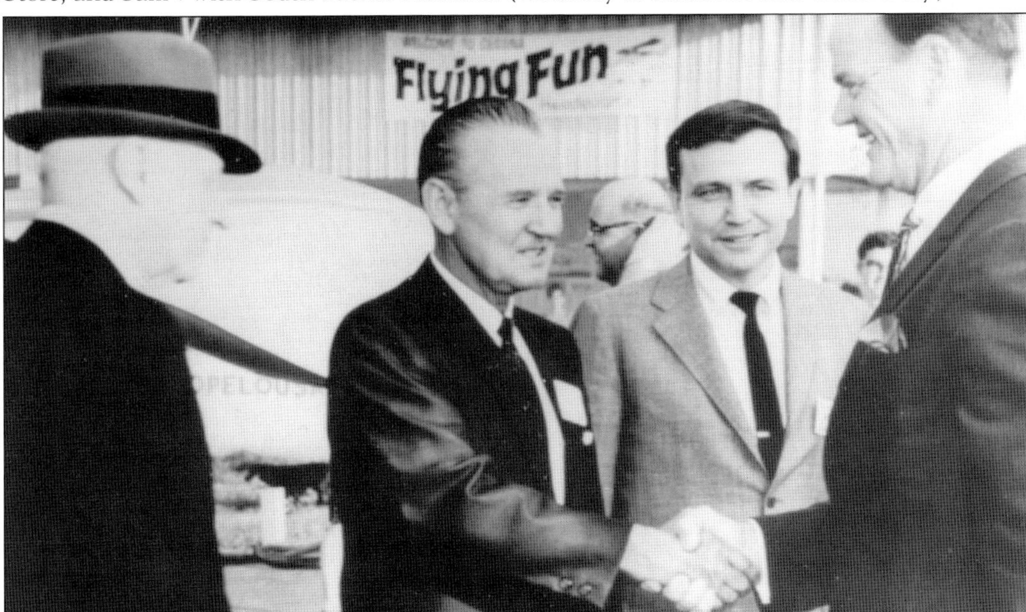

Mayor Wilfred Cortez, in the center of this photograph, welcomes radio personality Paul Harvey to Opelousas on November 21, 1966. Cortez served as mayor of Opelousas from 1966 to 1974. Paul Harvey was in town to speak at the annual Opelousas Chamber of Commerce banquet held that evening. Also part of the welcoming committee was W.E. Jones, owner of KSLO Radio, pictured at left, and Chamber of Commerce president John Shaw, pictured to the right of Cortez.

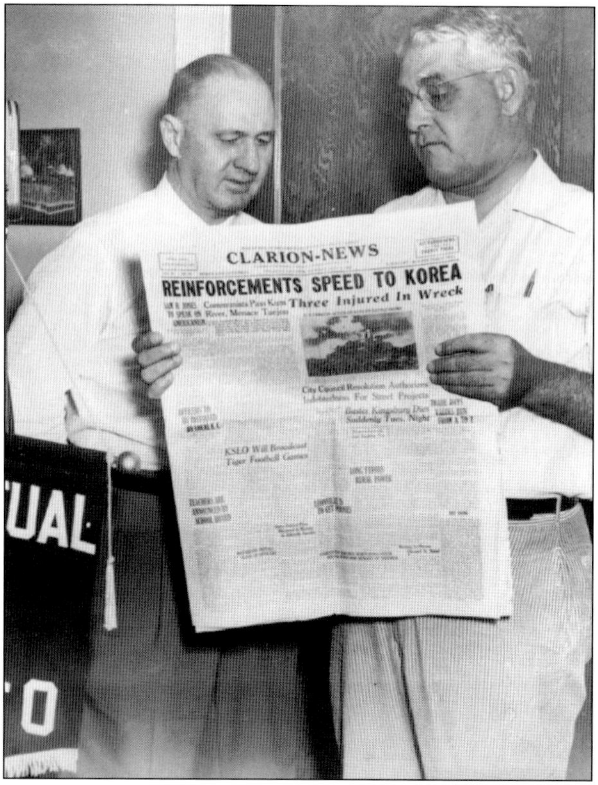

On September 1, 1947, W. Eugene Jones started KSLO, the first radio station in Opelousas, in a new brick building on North Court Street. In this photograph, Jones looks over the July 13, 1950, edition of the *Clarion-News* in Opelousas. Holding the newspaper is A.B. Reed Sr., the owner of the *Clarion-News*.

Johnny Wright with KSLO Radio interviews Opelousas business owner Anthony "Tony" Abdalla for an event during the 1950s while Mayor Percy LeDoux looks on. Johnny Wright, whose given name was Lloyd Wandell Allegood (1929–2005), was the general manager and part owner of the radio station. Known as the voice of the Opelousas area, he was trusted and beloved by all who listened to his broadcasts on KSLO Radio for over 50 years. He died in Opelousas on July 25, 2005.

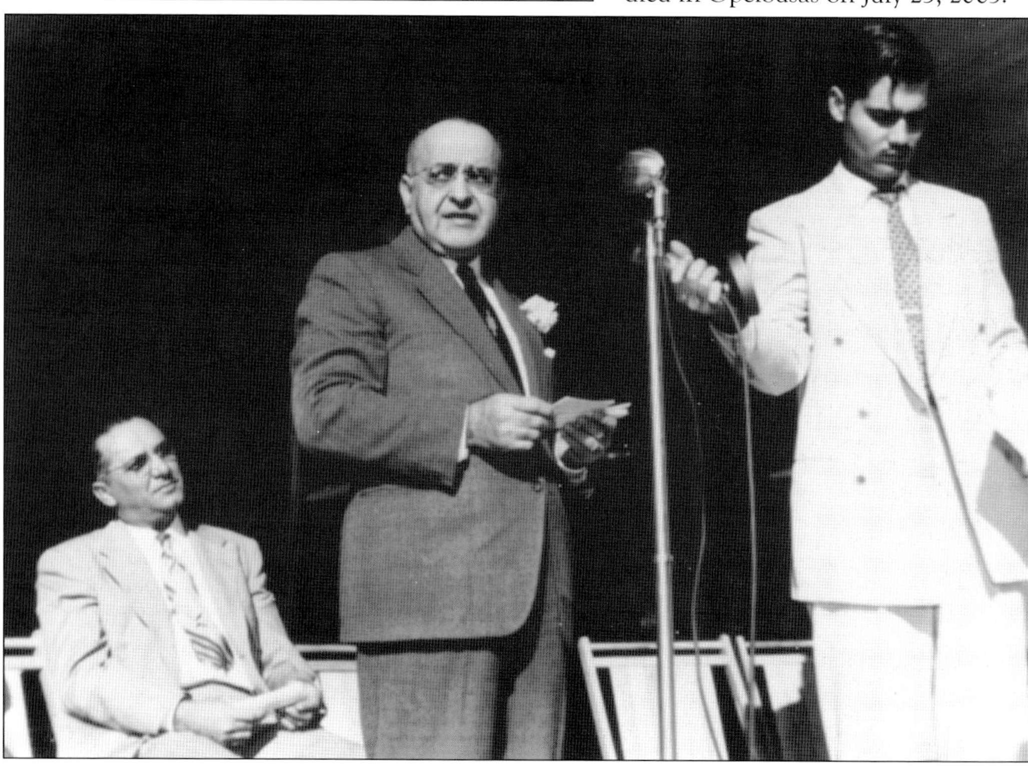

First organized as the Opelousas Junior Chamber of Commerce in 1944, the organization later became the Opelousas Jaycees. That organization, along with its sister group, the Jaycee Jaynes, served the Opelousas community for about five decades. Pictured in this June 1969 photograph are Frank Primeaux, newly elected president of the Opelousas Jaycees, and Carola Lillie Andrepont (now Hartley), recording secretary of the Opelousas Jaycee Jaynes. Each received an award as outstanding Jaycee and Jaycee Jayne for their work with the organization in 1968–1969.

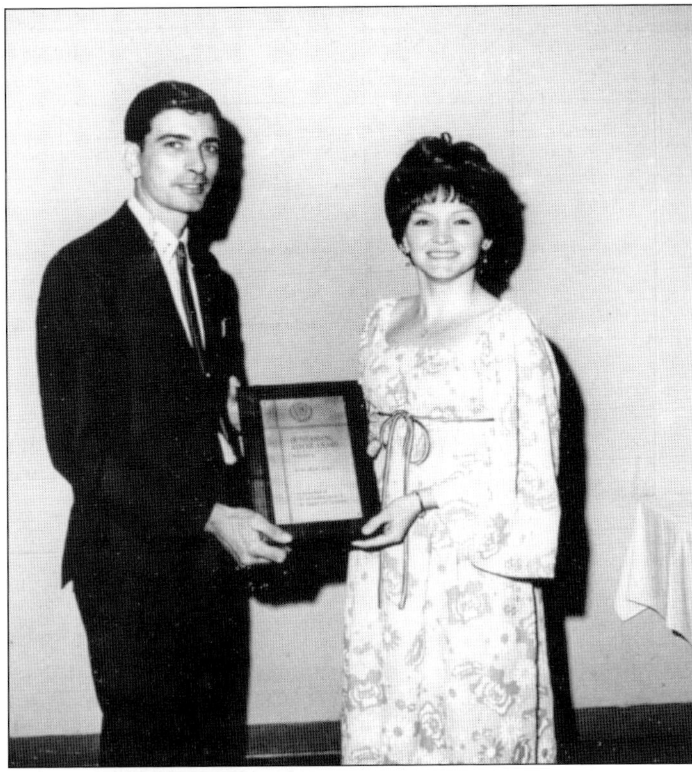

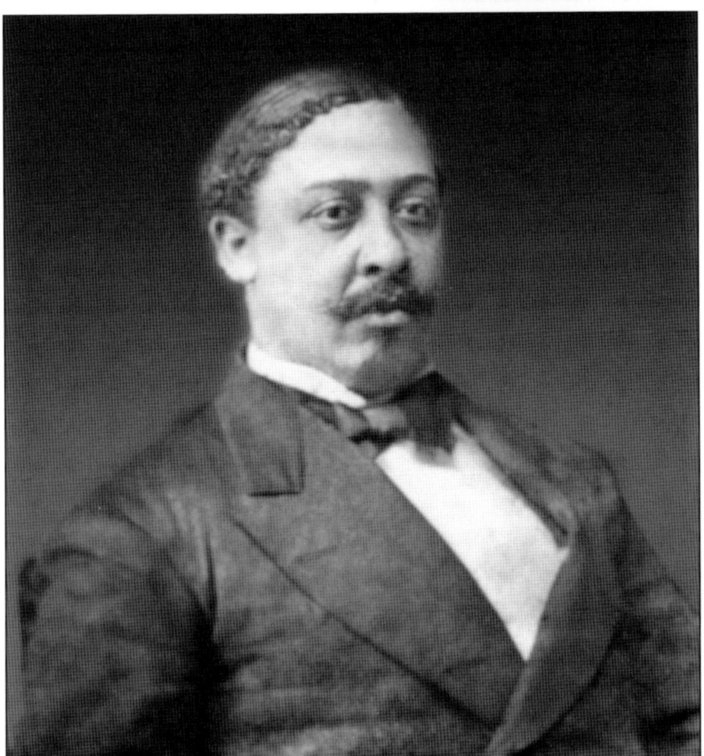

The Opelousas community is proud of its citizens who work hard and achieve great things during their lifetimes. Charles Edmund Nash (1844–1913), who was born in Opelousas, became the first African American US congressman from Louisiana in 1870. He was elected to Congress during the period of Reconstruction.

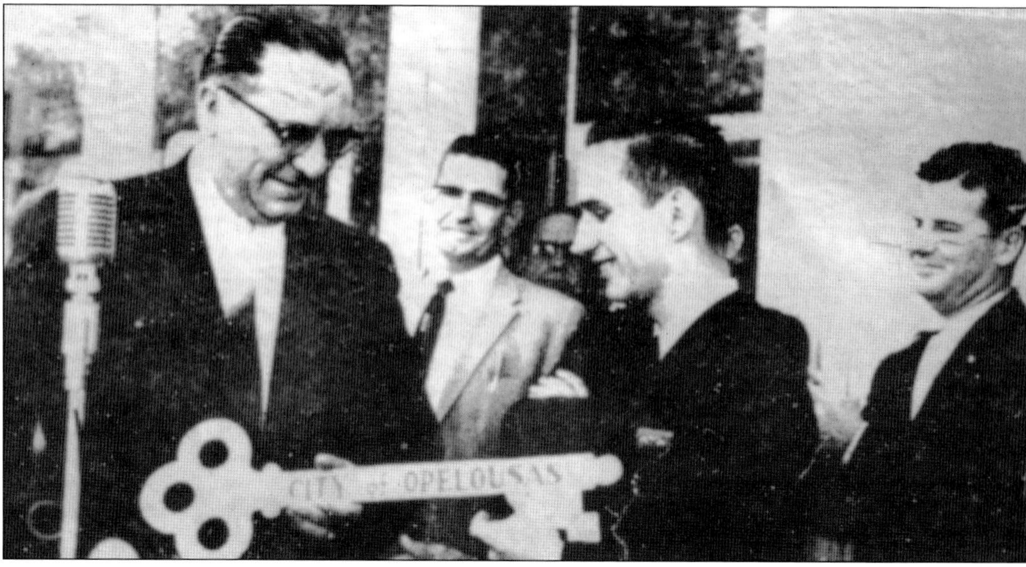

Often the people of Opelousas come together to celebrate citizens who have brought honor to the community. In the above photograph, nationally known swamp pop music artist Rodney "Rod" Bernard is honored during "Rod Bernard Day" on Friday, March 6, 1959, when he returned from a three-week radio and television tour of the eastern states. That tour included an appearance on the popular television show *American Bandstand* hosted by Dick Clark, where he sang his hit "This Should Go On Forever." Pictured at left in the photograph is Mayor Percy LeDoux who presented Bernard with a key to the city. Between the two are Harvey Gardiner (center left) and J.A. Allen (center right). In the photograph below, Remi Prudhomme addresses the large crowd that gathered on the St. Landry Parish Courthouse Square to welcome him back to Opelousas on February 27, 1965. Prudhomme, who was a star football player for Opelousas High School and Louisiana State University, was honored as the first from Opelousas to be selected as an All-American football player.

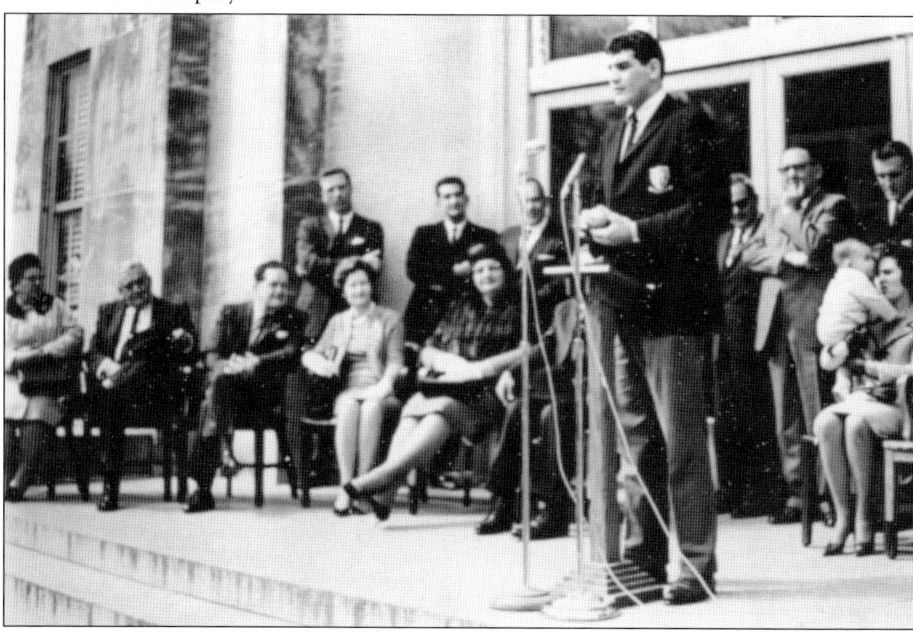

Opelousas native Rodney "Rod" Milburn, a track star at J.S. Clark High School and Southern University in Baton Rouge, dominated the 110-meter hurdles during the 1970s. He tied the world record three times and won the gold medal at the 1972 Summer Olympics in Munich, Germany. He received many honors over his career, including the 1971 and 1973 James J. Corbett Memorial Award. He was elected to the Louisiana Sports Hall of Fame in 1988 and the National Track and Field Hall of Fame in 1993. This photograph shows Milburn on the ladder during the naming of Rodney Milburn Boulevard in North City Park on July 3, 1992. With him are Opelousas city councilmen Walter Richards, left, and Mike Thibodeaux, right. Milburn died on November 11, 1997, in a work-related accident in Baton Rouge, Louisiana. (Courtesy of Mike Thibodeaux.)

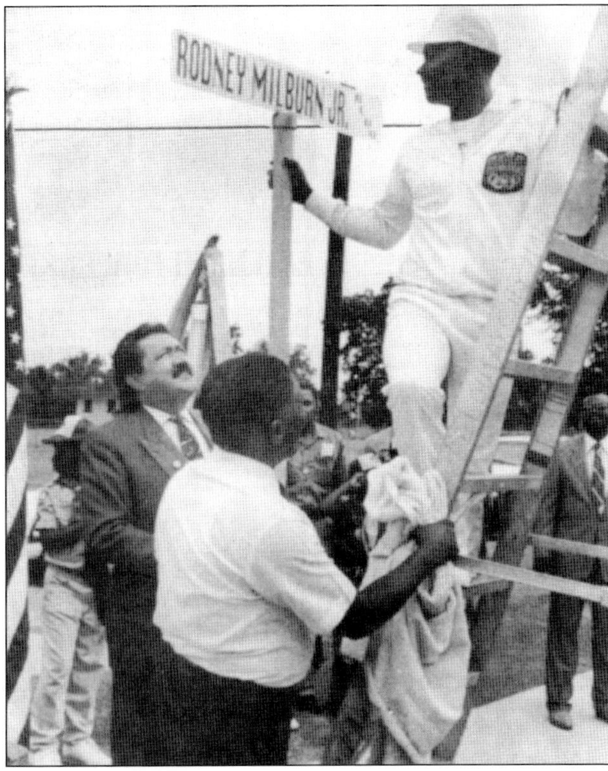

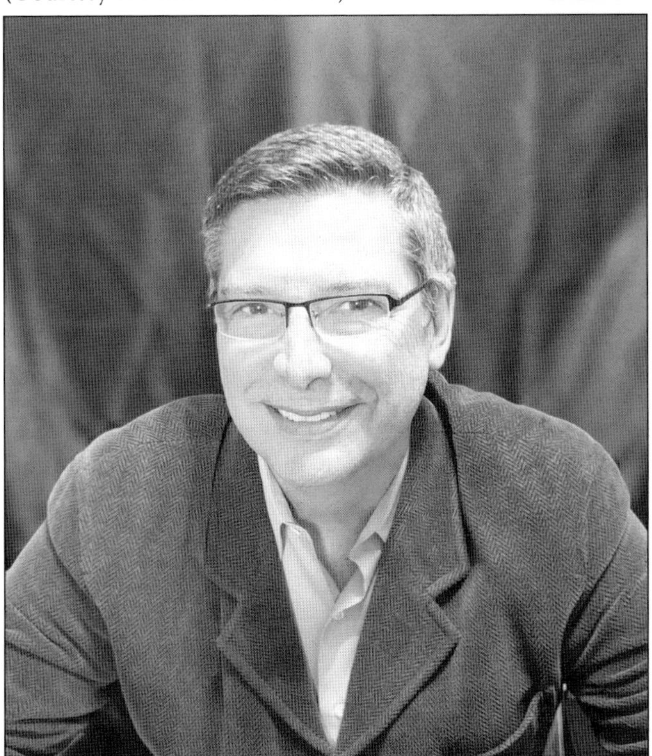

The son of John Bradley and Virval Fontenot, John Ed Bradley was born in Opelousas in 1958. He played football for Opelousas High School and Louisiana State University (LSU), where he was a starting center in the late 1970s. He received his bachelor of arts from LSU in 1980. Bradley is the author of several novels, a memoir, and other written works for *Esquire*, *Sports Illustrated*, GQ, *Louisiana Life*, and *Play* magazines. Early in his career as a reporter for the *Washington Post*, he was nominated for a Pulitzer Prize. (Courtesy of John Ed Bradley.)

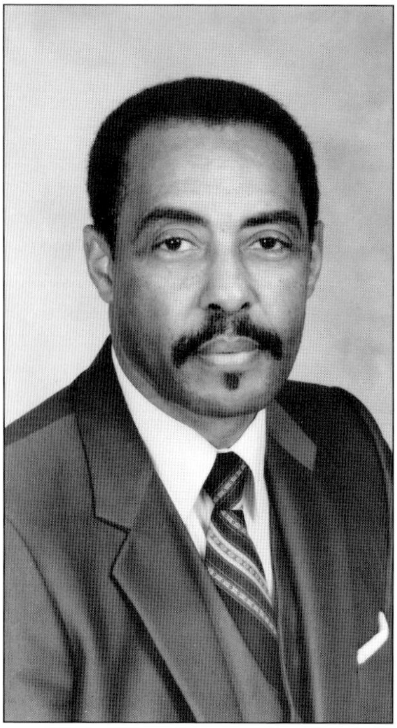

The year 1986 was a historic one in Opelousas. In November, the city election was held with historic results when John Wilfred Joseph (1933–2017) was elected mayor of Opelousas. Joseph, the son of Rev. Adam Joseph and Julia Lee Jones, was born in Plaisance, Louisiana, and later moved with his family to Opelousas. He graduated with honors from St. Landry Training School in 1951 and furthered his education at Leland College, Southern University, University of Southwestern Louisiana, Louisiana State University, and Clark Atlanta University. He married Cecile Catherine Slaughter in 1955; the couple had eight children. He worked for the St. Landry Parish school system for 32 years serving as teacher, coach, guidance counselor, assistant principal, principal, supervisor, and director of federal programs. Following his retirement, he ran for mayor and won the election in November 1986. Joseph was reelected to a second term in 1990 and served until 1994 when he retired. Mayor Joseph is pictured at left in the 1980s. The photograph below shows the mayor with some of his administration in the early 1990s. From left to right are (seated) Cam Leach, Mayor John W. Joseph, and Richard Millspaugh; (standing) Leroy Payne, Mike Thibodeaux, Louis Butler, Dale Pefferkorn, Charlie McKinney, and Ceasar Veazie.

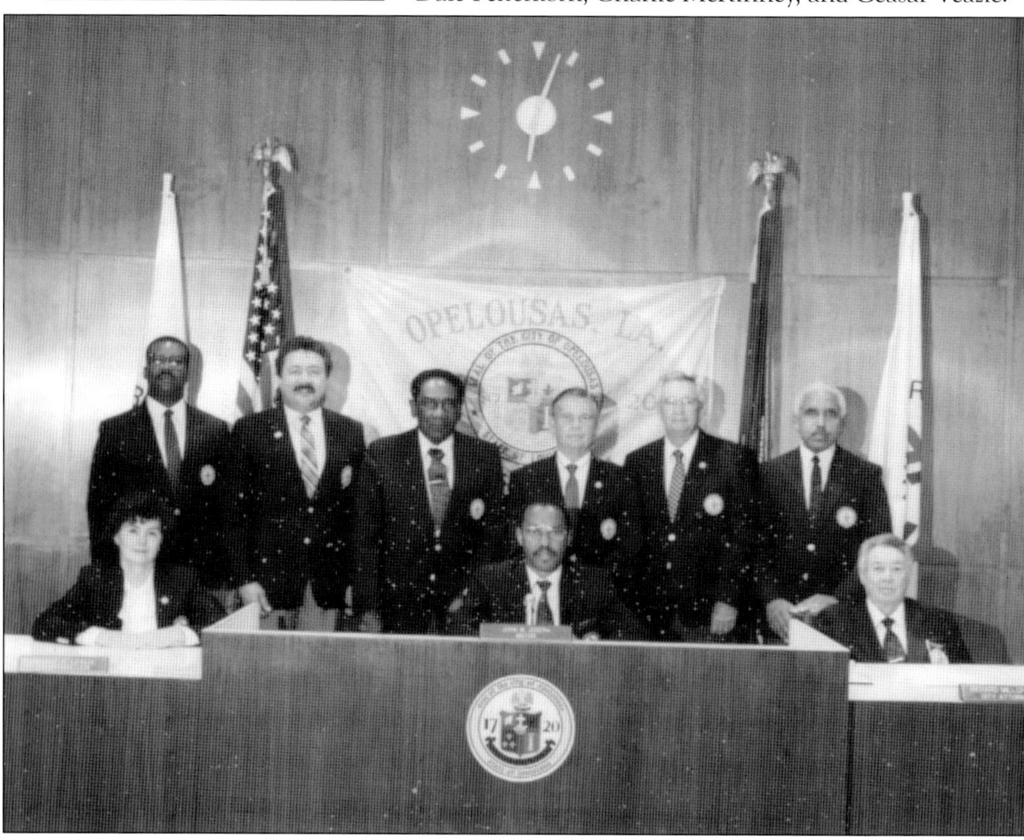

Three

EVENTS AND ACTIVITIES

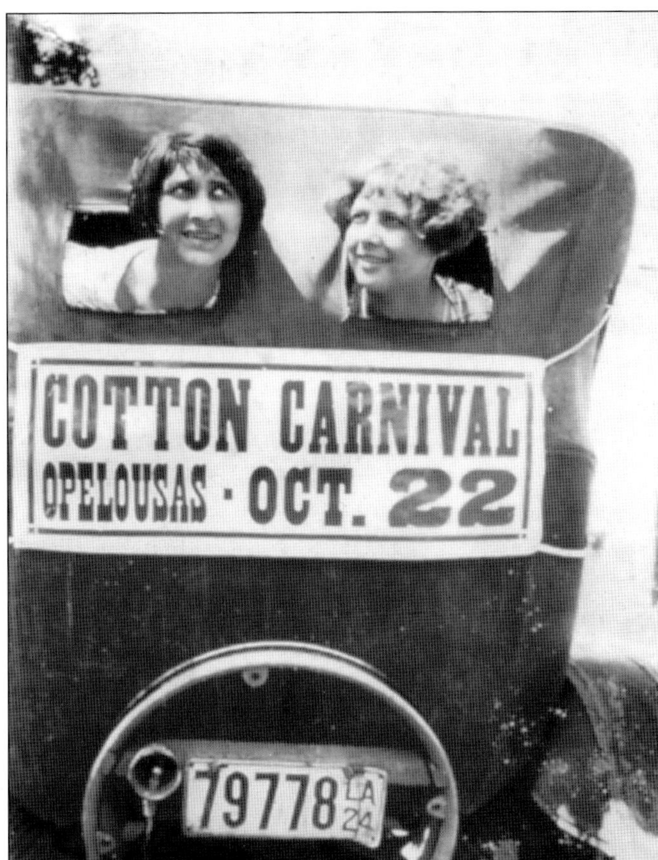

Fairs, festivals, events, and activities made Opelousas the place to be for fun and entertainment. From its very beginnings over two centuries ago, the town has been known for its Southern hospitality and joie de vivre (the joy of living). Over the years, many fairs, festivals, and events helped entertain the town and its visitors, including the Cotton Carnival, an annual event from 1922 to 1924. The photograph at right advertises the 1924 Cotton Carnival.

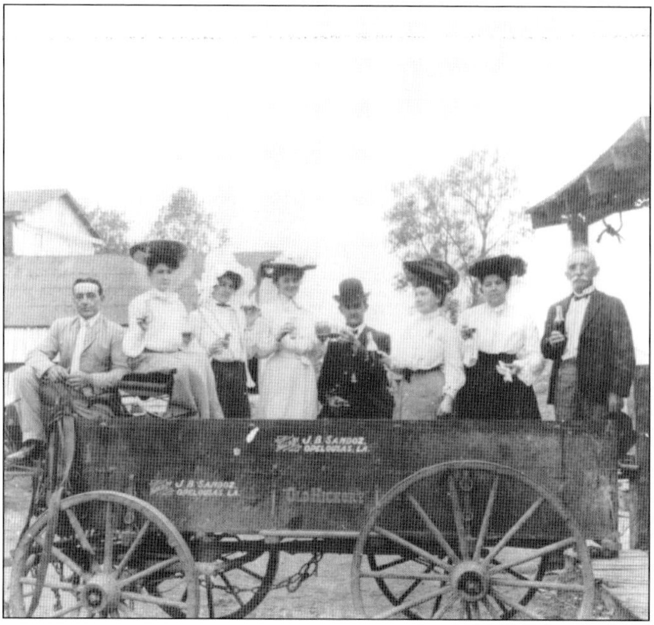

Entertainment in Opelousas from 1880 to 1900 included going on excursions. Sometimes the excursions required trips to other areas by train. Other times people jumped on wagons to ride around Opelousas and to other area towns. Some of these wagon rides were included in the town's celebrations. In this photograph, residents are enjoying an excursion during one of the many celebrations of that time. The wagon is sponsored by J.B. Sandoz, one of the largest and most successful businesses in Opelousas at the turn of the 20th century.

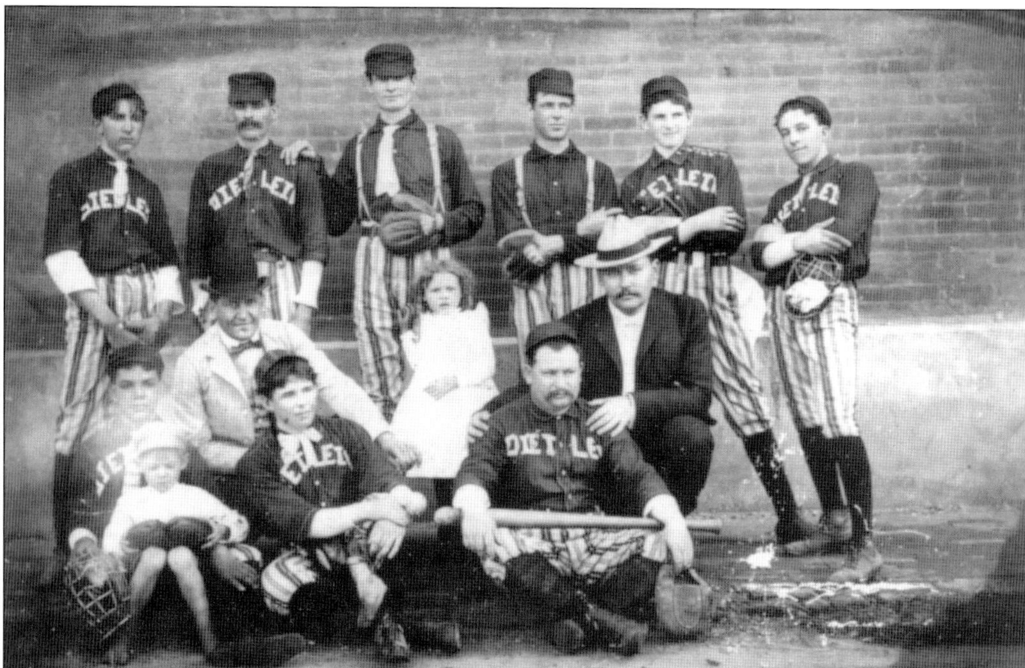

Baseball came to Opelousas at the end of the 1880s. During the 1890s, the game became very popular, drawing hundreds of Opelousas citizens to Haas Park to cheer on the local teams. Local businesses sponsored teams that played each other as well as teams from other area towns. One of the teams was sponsored by Dietlein and Jacobs Wholesale located on Railroad Avenue in Opelousas. Members of that team are pictured in 1895. From left to right are (first row) ? Dietlein, F. Cliff Allen, and Octave Durio; (second row) Charlie Heno, Fritz Dietlein, Mary Hollier (mascot), and Isidore "Issy Do" Isaac; (third row) Willie Eckert, A. Halphen, "Hop" Hollier, ? Hollier, J. Arthur Allen, and Clarence Reynolds.

Opelousas had a few parks in and around the town during the early part of the 20th century, including Haas Park and Comeau Park. Spending leisure time in one of those parks was a fun activity for local and area citizens. This photograph shows two unidentified young Opelousas women of that time enjoying the swing at one of the local parks.

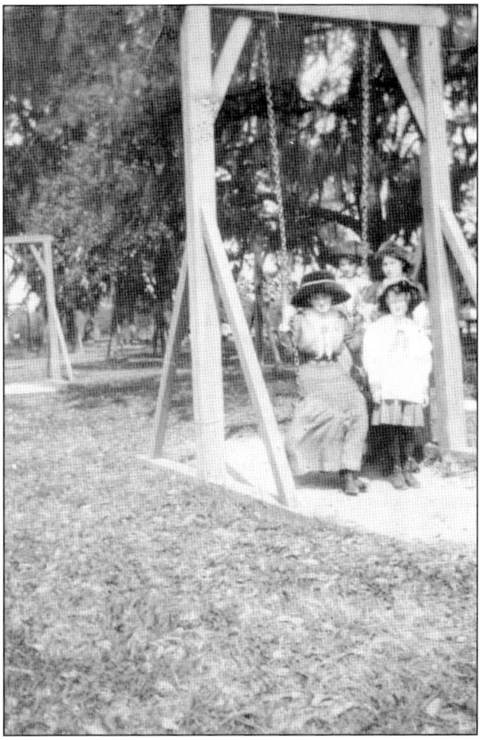

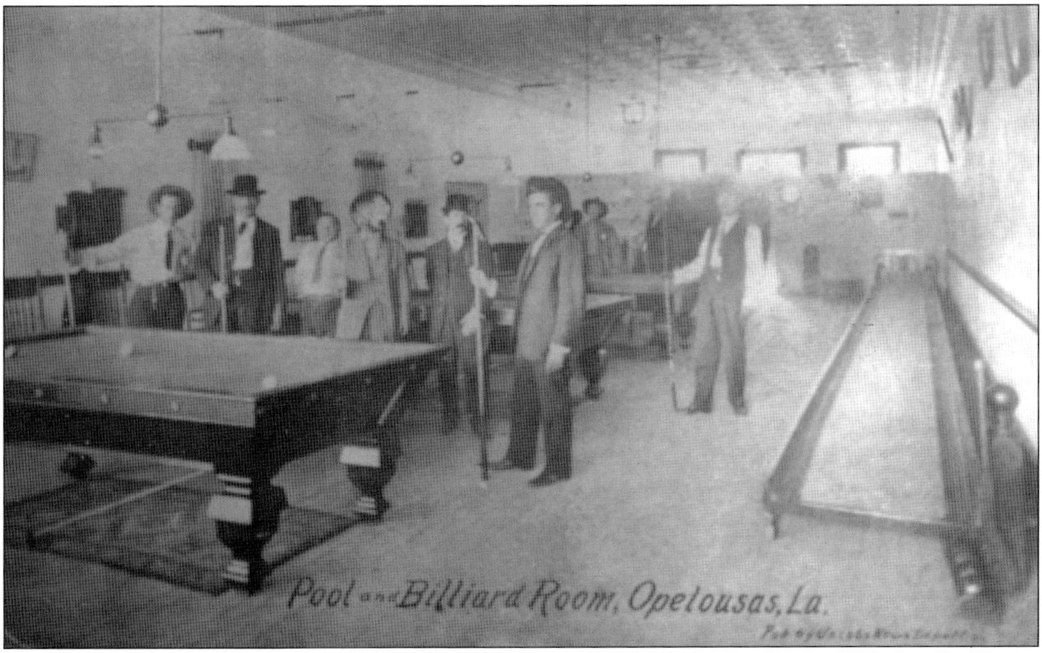

Billiards, or pool, was an early form of entertainment for the men of Opelousas. One of the Opelousas pool rooms at the beginning of the 1900s was in the Eddy Saloon, Pool Hall, and Hotel, operated by F.H. Eddy. Eddy's business was in a building owned by Charles Pitre on the southeast corner of Court and Bellevue Streets. This c. 1909 postcard produced by *Jacobs News Depot* shows a group of local men enjoying a game of pool at one of the town's pool and billiard rooms.

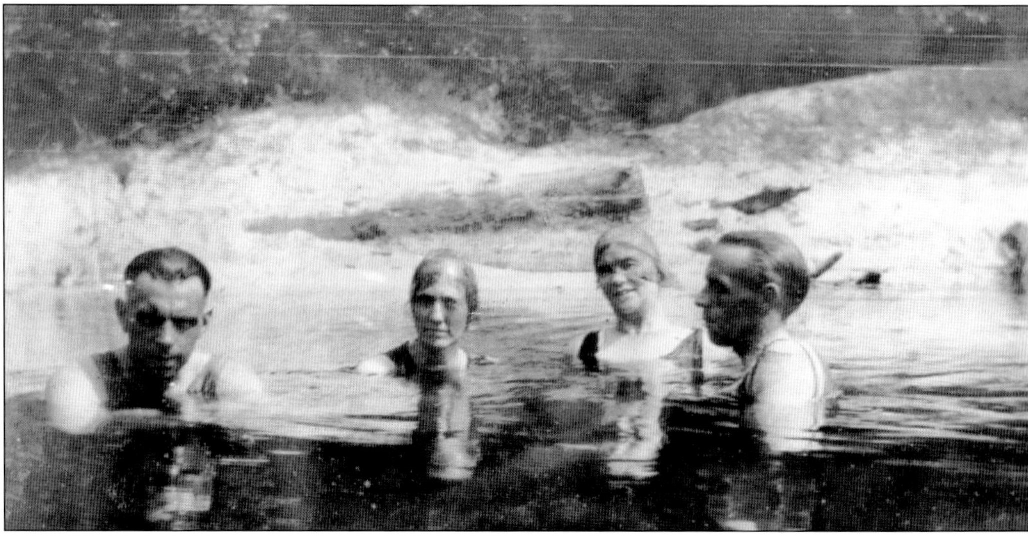

Although there were probably swimming holes in the waterways in and around the Opelousas area throughout prehistory and history, the first known swimming pool in Opelousas was the Wallior Swimming Pool located on the east end of Grolee Street. Owned by Remy Wallior, it measured 75 by 150 feet, with cypress walks, sides, and a gravel bottom. When it opened in 1920, it claimed to be one of the most up-to-date equipped pools in south Louisiana. The above photograph, taken in 1912, shows Opelousas folks enjoying the swimming hole at Swayze Lake, a resort area near town. The photograph below shows a group of young ladies from Opelousas enjoying the Wallior Swimming Pool during the 1920s. From left to right are Myrtle Andrus, Mary Boutte, Aurelina Campbell, Vernie St. Cyr, and Mary Alice Andrus.

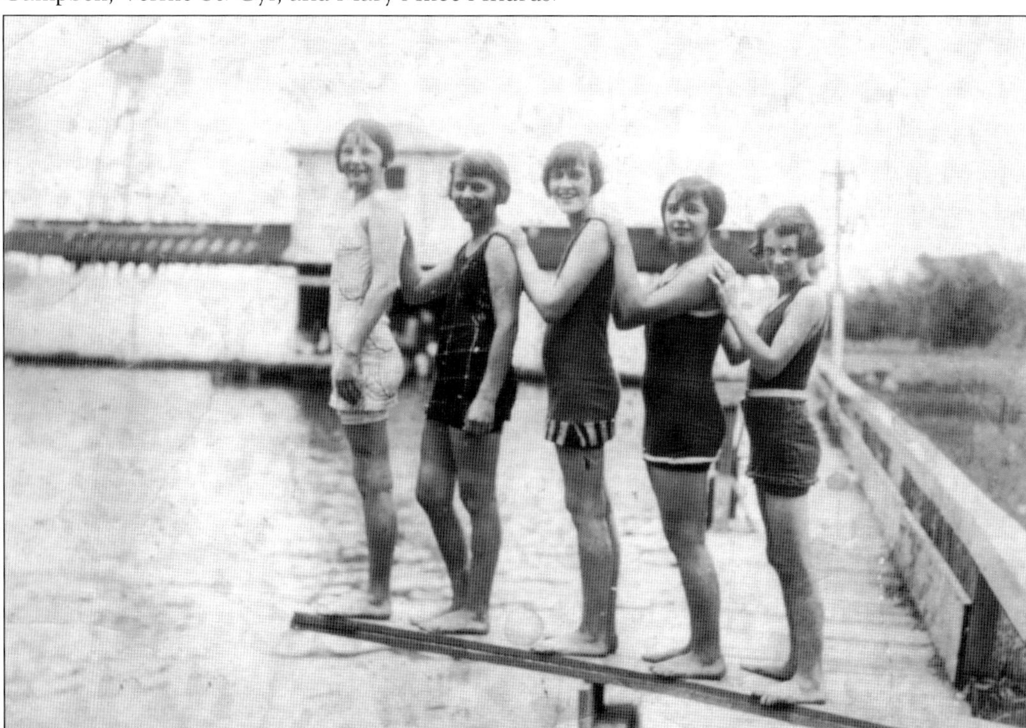

A popular activity in Opelousas a century ago was the Children's Mardi Gras Ball, sponsored annually for decades by the Women of the Episcopal Church. The Mardi Gras Ball Committee worked on the event for months, with many children participating each year. Marynia Comeau, the daughter of Arthur Alexandre Comeau Sr. and Margaret Mitchell Mornhinveg, born in 1916, was one of the girls who entered the contest each year. For one of the balls, she served as a page, and during a later year, she won first prize dressed as a bridal bouquet, as pictured here. (Courtesy of Thom and Madeline Daly.)

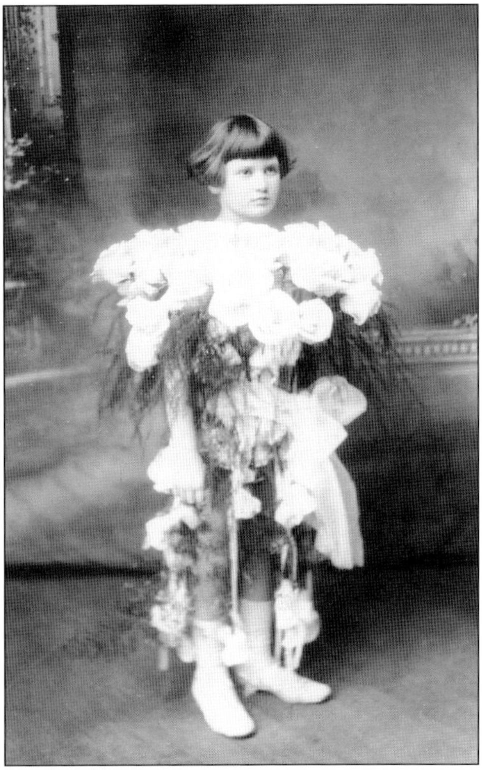

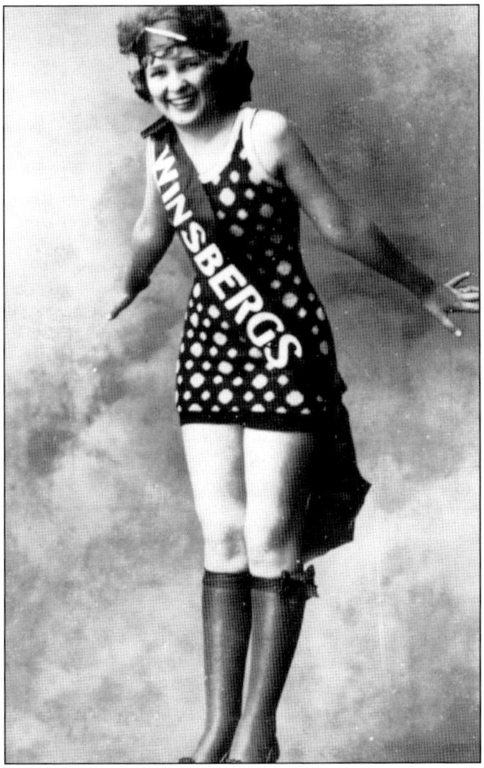

During the 1920s and through the beginning of the 1940s, some of the area department stores used models in their windows and held events and style shows with these models. One of the models for Winsberg's, the largest department store in the Opelousas area, was Marguerite Fontenot (1910–2004), who later became the wife of Charles Boagni Jr. Marguerite is pictured here on a postcard used by the store for advertising purposes.

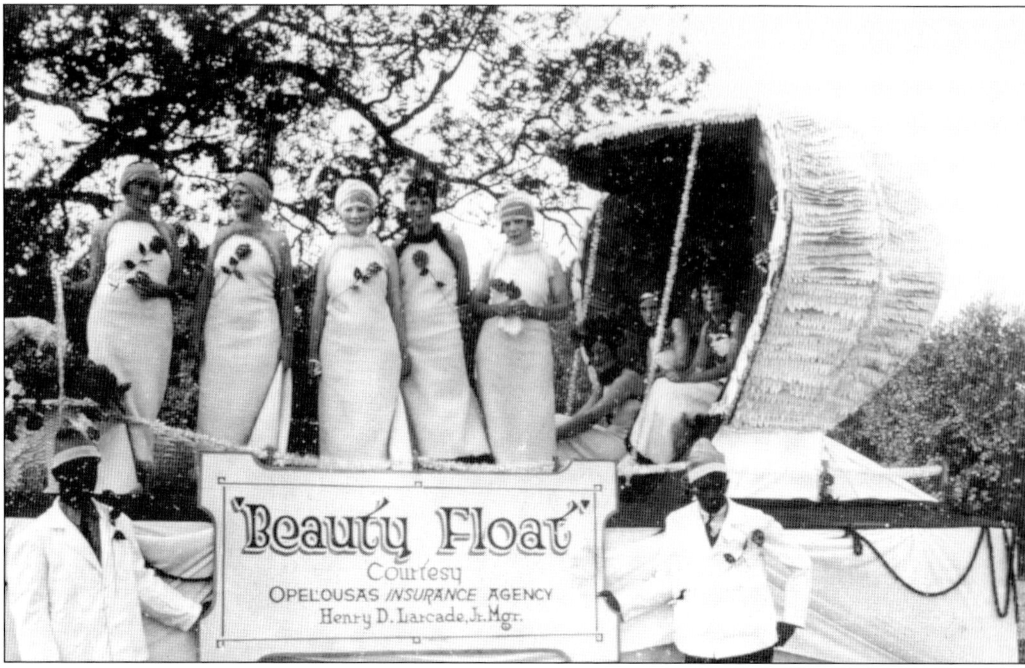

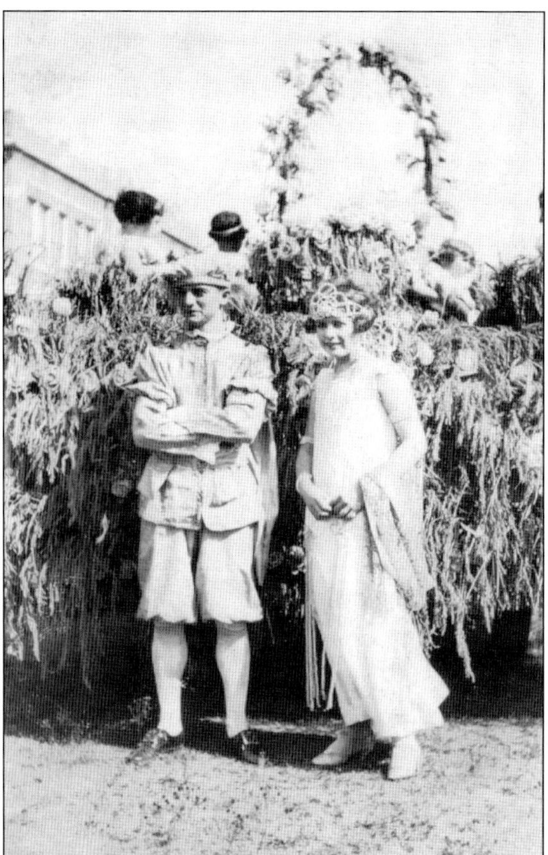

Throughout its long history, fairs, festivals, and celebrations in Opelousas were always an important part of local culture. One of the most successful festivals during its time was the Cotton Carnival, held in the town in the fall from 1922 to 1924. This event, which included a long parade, a fair, and grand ball, was well promoted, drawing thousands of outsiders to the town each year. These two photographs present a glimpse of that jubilant event in the town. Above is the float for the Larcade Insurance Agency that featured a group of Opelousas beauties. At left is the 1922 Cotton Carnival queen, Yvonne Dejean, daughter of Mr. and Mrs. Armand L. Dejean, pictured with the Cotton Carnival king C. Willis Roy.

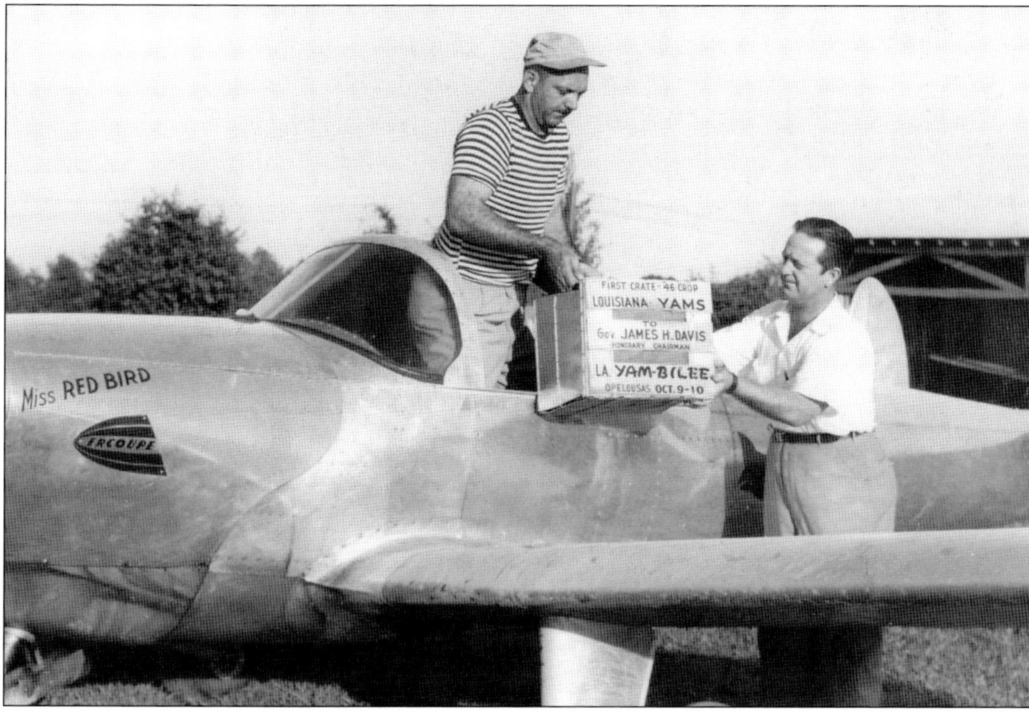

A local festival that continued for over five decades was the Louisiana Yambilee, used to promote the yam industry in Opelousas. Born over a cup of coffee while Felix Dezauche and J.W. Low were having a conversation in 1946, the Yambilee grew to be one of the most successful agriculture festivals in Louisiana, attracting thousands to the town each year. This photograph shows yams from St. Landry Parish being loaded on an airplane to be delivered to Jimmy Davis, Louisiana's governor who was a special guest for the first festival held October 9–10, 1946. Pictured loading the yams into the airplane are, from left to right, pilot John W. Dezauche and J.W. Low, Yambilee president.

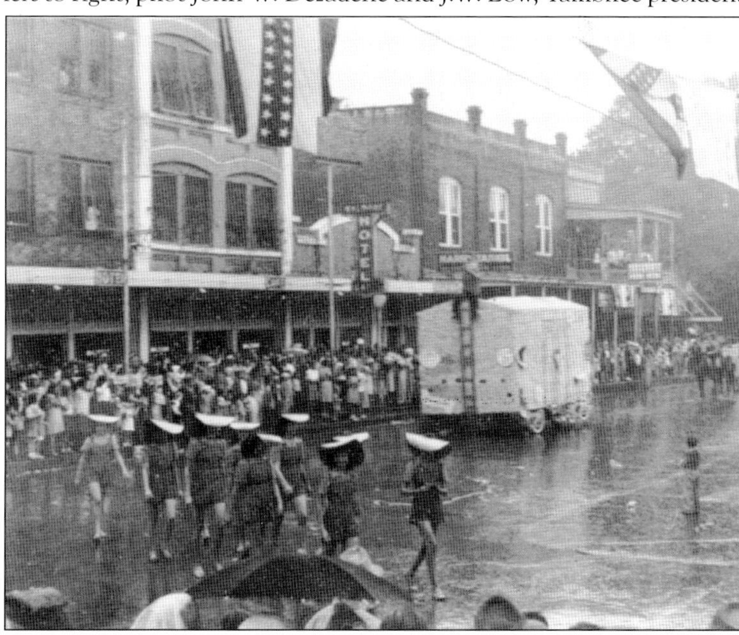

It poured down rain for the first Grand Yambilee Parade, which was held in Opelousas on October 9, 1946, but that did not prevent the parade from rolling through downtown Opelousas. As this photograph shows, hundreds of people turned out to view the Grand Yamland Parade as it moved past the businesses on Landry Street. Despite the rain, the festival was a huge success and continued in Opelousas for over five decades.

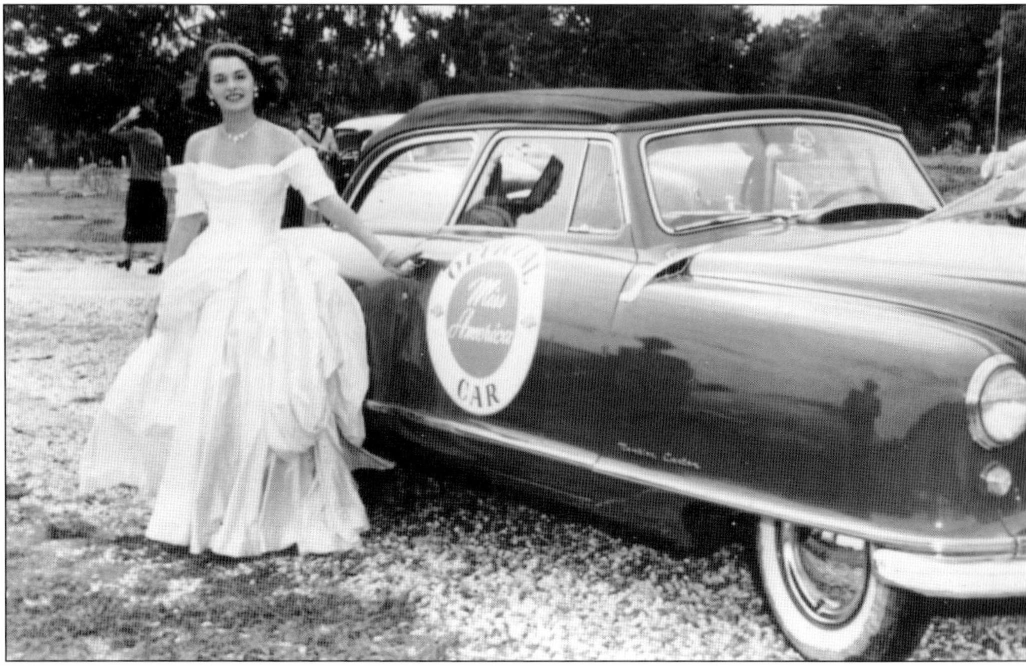

The special guest for the 1950 Yambilee Festival was Yolande Betbeze (later Fox), Miss America 1951, shown here as she arrived in Opelousas on Tuesday, October 17, 1950. She appeared at most festival events over the next two days. When leaving Opelousas, Betbeze said, "That Yambilee is a credit to the Yam industry and the whole south and is something we should all truly be proud of. I had a most wonderful time and hope to come back again."

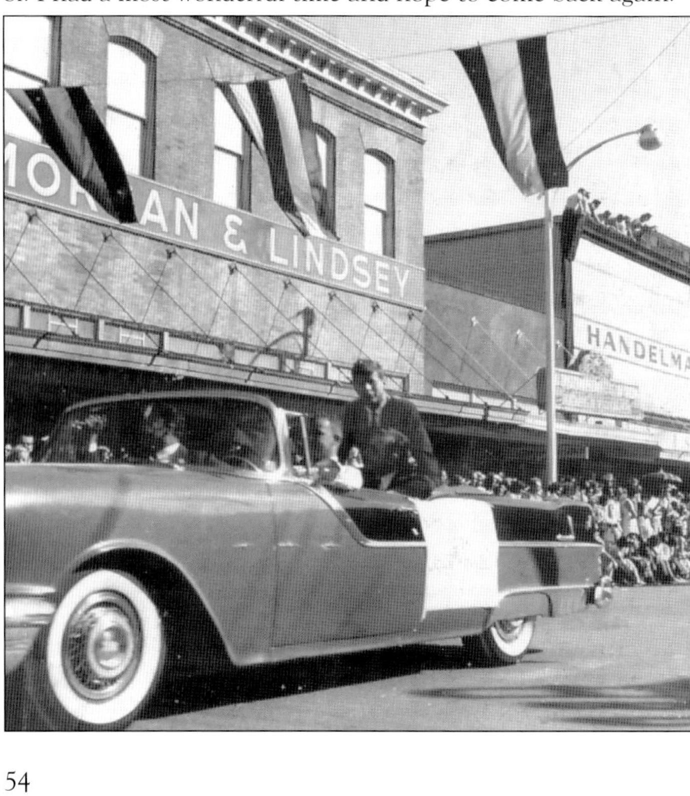

Sen. John F. Kennedy rides down Main Street for the Grand Yambilee Parade held in Opelousas on October 6, 1956. Allen Penick of Opelousas was the lucky volunteer who got the most sought-after job in the parade—driving the car with the senator from Massachusetts. As he rode through the town, there were waves and yells of approval from the crowd. People were excited to see the young politician, who had been described in a local newspaper article as "something new in politics, combining a scholarly and penetrating mind with a deep sense of needs of the people, and a radiating personality."

Scott Forbes starred as Jim Bowie in the ABC television series *The Adventures of Jim Bowie* from 1956 to 1958. The series was set in 1830s Louisiana and often featured Bowie riding his horse through the wilderness near his home in Opelousas. This photograph shows Forbes in his role as Bowie in front of the Jim Bowie Oak in downtown Opelousas in 1958. On October 5, 1958, Forbes rode as a special guest in the Grand Yambilee Parade. (Photograph by J.A. Bourdier for the *Daily World*.)

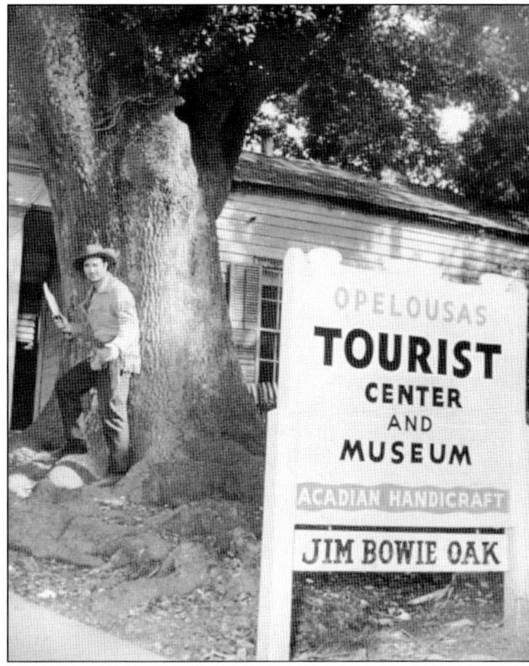

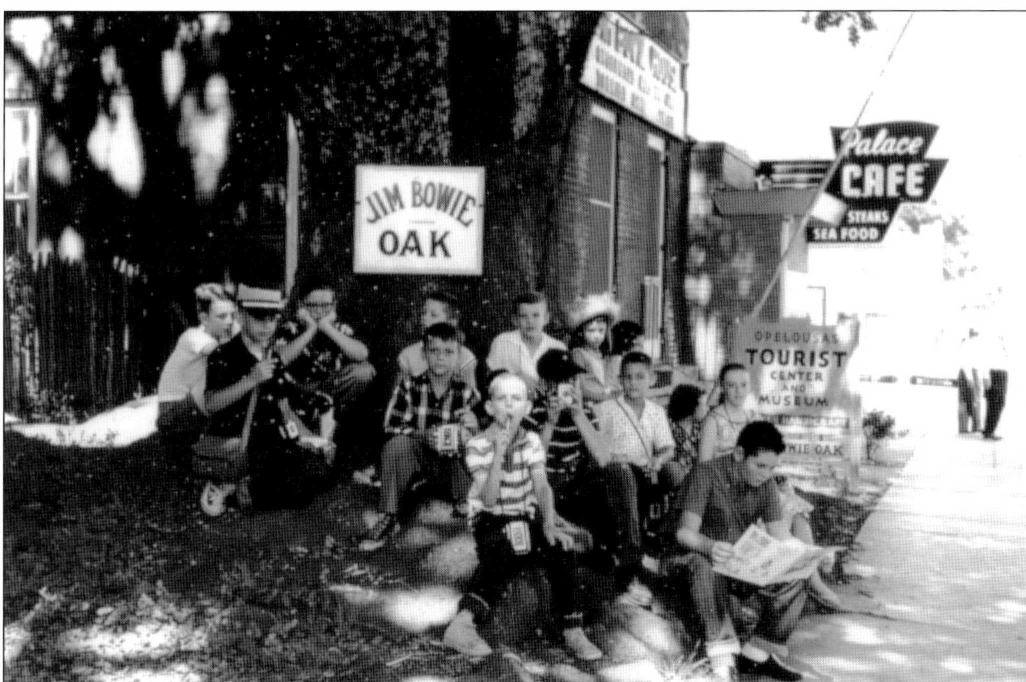

It was all lollipops, newspapers, and Brownie cameras with this group of amateur photographers as they toured downtown Opelousas in May 1960. A field trip to downtown always meant a stop at the Jim Bowie Oak. There were no cell phones to distract them from taking in all the history of the old village. As with other groups, the excursion included lunch at the Palace Café plus a visit to the tourist center and the Jim Bowie Museum. Some of those identified in the photograph are, in no particular order, Pat McDonald, Marty Roy, Steve Bienvenu, Andrew Myers, and Becky Pavy.

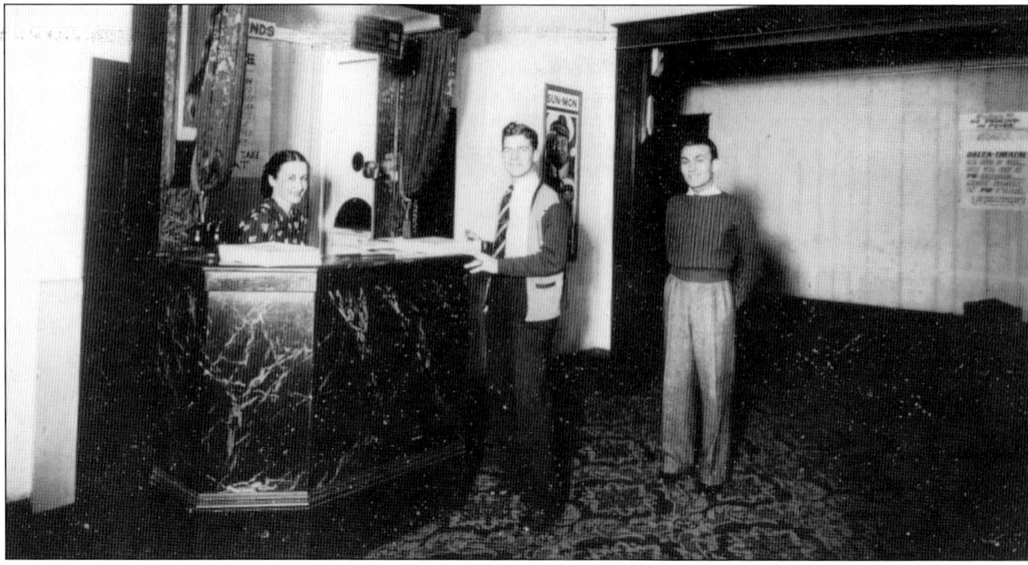

The first motion picture theater in Opelousas opened in 1906 when the Sandoz Opera House began showing moving pictures. By 1911, Opelousas had the Bon Ami Theater on Court Street, which by 1915 was known as the Princess Theater. Over the years, the Princess became the Bailey Theater and finally the Rex Theater, which operated for many years. This photograph shows the box office and lobby of the Delta Theater on Market Street in Opelousas around 1939. The theater originally operated as the Conrad Movie Theater, opened in 1933. It became the Delta Theater in 1935. Pictured seated in the box office is Angela Edwards. Standing from left to right are concessioner J.A. Allen and ticket taker Frank Onnebane.

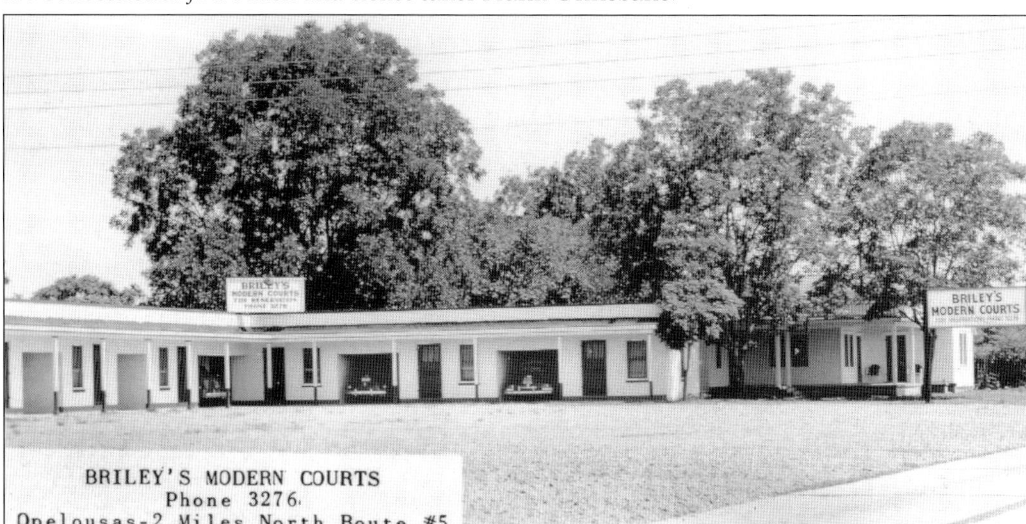

Briley's Modern Courts is pictured in this early-1950s postcard. In the late 1940s, Dudley Briley built the tourist courts about one and a half miles north of Opelousas on Washington Highway. Later, he added a store, and in 1950, with his partner L.D. "Tu Tu" Guidry, the Midway Drive-In Theater was built on the property. The drive-in theater, a popular form of entertainment at the time, operated until 1957 when Hurricane Audrey destroyed the screen, forcing it to close. According to grandson Donald Cropper, Dudley Briley also developed the Briley subdivision during that time.

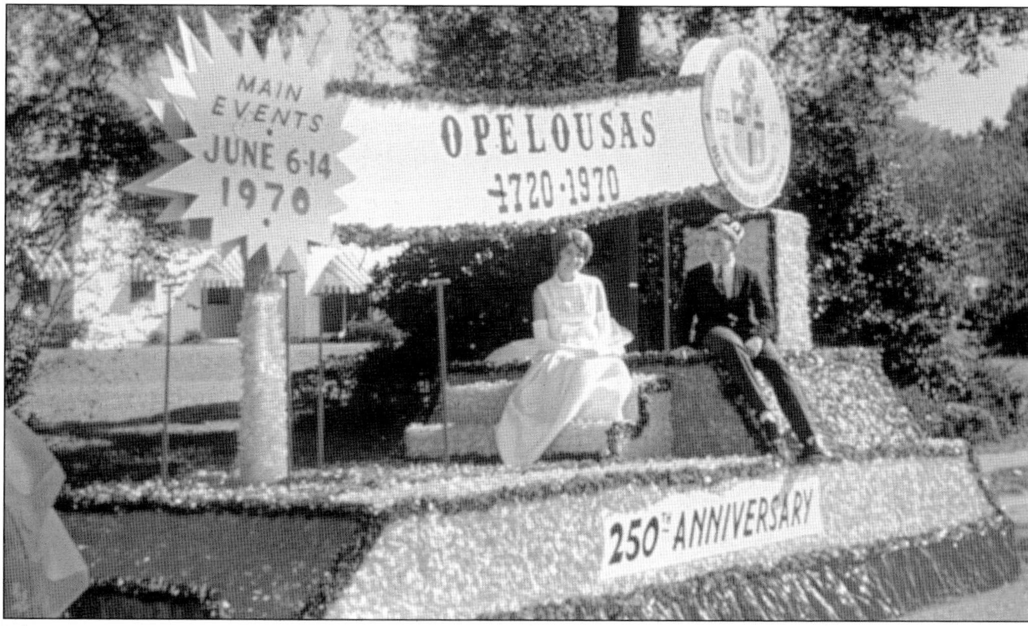

The year 1970 was an exciting one in Opelousas with events and activities held throughout the year for the celebration of the 250th anniversary of the historic town. The main event was held June 6–14 and included a gigantic parade that ran through downtown Opelousas on June 14. The float pictured above was in that parade and used in prior months to promote the event. The photograph below shows Huey Bourque, executive director of the Greater Opelousas Chamber of Commerce, with Marcel LeBlanc, one of the event organizers, displaying the special doubloons produced to commemorate the anniversary.

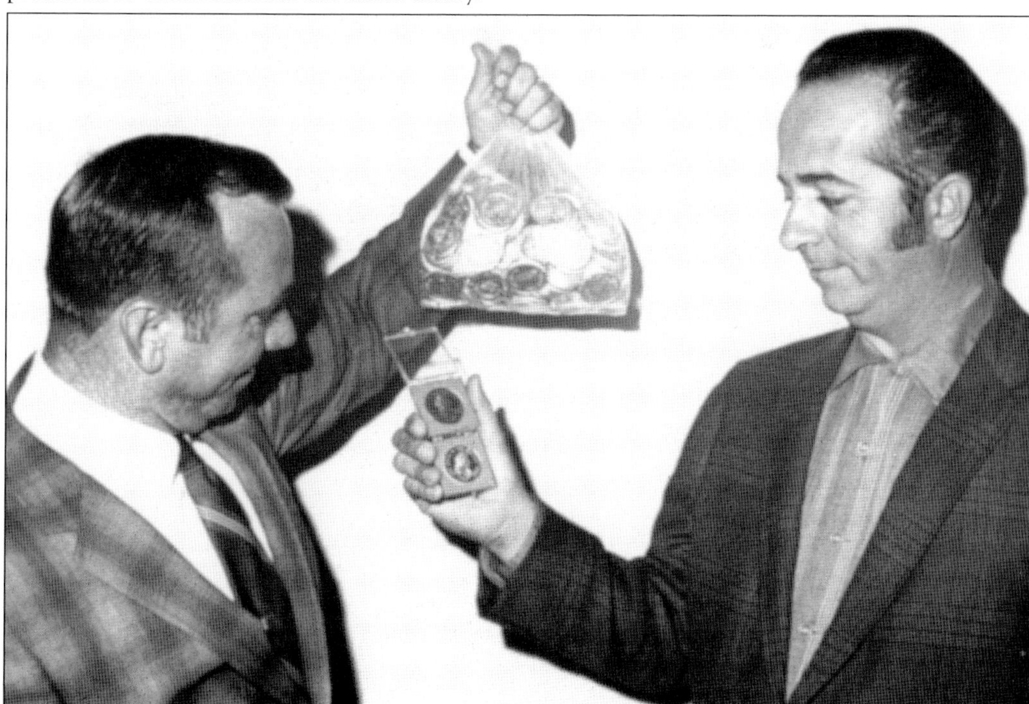

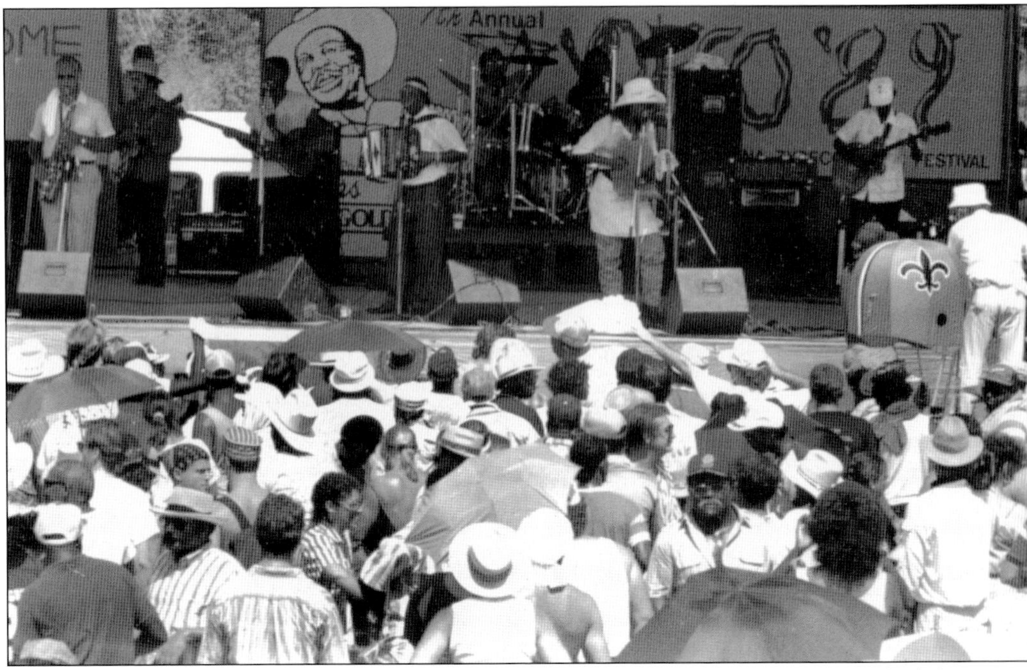

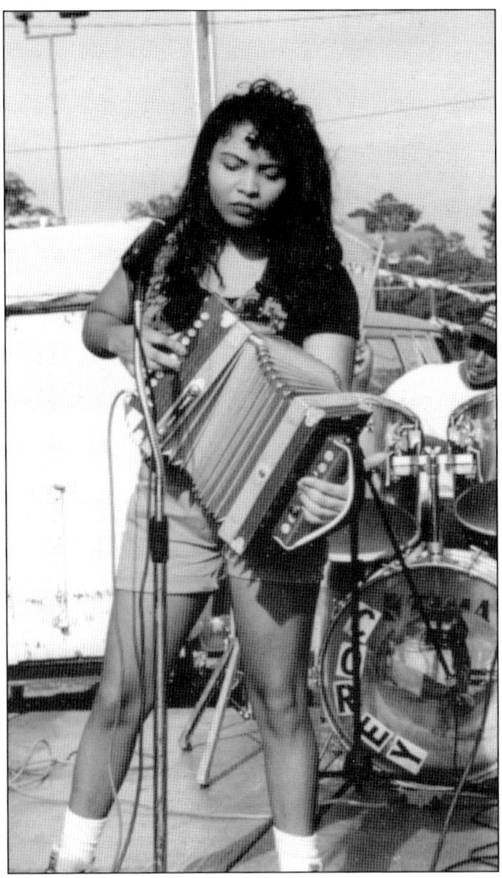

Opelousas is the "Zydeco Capital of the World," with the music of Southwest Louisiana celebrated each year at the annual Southwest Louisiana Zydeco Music Festival, pictured above. Originally known as Creole "La La" music, its name became zydeco when area musician and zydeco king Clifton Chenier called it that many years ago. The name comes from "les haricots," a modified pronunciation of the French phrase for beans, or snapbeans. To preserve the Creole culture and its zydeco music, in 1981 a group of concerned citizens called The Treasures of Opelousas, with support and sponsorship from the Southern Development Foundation, organized the first Zydeco Music Festival in 1982 on a Plaisance farmer's field near Opelousas. It quickly grew to be one of the premier festivals in the state, with 20,000 plus in attendance by the 1990s. The festival, today known as the world's largest zydeco ("La La") music festival, is held in Opelousas on the Saturday before Labor Day each year. The photograph at left shows zydeco musician Rosie LeDay performing zydeco music for the Main Street Revived concerts held in downtown Opelousas during the 1990s. (Above, courtesy of Wilbert Guillory; left, photograph by Sherri Landry.)

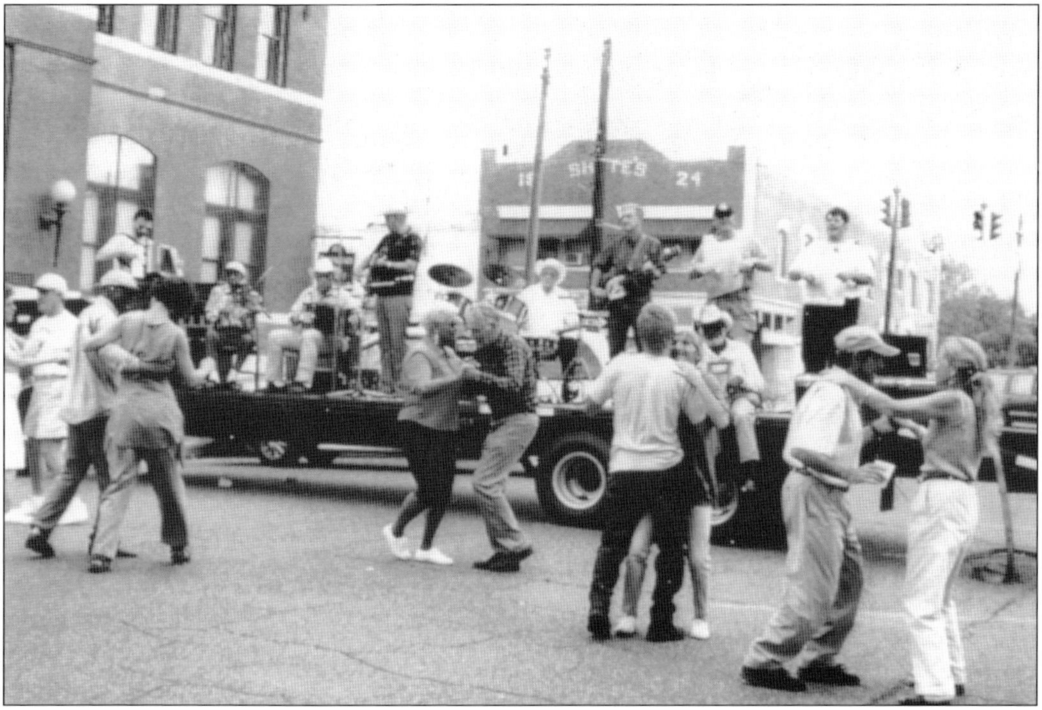

During the 1990s, hundreds of people turned out on Friday evenings for the Main Street Revived concert series in downtown Opelousas, sponsored by the Opelousas Tourism and Activities Committee. This photograph from the latter part of that decade shows a group of dancers enjoying some of the music of Southwest Louisiana on the corner of Court and Landry Streets. (Photograph by Vicki Kennedy Bergstrom.)

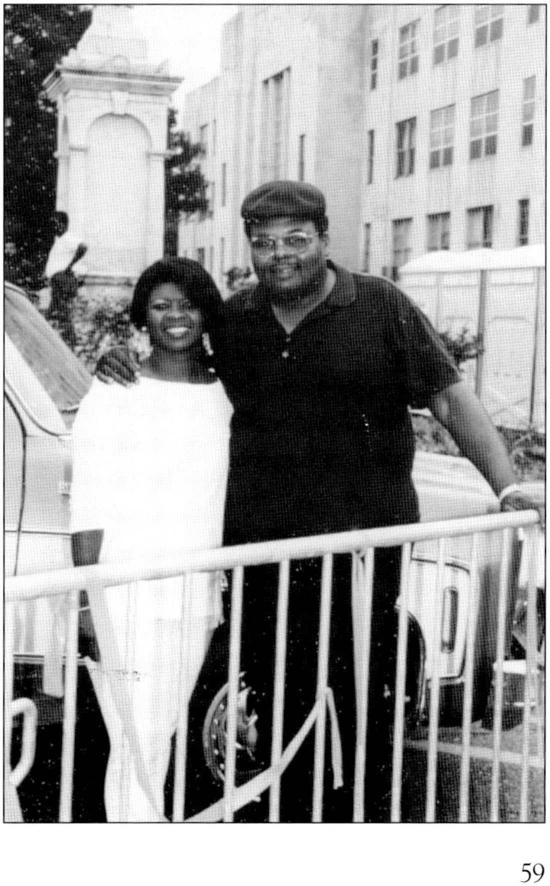

Irma Thomas, the soul queen of New Orleans, poses for a photograph with local musician Rosco Chenier on the courthouse square in downtown Opelousas just before her performance in 1992. Thousands of people from the Opelousas area came out to see Thomas perform with her group The Professionals for the Main Street Revived concert held on May 15, 1992.

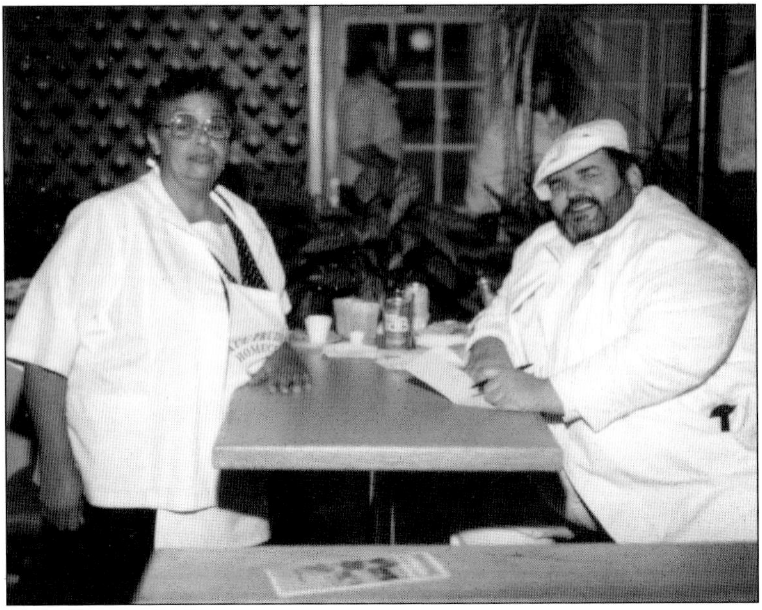

Internationally known Cajun chef Paul Prudhomme is pictured with Opelousas chef Shirley Lemelle during the Paul Prudhomme Homecoming celebration. Sponsored by the Opelousas Tourism and Activities Committee, the event was held on March 7, 1988, to honor the Opelousas native, and various activities could be found in Opelousas throughout the day. (Photograph by Sherri Landry.)

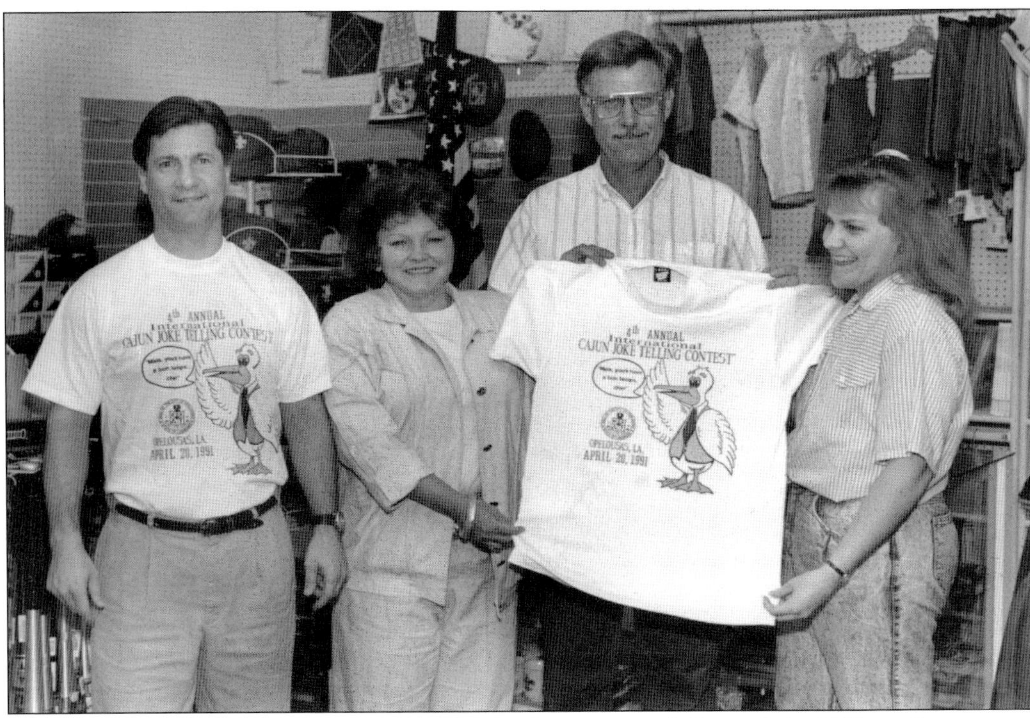

An annual event that attracted hundreds, the International Cajun Joke Telling Contest was held in Opelousas each April for over two decades. Pictured here are some members of the event committee displaying the 1991 official T-shirt for the fourth annual contest. From left to right are Fred Credeur, T-shirt manufacturer; Carola Andrepont (now Hartley); Ken Vidrine; and Sherri Landry. (Photograph by Freddie Herpin.)

Four

Religion

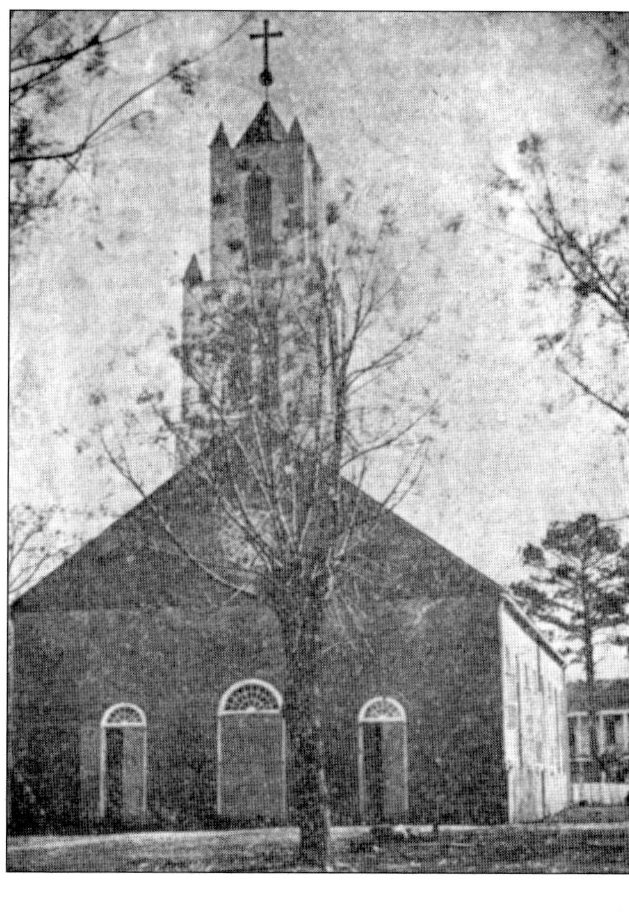

Religion played a major role in the development of Opelousas. The first settlers to arrive were of the Catholic faith. The first church in the greater Opelousas area was the Church of the Immaculate Conception, established in the 1770s at Church's Landing on the Bayou Courtableau near what is today Washington, Louisiana. By the 1790s, the church was called St. Landry Catholic Church, named for the bishop of Paris who served around 650. This photograph shows the church built in 1827 on land donated by Michel Prudhomme and Madame Tesson in north Opelousas in 1798. The present church sits on that same property.

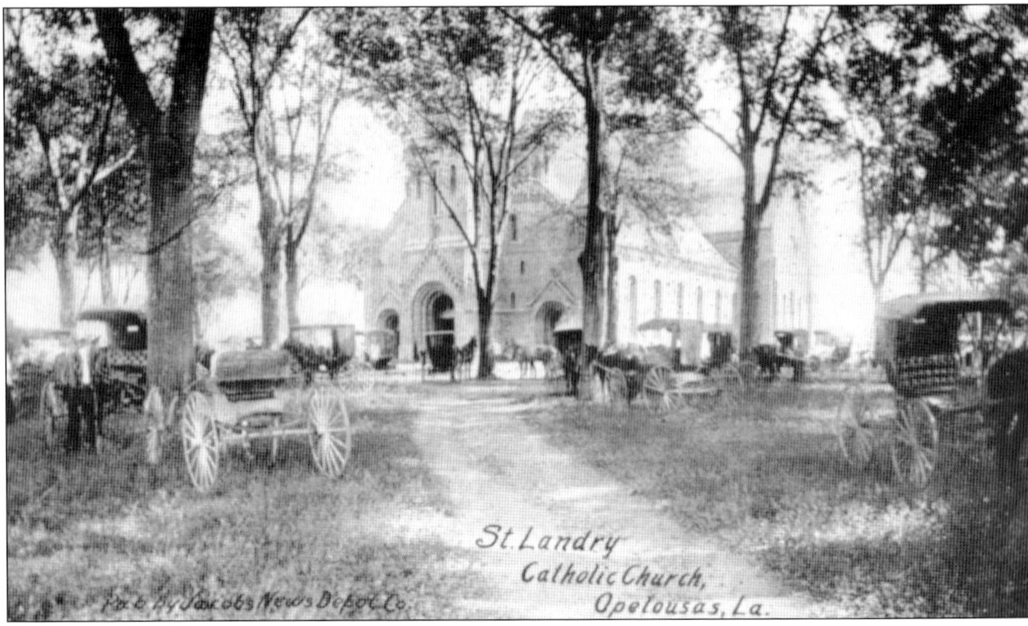

The new St. Landry Catholic Church building at the corner of Church and Main Streets in north Opelousas was dedicated in 1909. This photograph, taken by Aaron Jacobs around 1910, shows buggies parked in the church yard as mass was celebrated inside the church by Rev. John Engberink. On May 3, 1982, the church was listed in the National Register of Historic Places.

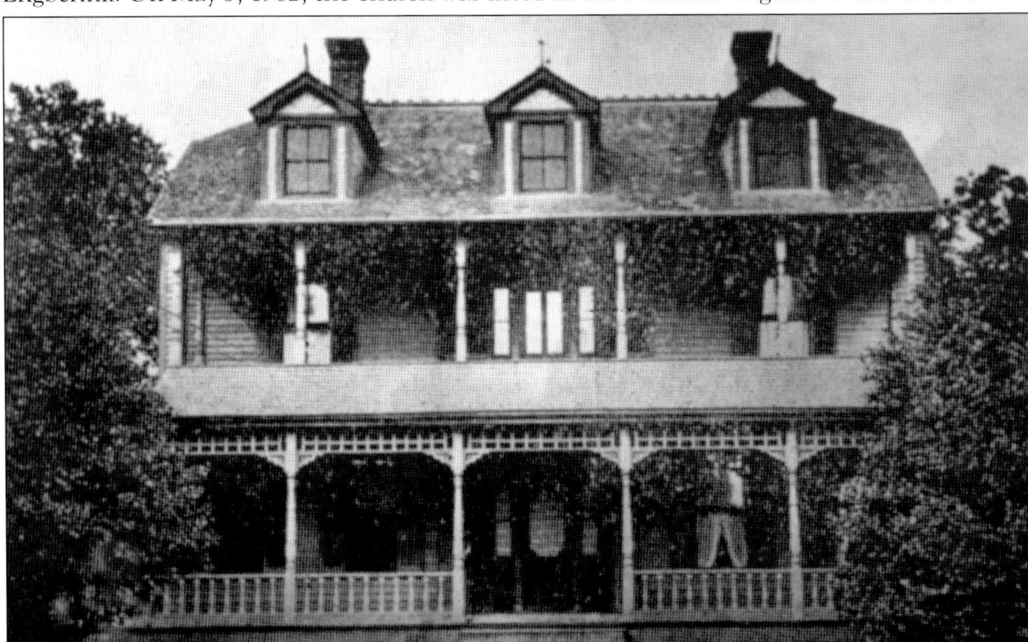

The St. Landry Catholic Church rectory sat on property to the east side of the church for many years. The building, pictured here around 1914, was sold in 1956 and dismantled and removed from the property. During that year, a new church rectory was built on the north side of the church, where it remains today.

Fr. Joseph Verbis Lafleur (1912–1944), priest and soldier, was an Army chaplain from Opelousas who became a prisoner of war in the Philippine Islands. He lost his life serving his country on September 7, 1944. The cause for canonization of Lt. Fr. Joseph Verbis LaFleur was officially opened by Bishop Douglas Deshotel of the Diocese of Lafayette on September 5, 2020. In 2021, he became a Servant of God. The beatification process is currently ongoing.

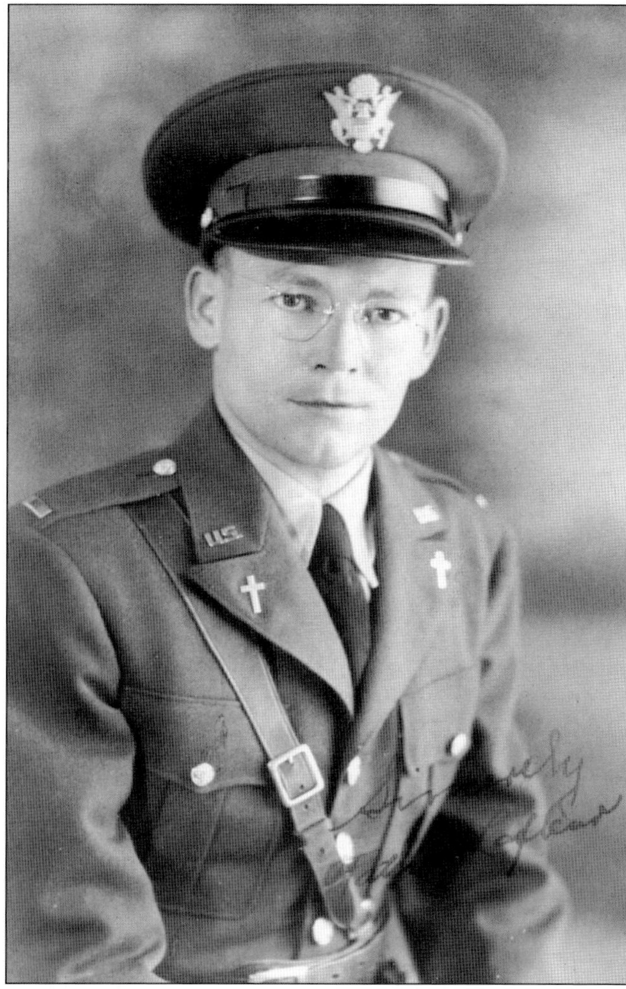

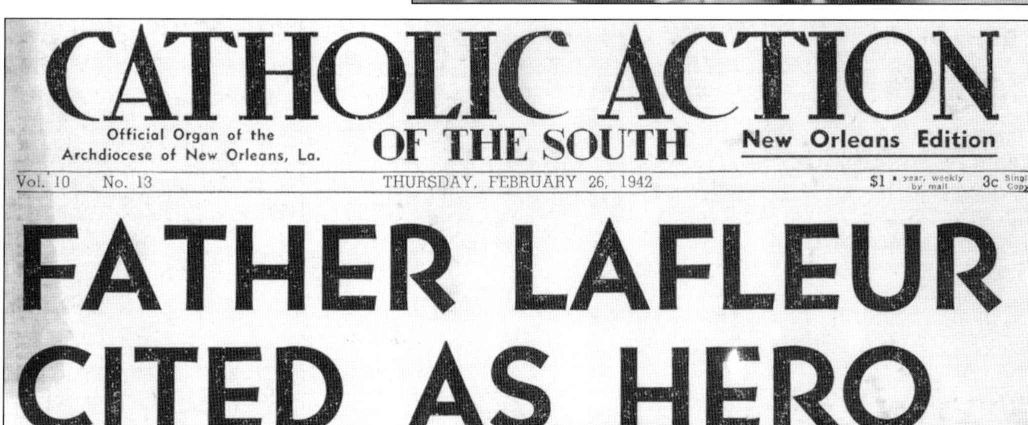

CATHOLIC ACTION OF THE SOUTH

Official Organ of the Archdiocese of New Orleans, La.

New Orleans Edition

Vol. 10 No. 13 THURSDAY, FEBRUARY 26, 1942 $1 a year, weekly by mail 3c Single Copy

FATHER LAFLEUR CITED AS HERO

The bold headline in the *Catholic Action* newspaper of February 26, 1942, announced Fr. Joseph Verbis Lafleur of Opelousas was cited as a hero. Father Lafleur, who fought in the Pacific theater during World War II, was eventually captured in the Philippine Islands and became a prisoner of war. He died at sea while being transported with other prisoners to Japan on September 7, 1944.

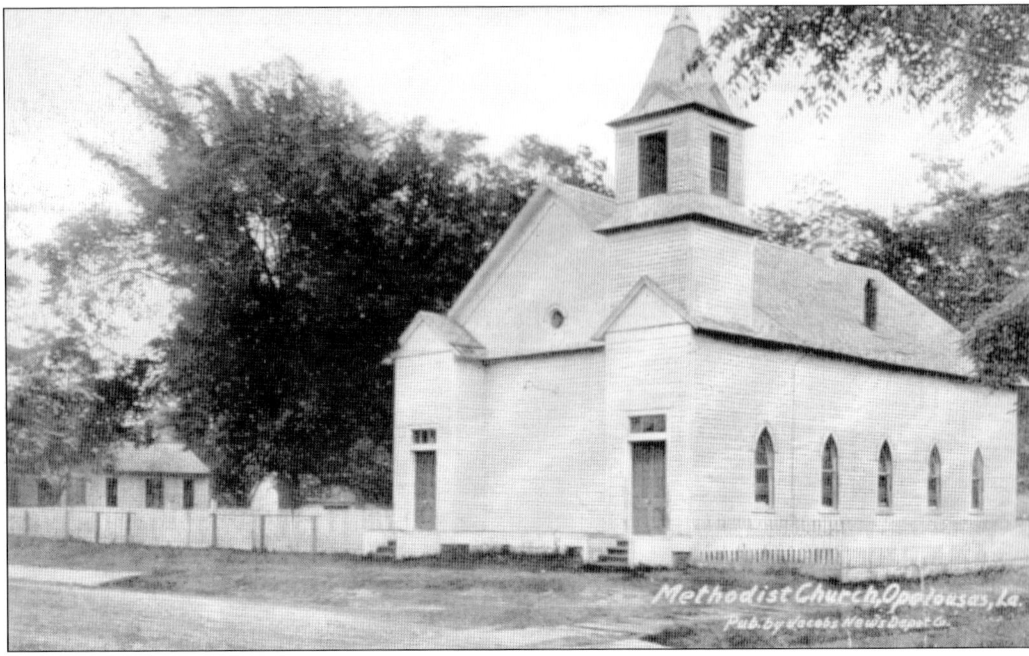

After the Louisiana Purchase of 1805, people from other areas of the United States came to Opelousas. Elisha Bowman was one of the men who arrived in Opelousas in 1806. He organized a Methodist society and accepted 17 members into the new church, the first Methodist church founded west of the Mississippi River. That church today is known as the Louisiana Memorial United Methodist Church. The new church building erected on the corner of Lombard and Bellevue Streets in 1907 is pictured here in this 1909 postcard produced by *Jacobs News Depot*.

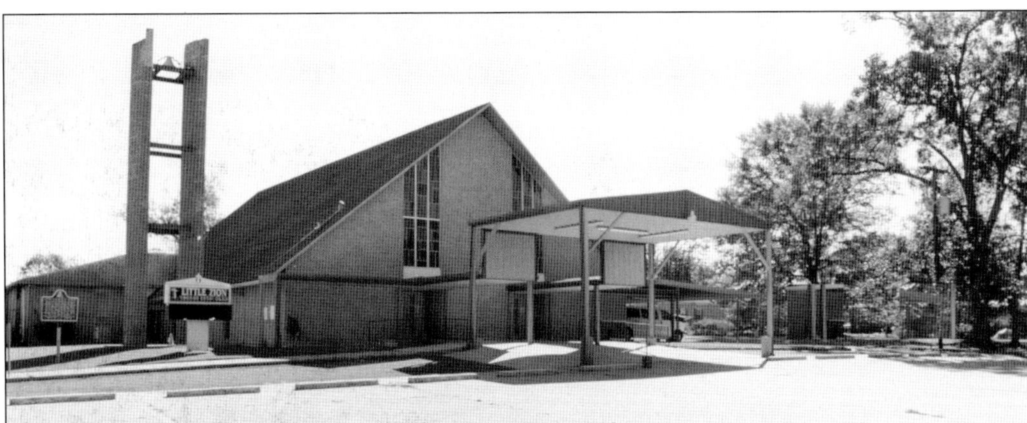

The first Baptist church in Opelousas was the Opelousas African Baptist Church, organized in a blacksmith shop on June 29, 1867. On August 16, 1869, Rev. J.P. Davenport asked the St. Landry Parish Police Jury for a donation of land to build a church, parsonage, and graveyard. James Thompson, police jury president, located and marked off the land, and it was transferred to the church on that same day. The first church building was constructed soon after, and it became Little Zion Baptist Church. In 1968, the old building was moved from the property. Groundbreaking ceremonies were held on January 21, 1968, and a new brick church was constructed for the congregation. That building is pictured on North Academy Street in this present-day photograph. (Photograph by Sherri Landry.)

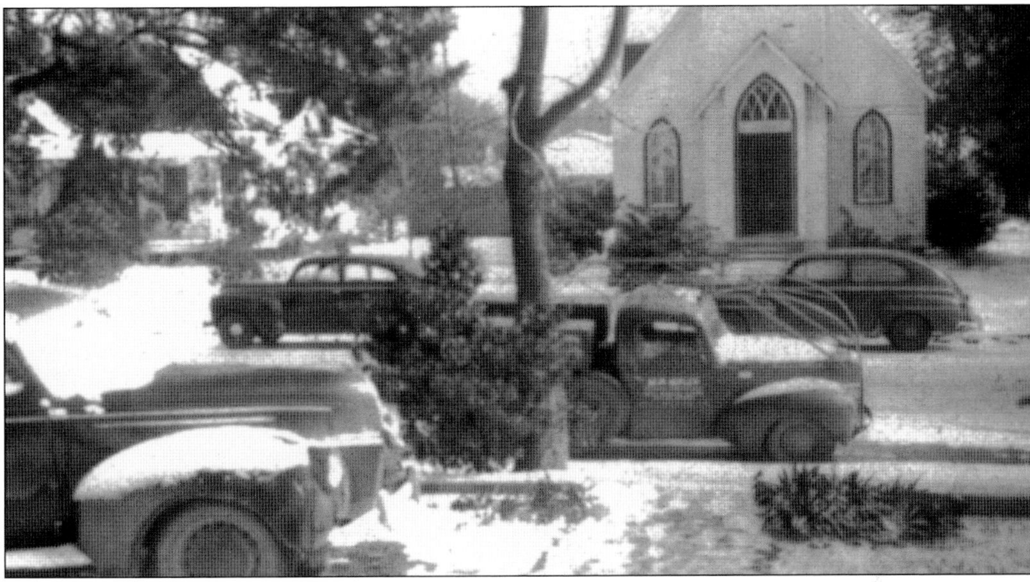

In 1845, the Right Rev. Leonidas Polk, DD, the bishop of the Diocese of Louisiana, visited Opelousas, preached in the protestant chapel, and administered the rite of confirmation. Ten years later, he returned to organize the first Episcopal Church in Opelousas. The first pastor was Rev. David Kerr, who preached his first sermon on June 15, 1855, in the courthouse. The first church building was erected in the early 1860s on the corner of Union and Landry Streets. It was consecrated by Bishop Polk on March 1, 1861. A new church building was constructed in 1880 and sat on that corner for decades, until 1959 when it was dismantled and moved to South City Park. It is now used by the Opelousas Little Theater. The new Episcopal Church of the Epiphany building, constructed in 1959–1960, is located on South Union Street in Opelousas. These two photographs show the old church building during a snowfall in 1947 (above) and in the 1950s (right).

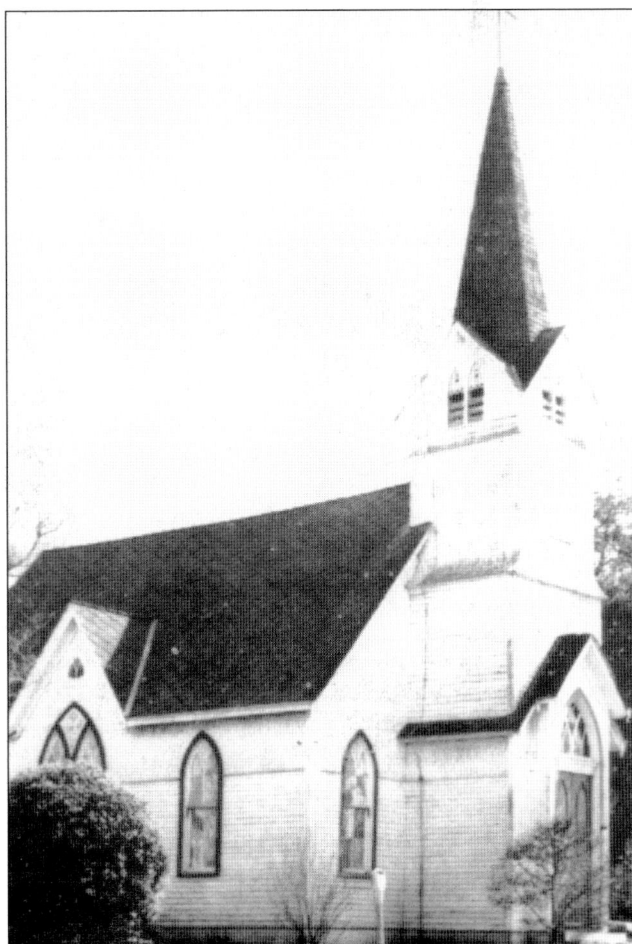

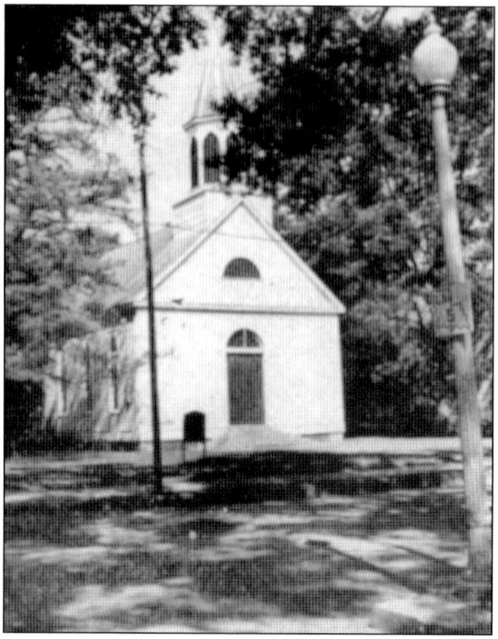

The First Presbyterian Church in Opelousas is pictured in this 1950s photograph. The old church building was constructed on the corner of Main and Cherry Streets. The First Presbyterian Church was organized by Dr. Louis Hadden. Members who signed the church charter on May 20, 1871, were James A. Houston, Mary A. Houston, Kate Houston, Dr. Louis Hadden, Cora Hadden Truman, John B. Wilson, Louise E. Wilson, and Annie E. Wilson. The first minister was James A. McConnell, who was appointed on May 30, 1871. He preached until August 1872. Following the construction of a new church building, it was renamed Hope Presbyterian Church. (Courtesy of Jo Ann Caillouet.)

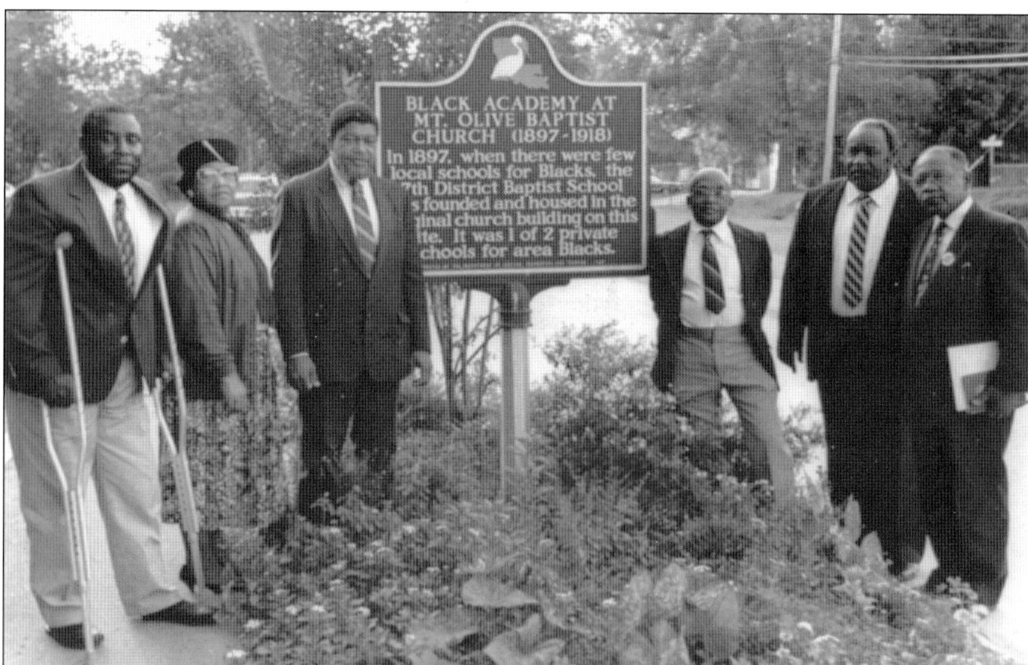

In 1991, Mount Olive Baptist Church in Opelousas celebrated its centennial. In October, the church's board of trustees gathered in front of the historic marker erected by the Louisiana Department of Culture, Recreation, and Tourism in 1985. The marker highlights the spot where the Black Academy of Mount Olive Baptist Church once stood on West Church Street. The 7th District School was founded in 1897 when there were few schools for Blacks in the area. It operated until 1918. Trustees pictured are, from left to right, Donald Greene Sr., Gladys Cunningham, Dr. Lionel Daniels, Willie Norman, Hebrard Greene Jr., and Rev. Joel S. Greens Sr.

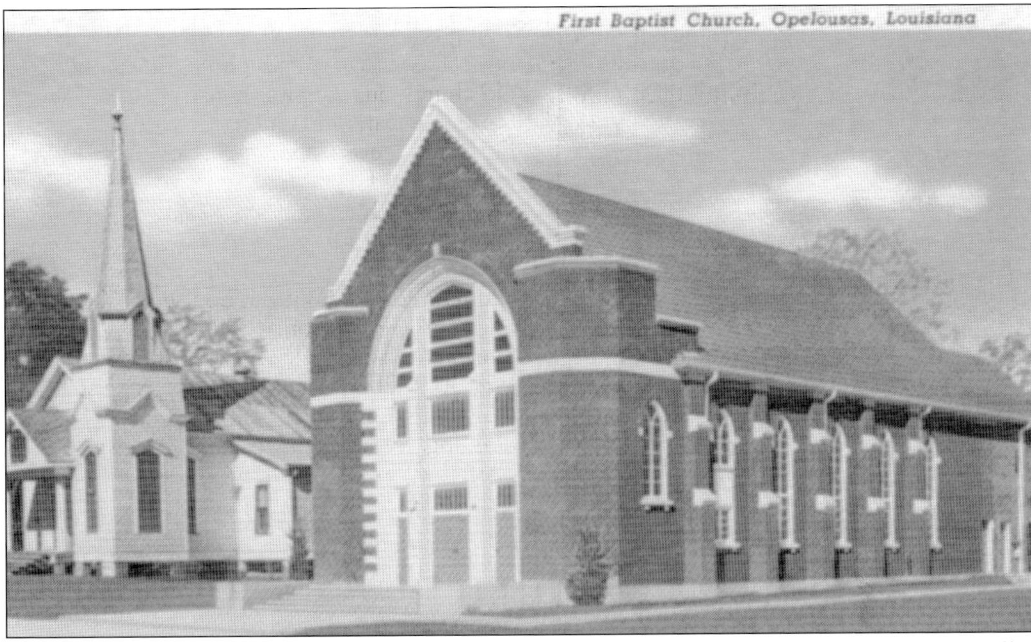

The First Baptist Church of Opelousas, organized in 1880 by Dr. W.C. Friley and Rev. Ed W. Kelley, had Rev. W.P. Carter as its first pastor. A church building was constructed on Bellevue Street in 1883 on property acquired by W.L. Truman, a cousin of Pres. Harry S. Truman. As shown in this photograph, a new brick church building was constructed in 1952, with the old wooden church still on the property. Today, the 1952 building houses the Bellevue Street Baptist Church, and the congregation of the First Baptist Church worships in a new structure located on Interstate 49 south.

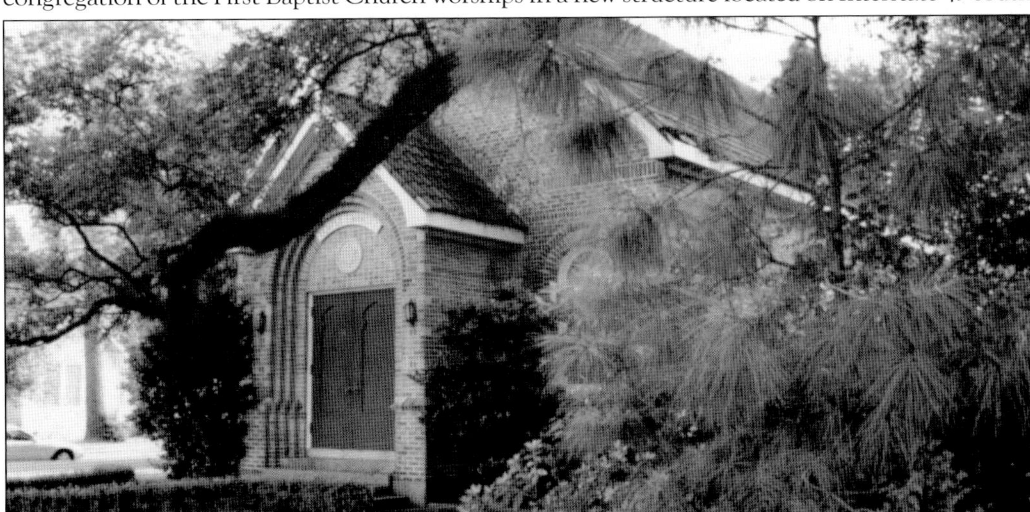

As more Jewish immigrants came into the Opelousas area, the Jewish community established its own cemetery by 1865. In 1877, holding services at the Masonic Lodge, the community formed a congregation with Joseph Bloch as president and Emanuel Phillips as secretary. A small temple was later built for the congregation that lasted until the 1920s. In 1929, Temple Emanuel was founded with 65 members, absorbing the earlier congregation. In 1930, a brick synagogue was erected on land donated by the Haas family on South Main Street. That building, no longer used for services, is now privately owned and will be restored for commercial use. (Photograph by Sherri Landry.)

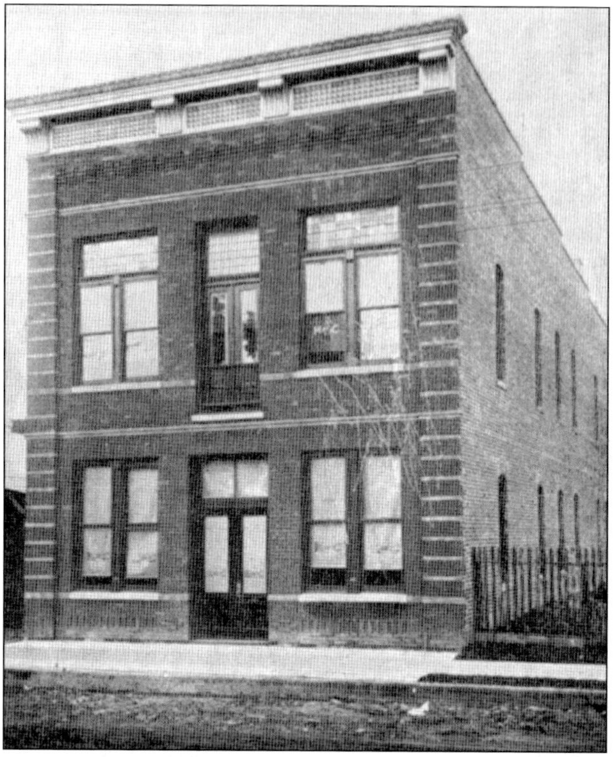

On November 25, 1906, what would become Knights of Columbus Council No. 1173 was organized in Opelousas. The Knights of Columbus Hall, shown in the 1915 photograph at left, was built on Main Street in 1908. The first floor had a reading room, a banquet hall, and a reception room. The second floor was the lodge room. It stood on Main Street until 1941 when it was sold and attached to the Bordelon Motors Inc. building. The photograph below, taken on May 12, 1908, shows members of the Louisiana Knights of Columbus meeting for their convention held at the new Knights of Columbus Hall in Opelousas.

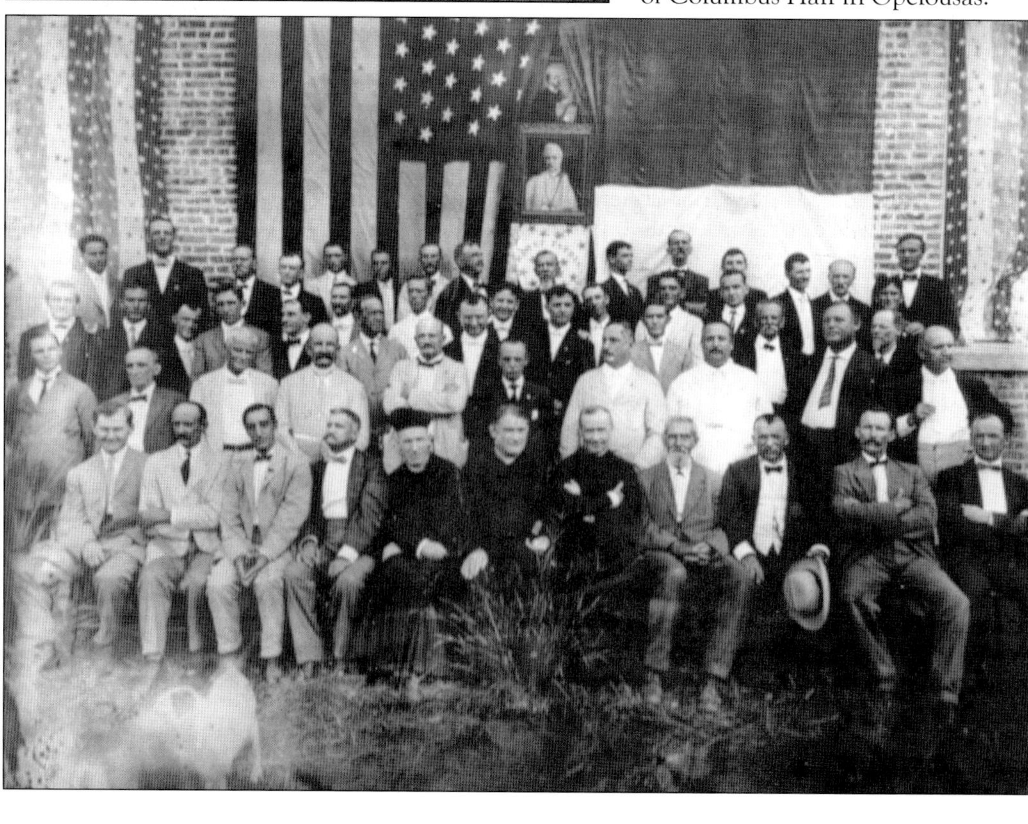

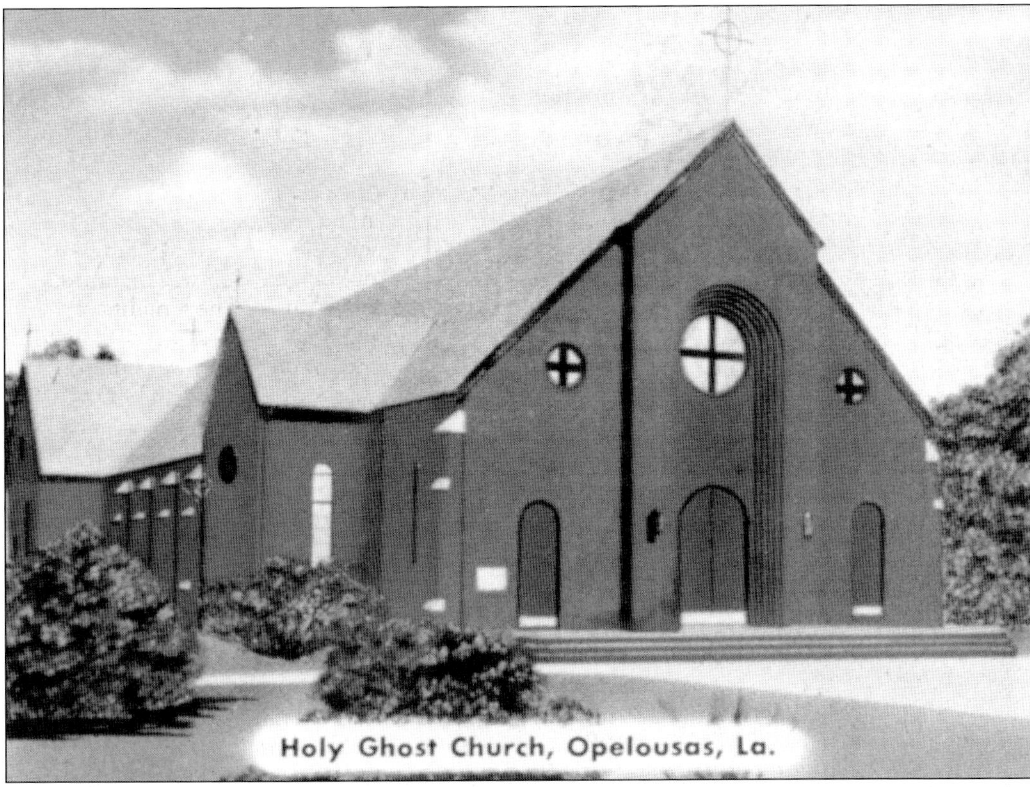

In 1919, the Diocese of Lafayette established a new church parish in Opelousas dedicated to the African American population. The new church was named Holy Ghost Catholic Church with Fr. James Hyland as pastor. Since there was no church building or rectory, the celebration of mass and church services were held in the auditorium of the St. Joseph Catholic School on Union Street, with Father Hyland living in a classroom. The first church, completed in March 1921, was constructed on Walnut Street and blessed by Bishop Jules Jeanmard of the Diocese of Lafayette. In 1949, a new brick church building, shown in this photograph, was constructed on Union Street, where it remains today.

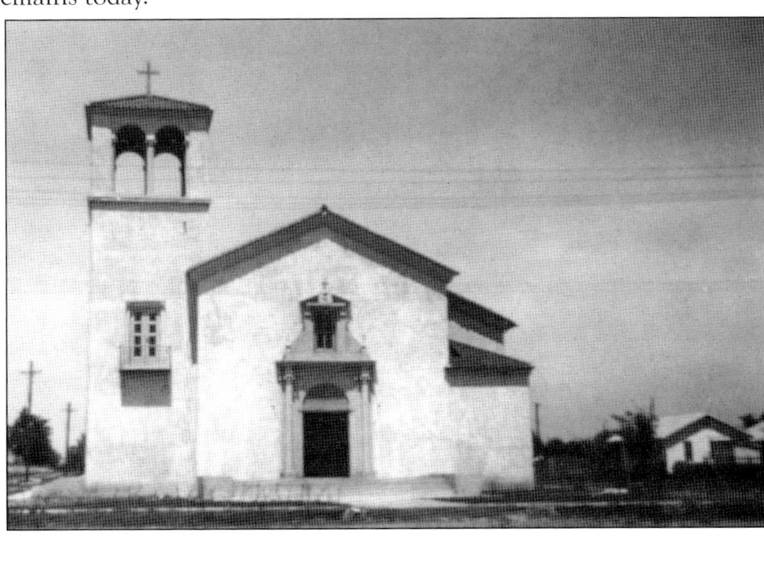

In 1948, Opelousas had a third Catholic church parish when Our Lady of Mercy Church opened on the west side of town. The church is shown in this photograph taken shortly after it was constructed. Two decades later, a fourth church parish was organized on the south side when Our Lady Queen of Angels Catholic Church was created.

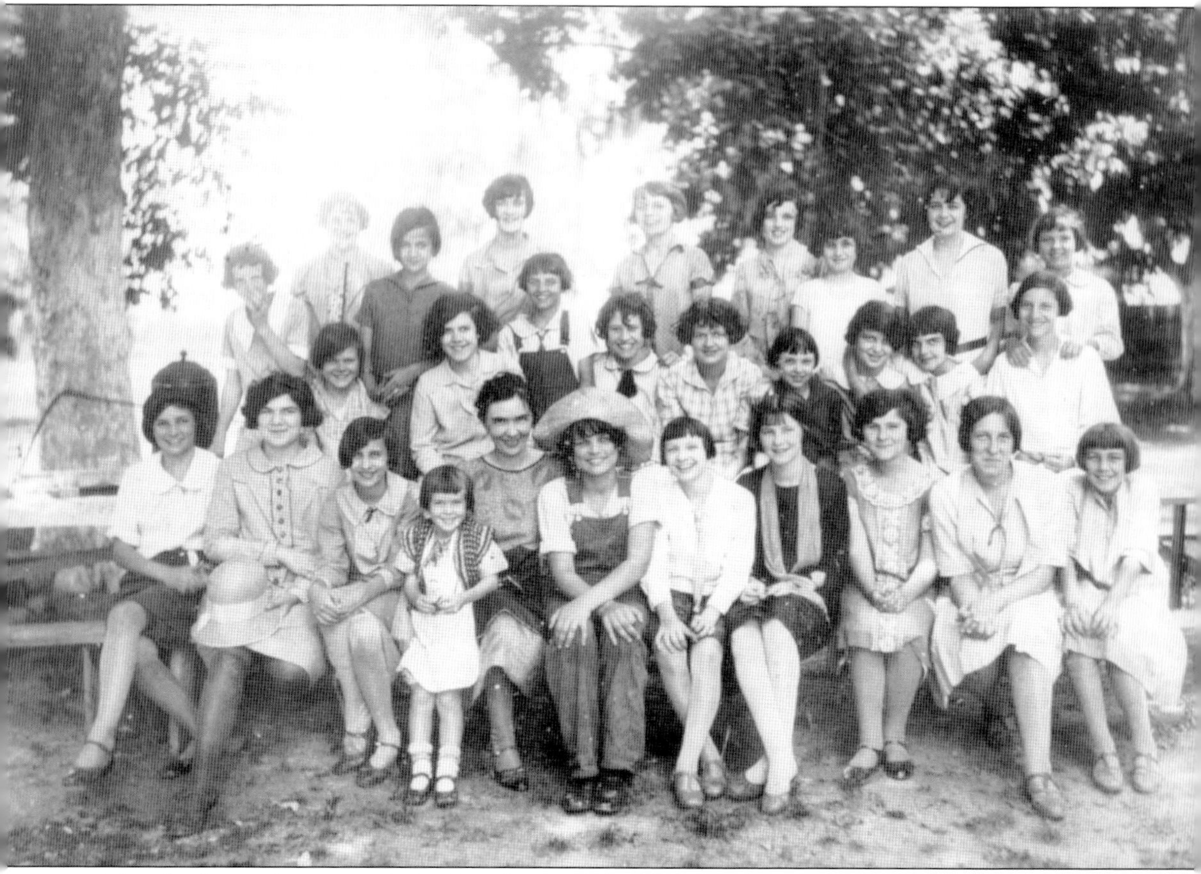

The Opelousas Junior Catholic Daughters of America with sponsor Fannie Bowden visited the Suburban Gardens, a popular resort area off the old Port Barre Highway near Opelousas around 1926. The Suburban Gardens, owned by Simon Stelly and Lee Danel, operated from 1926 until the flood of 1927 forced it to close. Pictured in this group are, from left to right, (first row) Dee Dee Garland, Marie Pavy, Helen Ventre, Marian Barnett, Fannie Bowden, Lillian Barnett, Myrtle Andrus, Juanita Richard, Celeste Lafond, and Juliette Lafond; (second row) Edith Robinson, Rosa Boagni, Mazie Sonnier, Jessie Rosa Barnett, Aline Genin, Genevie Manouvrier, and Evelyn Haw; (third row) Agnes Titard, Ruth Robertson, Alice Garland, and Mary Louise Richard; (fourth row) Romaine Dejean, Orelena Campbell, Mary Boutte, Alice Boagni, Verna St. Cyr, and Marynia Comeau.

Five

Education

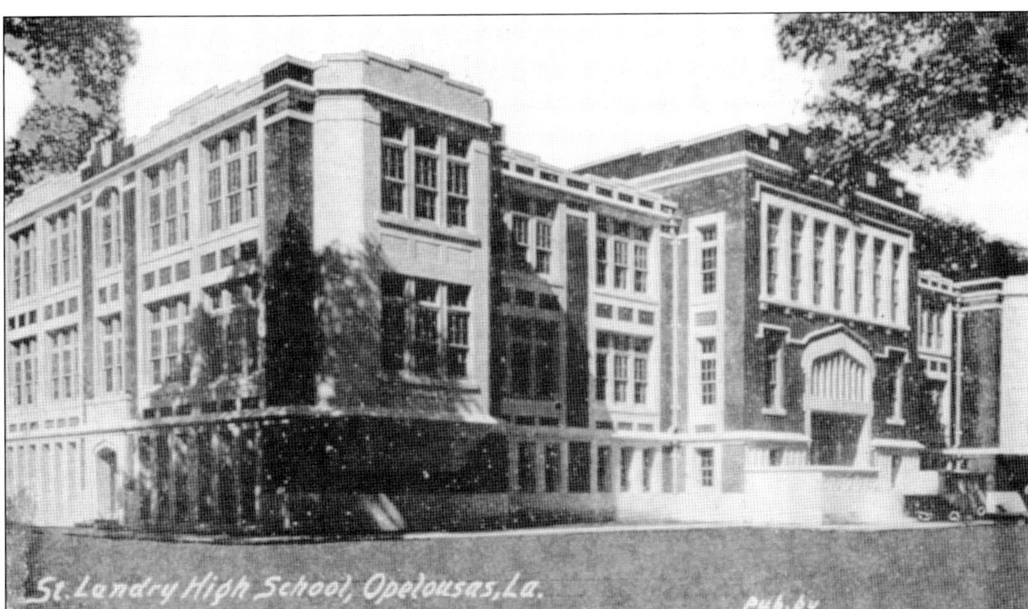

Although there were educational opportunities in St. Landry Parish going back to the early part of the 1800s, public education as it is known today began with the creation of the St. Landry School Board in the latter part of the 19th century. The year 1893 saw the opening of the newly constructed Washington High School in the neighboring town and the construction of St. Landry High School in Opelousas, which opened in January 1894. By 1915, Opelousas had a new brick school building located on South Street, pictured on this postcard by *Jacobs News Depot*.

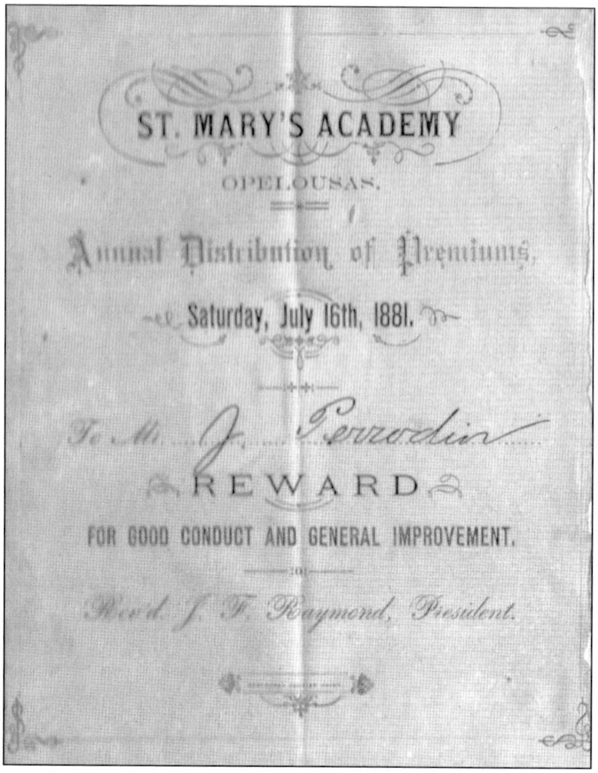

ST. MARY'S ACADEMY

OPELOUSAS.

Annual Distribution of Premiums,

Saturday, July 16th, 1881.

To Mr. J. Perrodin

REWARD

FOR GOOD CONDUCT AND GENERAL IMPROVEMENT.

Rev'd J. F. Raymond, President.

During the 1850s, the St. Landry Catholic Church in Opelousas established two schools, St. Mary's Academy for boys in 1855 and Academy of the Immaculate Conception for girls in 1856. These two schools eventually merged to become the Academy of the Immaculate Conception (AIC). In 1971, the school merged with the Holy Ghost School in Opelousas and became Opelousas Catholic, which continues to operate today. The image at left is a certificate awarded to J. Perrodin, a student at St. Mary's Academy, on July 16, 1881. The photograph below shows the new Academy of the Immaculate Conception building on the corner of Main and Church Streets, constructed in 1908.

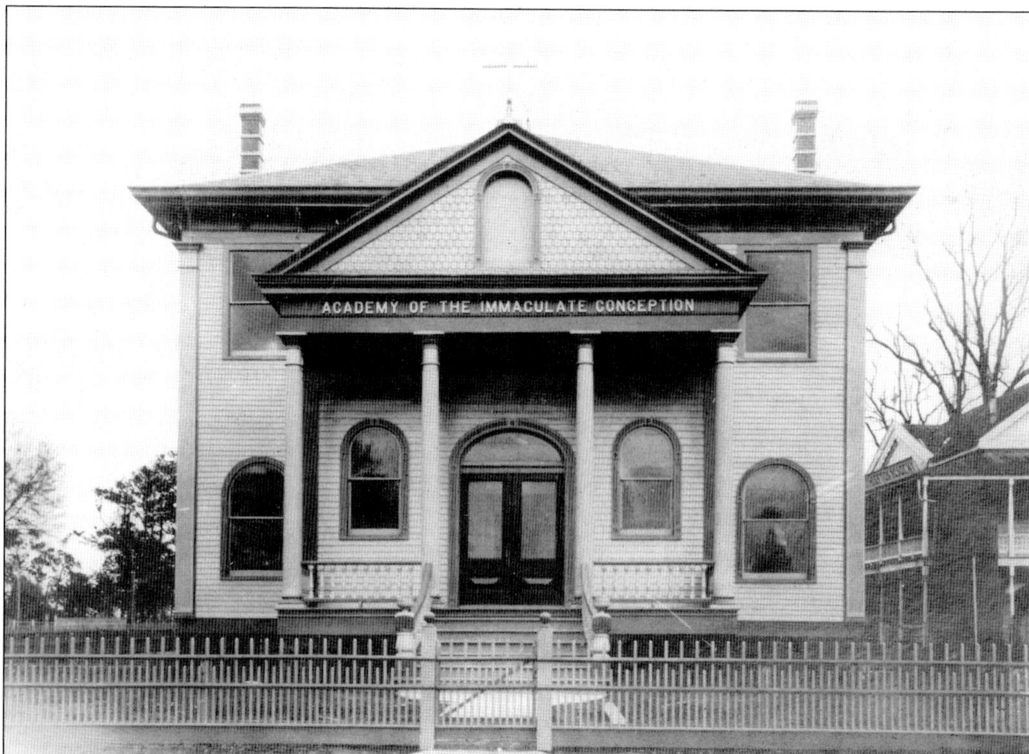

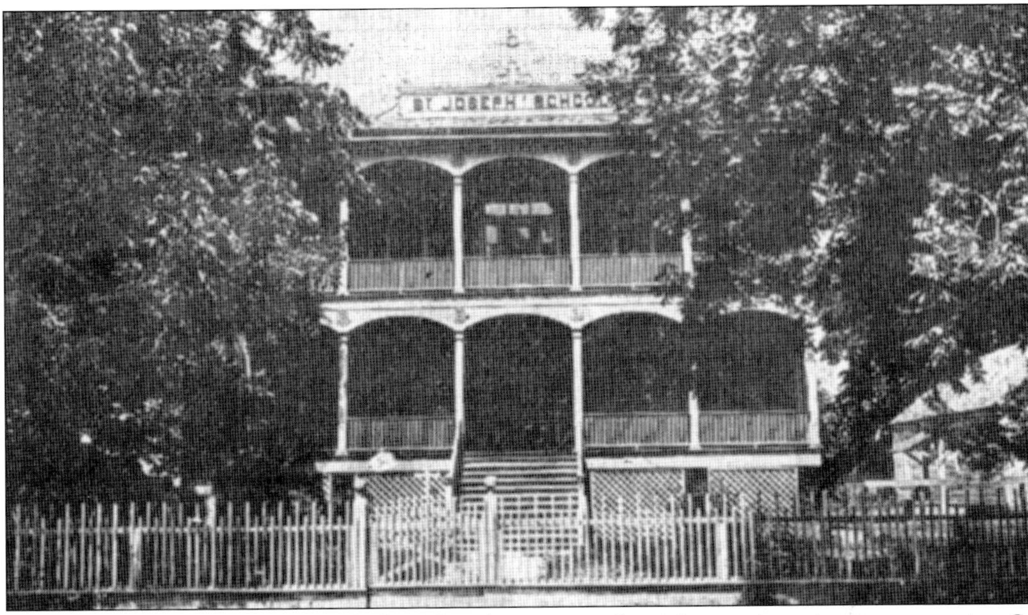

Established in 1874 by the Catholic Church to serve the African American community, St. Joseph's Academy was also called St. Joseph Convent or St. Joseph School. It was run by the Sisters of the Holy Family, who came to Opelousas from New Orleans. In 1920, when the new Holy Ghost Catholic Church was organized, the school's name was changed to Holy Ghost Catholic School. In 1971, the school merged with the Academy of the Immaculate Conception to become Opelousas Catholic, operating in Opelousas today. St. Joseph's School is pictured on Union Street in this photograph taken around 1915.

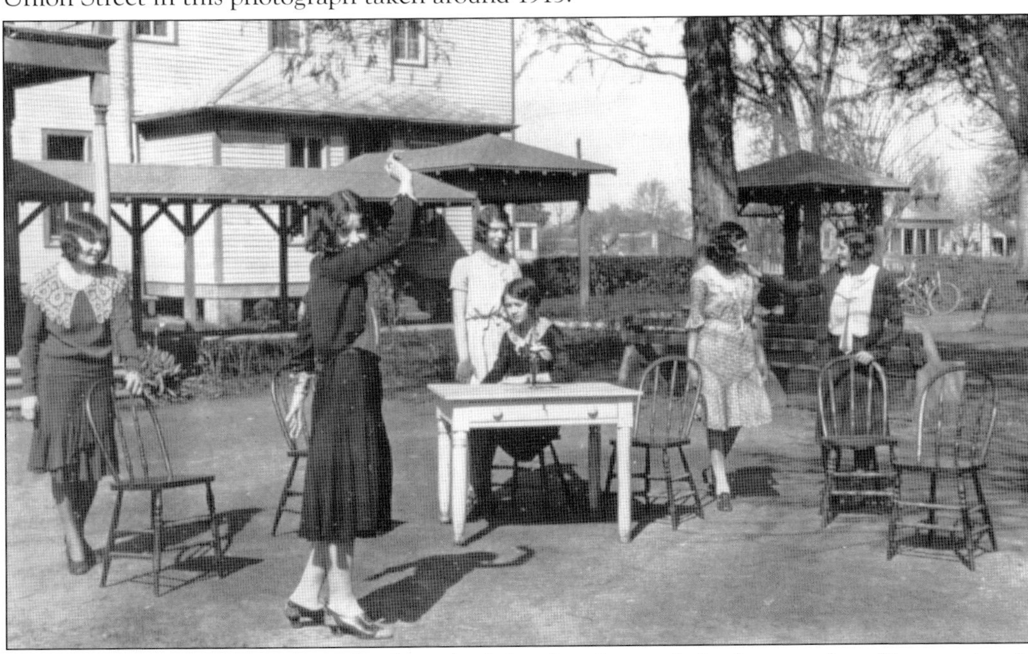

During the early 1930s, the school yard of the Academy of the Immaculate Conception in Opelousas was the perfect place to practice for the school play. As her classmates practice, Marie Beah Andrepont, far left, is watching with interest.

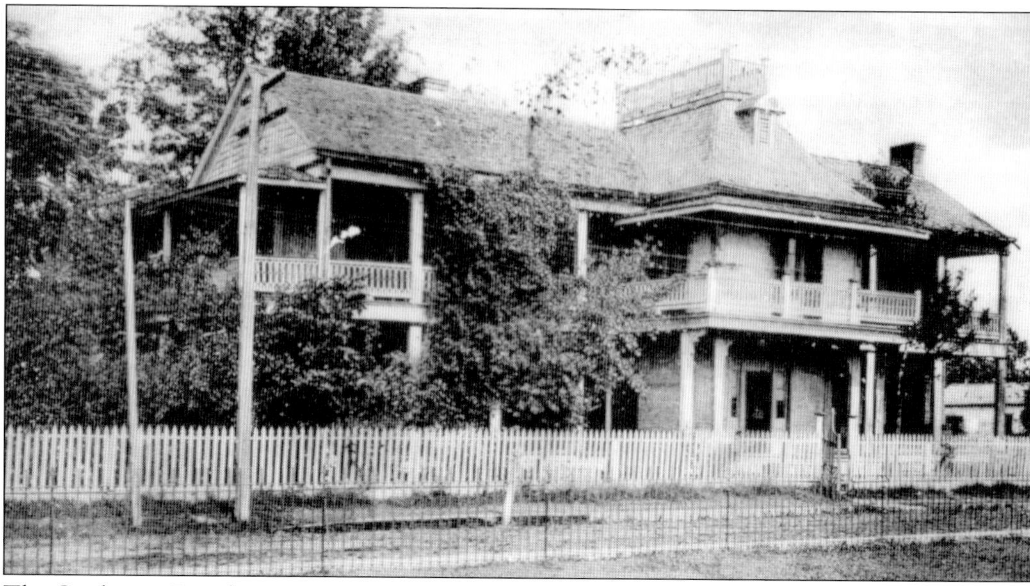

The Opelousas Female Institute sat on the corner of South and Court Streets for several decades. It was started in 1871 by Margaret M. White Hayes, who was known as "Mattie" and also as "Aunt Mag." At first it was called the School for Young Ladies, but by 1888, it became the Opelousas Female Institute. Although it was strictly a girls' school when it first opened, by the start of the 20th century, boys were allowed to attend. The school continued to operate until 1909. This photograph shows the school in the early 1900s. Several years later, it was demolished so that a private family home could be built on the property.

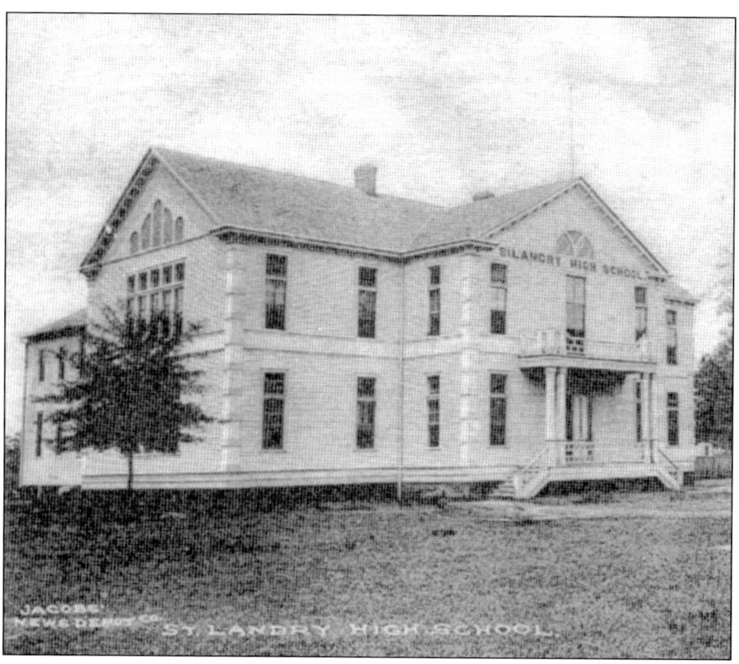

Although there were educational opportunities in St. Landry Parish going back to the early part of the 1800s, January 1894 saw the opening of the newly constructed St. Landry High School on North Market Street in Opelousas seen here around 1905. In 1915, a new brick high school was constructed, and in 1918, this school building was moved to Academy Street, near its intersection with Vine Street, and was used as the St. Landry Training School for the African American population.

Frances Emerson (1924–2012), second row, third from left, is pictured with her 1941 graduating class from Holy Ghost School in Opelousas. In 1945, she married Alvin A. Haynes Sr.; the couple had four sons, Alvin "Chubby" Haynes Jr., Vernon Haynes Sr., Karl Ray Haynes Sr., and Gregory Haynes Sr. Frances, an Opelousas businesswoman, teacher, and community leader, worked to build Williams Funeral Home in Opelousas into one of the most successful businesses in town, today operated by her sons Chubby and Vernon. She also served on the board of directors of Williams Life Insurance Company, one of the largest African American–owned businesses of its kind in the nation. (Courtesy of the Haynes family.)

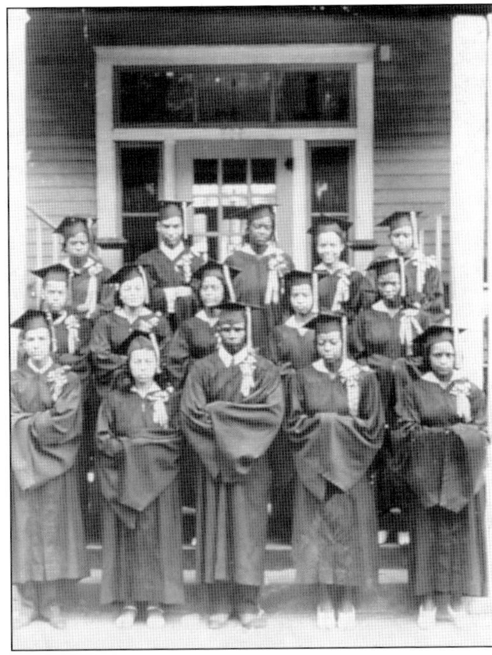

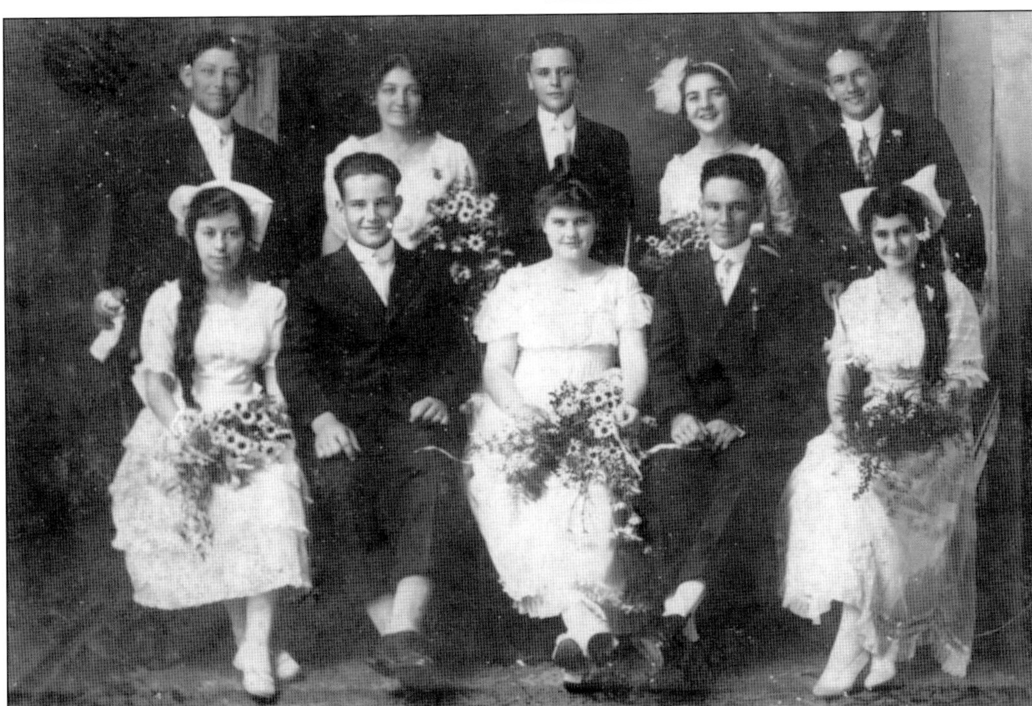

By 1915, Opelousas had a new brick public school building located on South Street. The first graduating class from that school in 1915 included five girls and five boys. Shown in the class picture are, from left to right, (first row) Myrtle Durio, Howard Voorhies, Pet Sanders, Edward Estorge, and Ruth Thompson; (second row) Preston Wyble, Noemie Burr, Lionel Castille, Corinne Trosclair, and Campbell Jones. In the early 1920s, St. Landry High School was renamed Opelousas High School. (Courtesy of Thom and Madeline Daly.)

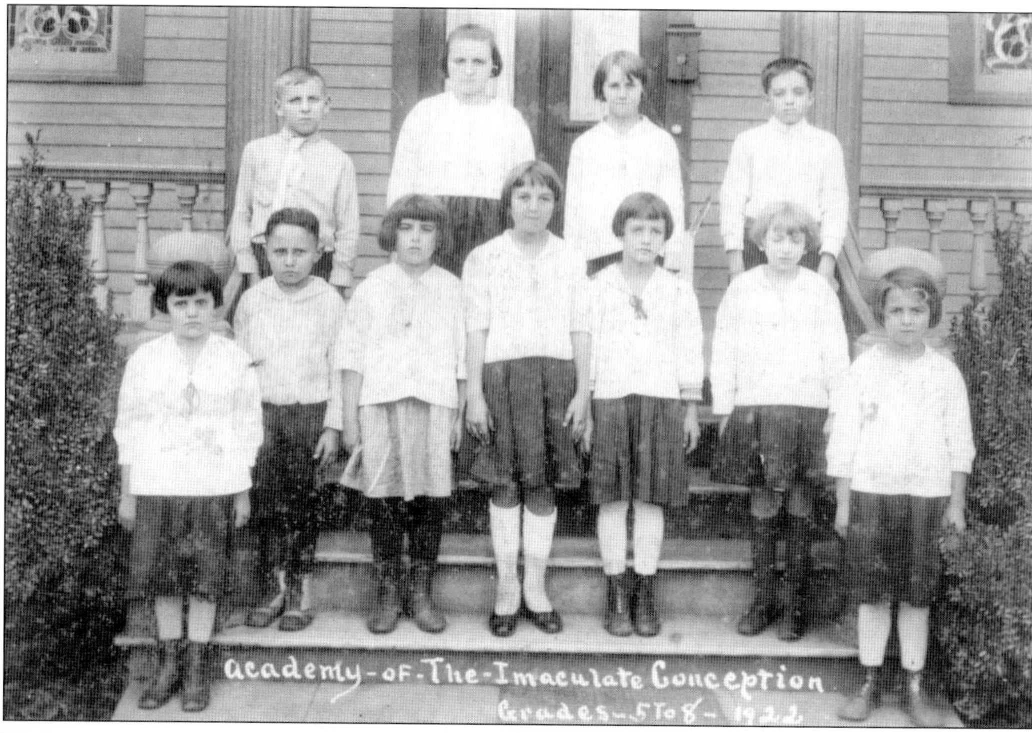

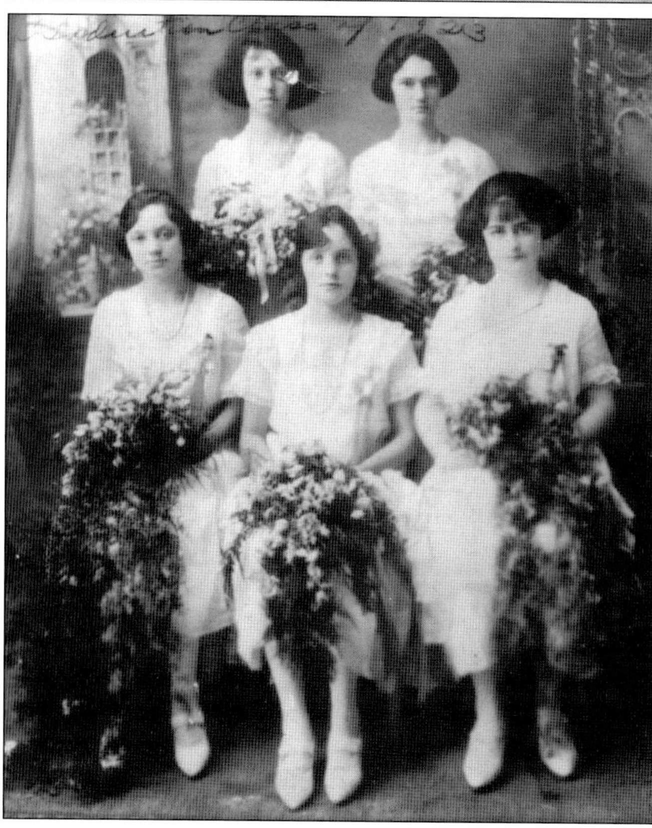

The fifth–eighth grade students at the Academy of the Immaculate Conception are pictured in 1922 on the steps of the school on Main Street in Opelousas. From left to right are (first row) Delores Sandoz, Earl Richard, Helen St. Cyr, Hazel Davy, Elodie Bernard, Rose Desipso, and Lucille Vidrine; (second row) Charles Ventre, ? Savoie, Aline Leger, and Lloyd Smith.

The 1923 graduating class of the Academy of the Immaculate Conception (AIC) held its commencement exercises on Tuesday, June 12 at the school auditorium on Main Street in Opelousas. Class members pictured here include, in no particular order, Lucille Danel, Gertrude St. Cyr, Carmen Mizzi, Georgie DeJean, and Bessie Ardoin.

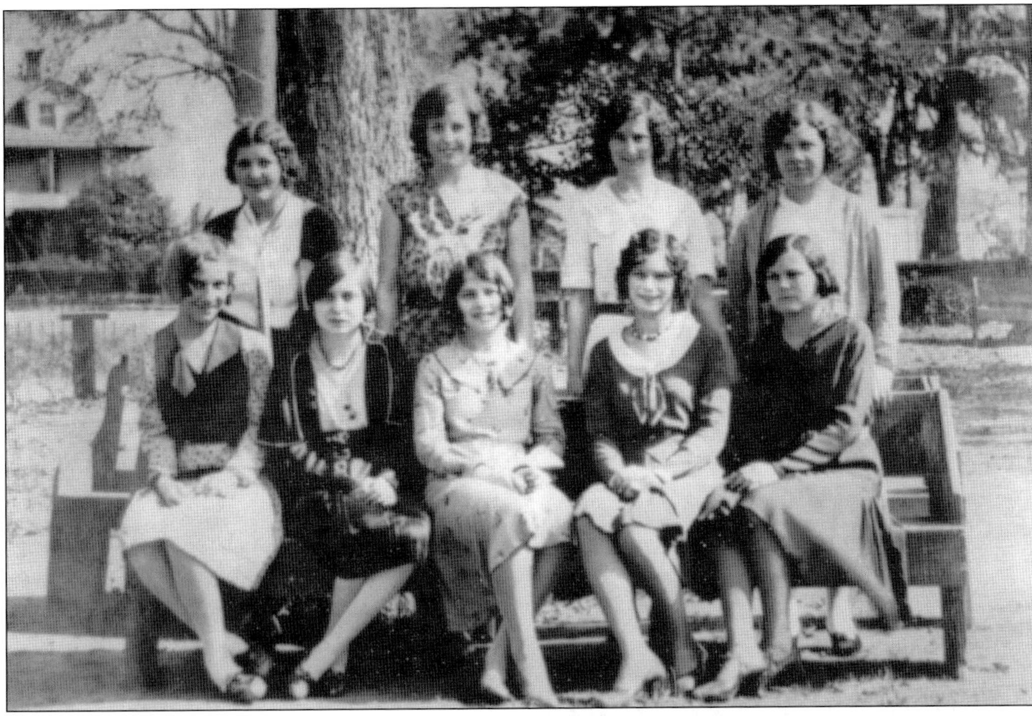

The 1932 graduating class of the Academy of the Immaculate Conception sits for its class picture on the school grounds in Opelousas. Pictured are, from left to right, (first row) Alice Evelyn Bordelon, Lucette Bernard, Wilda Chachere, Frances Reed, and Antonia Lafleur; (second row) Evelyn Fields, Aline Daigle, Rose Ledoux, and Barbara McMillian.

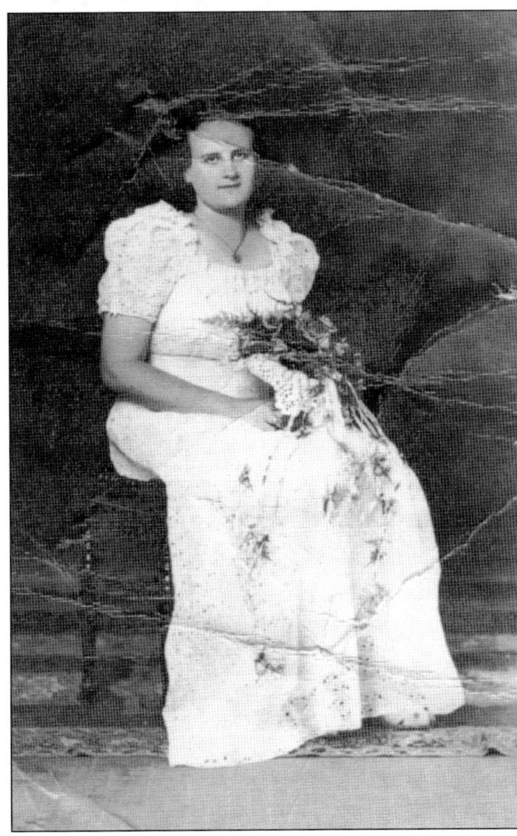

Dorothy Myrtle "Dot" Dunbar is pictured dressed for her graduation from Opelousas High School in 1939. Following her graduation, she worked for the newly opened *Daily World* newspaper. On March 1, 1947, Dorothy and her sister Ruth Dunbar Pavy opened a camera and bookstore in the Boagni Law office building on West Bellevue Street. After 12 years of developing their successful business, Dunbar Camera and Book Store moved to the larger Riseman Building on the corner of Market and Landry Streets in the heart of downtown. "Miss Dot," a well-respected community leader, continued in business until 1992. She died on July 17, 1998, and is buried in Myrtle Grove Cemetery in Opelousas.

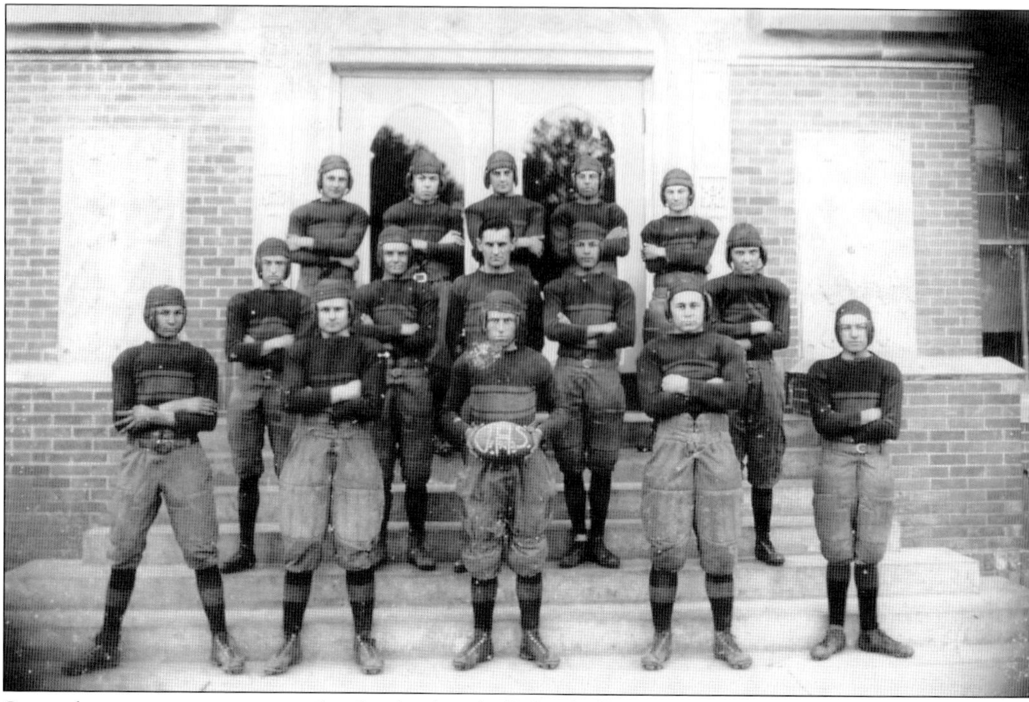

Sports became an activity at schools after baseball, football, and basketball came to Opelousas at the turn of the 20th century. St. Landry High School had a football team by 1900. In the 1920s, football and basketball were popular at public and private schools. When St. Landry High School became Opelousas High School, A.A. Mendoza was its first football coach. In 1922, with Sam Moncla as the coach, the school had a winning football team. Players were in uniforms for this photograph taken at the school. Identified by Miriam M. Roy, team members are, from left to right, (first row) Lee Garland, Earl Guedry, Lloyd Reynolds, Noah Guedry, and Sidney Bertheaud; (second row) Lee Robin, Edmond Pavy, Coach Sam Moncla, Havlin Haw, and Elden Voorhies; (third row) Arthur Sanders, Creighton Shute, Ivan Holman, Henry Pitre, and Victor Andrepont.

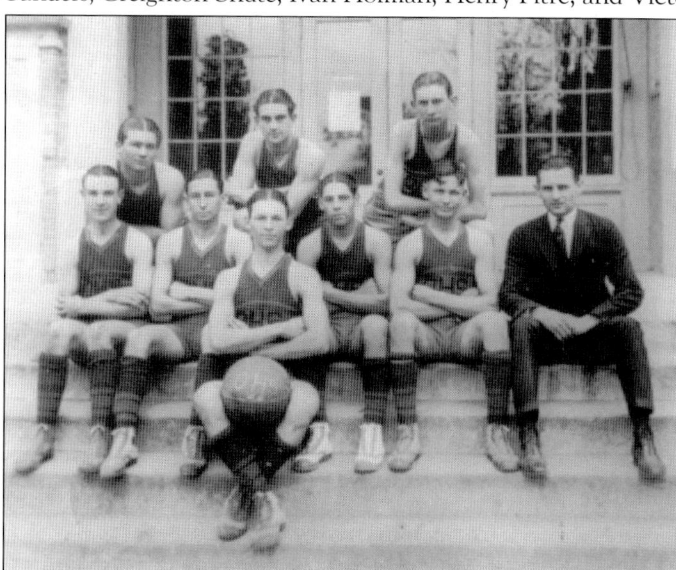

Basketball also became popular on school campuses during the 1920s. Posing for this photograph on the school steps on South Street is the 1922–1923 Opelousas High School basketball team. Members of the team are, from left to right, (first row) Havelin "Chicken" Haw, holding the basketball; (second row) Rupert Lyons, T.H. Littell, Henry Pitre, Lee "Brother" Garland Jr., and Sam Moncla, coach; (third row) Leon Tujague, Ivan Holman, and Anthony "Tony" Chachere.

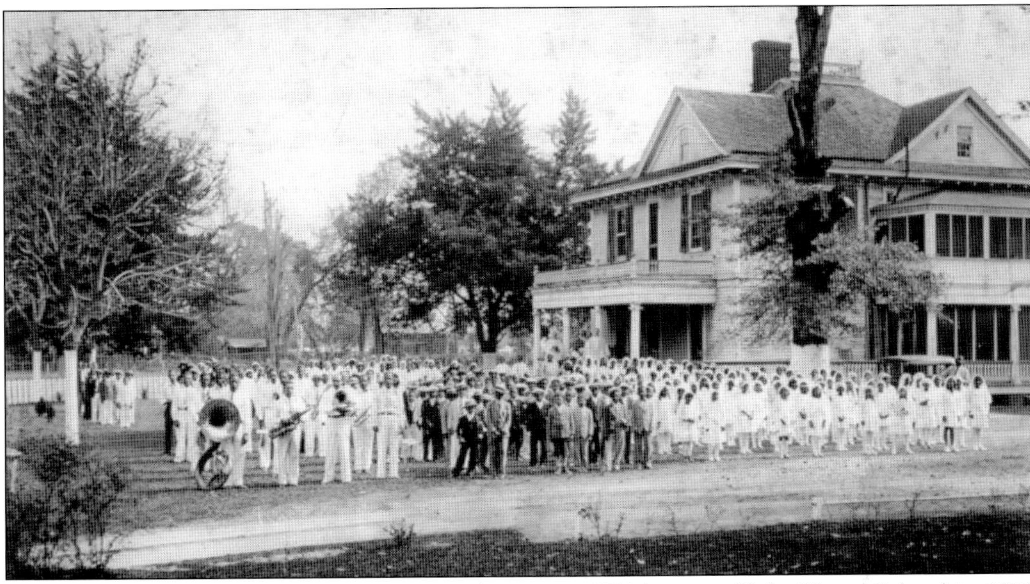

What began as St. Joseph's School in Opelousas in 1874 became Holy Ghost School in 1921, named for the new Holy Ghost Catholic Church Parish that was created in 1919. It continued to educate students as Holy Ghost School on North Union Street for over five decades until it merged with the Academy of the Immaculate Conception in 1971 to become Opelousas Catholic School, today located on Prudhomme Lane. This photograph is the Holy Ghost school band in the early days, pictured on the grounds of the Holy Ghost Catholic Church rectory on Union Street around 1928. (Courtesy of Frank Boudreaux and Opelousas Catholic School.)

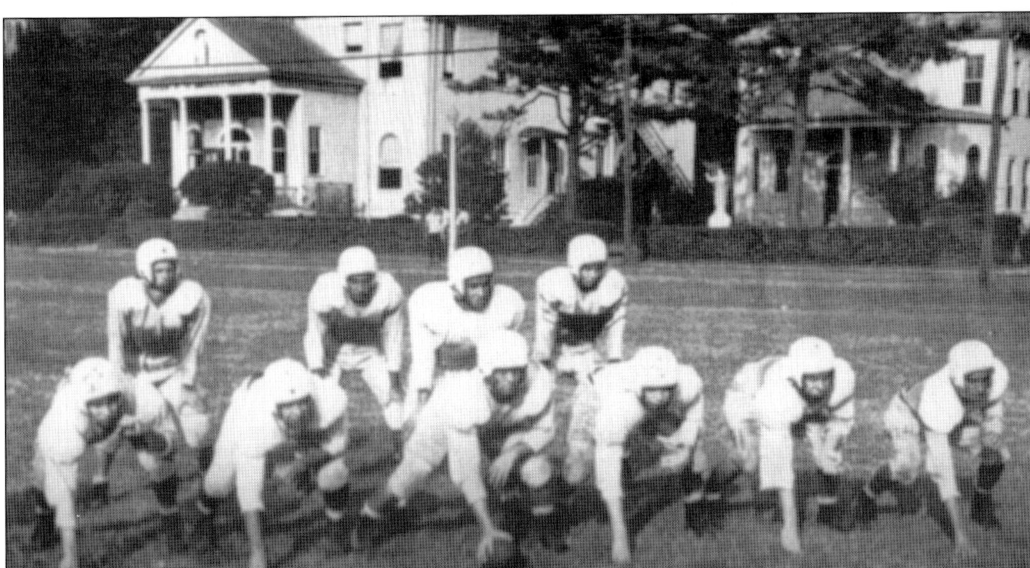

These unidentified members of the 1950 Academy of the Immaculate Conception football team pose for this photograph on Main Street with school buildings in the background. Some of the stars of Coach Warren Douglas's Wildcat squad that year included Donald Sebastien, Anthony Comeaux, Austin Wyble, Charles Hollier, Bobby Fontenot, Jimmy McCarthy, Herman Pellerin, C.J. Guilbeau, Charles Delahousaye, Sidney Bertheaud, and William Baque.

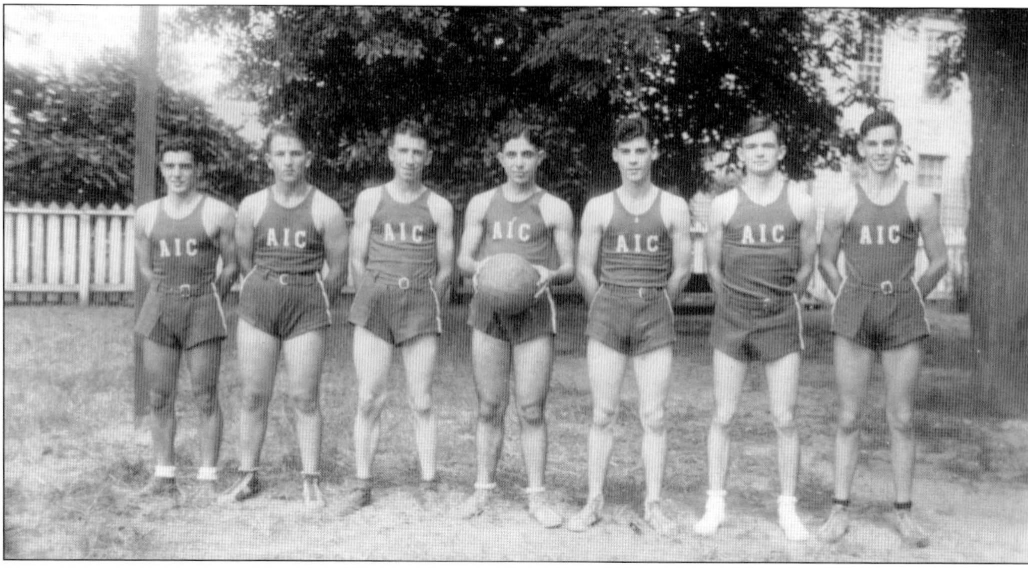

The Academy of the Immaculate Conception also had boys' and girls' basketball teams as early as the 1930s. The 1933–1934 boys' basketball team is pictured here wearing their uniforms on the school grounds. Pictured from left to right are Bernard Richard, Perry Moore, Beaty Herpin, Herbert Abdalla, George Ortego, Harold Comeau, and Charles Bordelon.

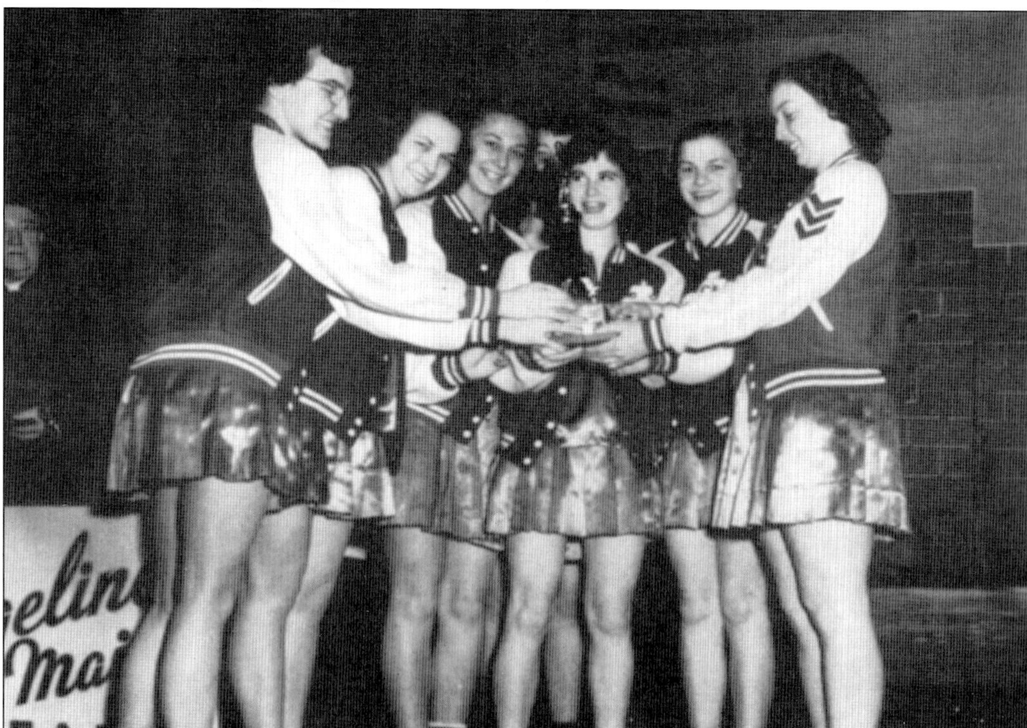

The 1950–1951 Academy of the Immaculate Conception girls' championship team, coached by Isabel G. Perry, posed for this photograph following one of their games. Identified by Virval Fontenot Bradley, in this photograph are, from left to right, Nira LeDoux, Jeanette Brinkman Landreneau, Verna Mel Christ, Jeanne Voitier, Ann Hollier, and Catherine Johnson.

Six

Culinary Culture

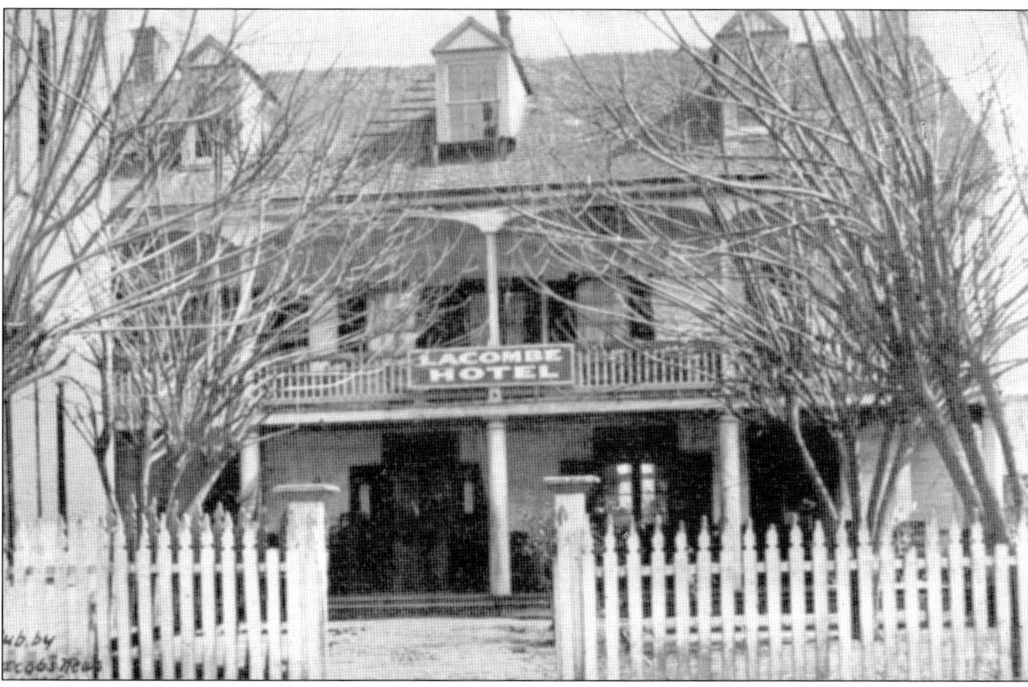

The Lacombe Hotel, originally established as the Eagle Hotel in the early 19th century, was operated in later years by Austin Lacombe, who was known as a perfect mine host. He branded his business as the most hospitable in the state. He was also known for the great meals he served to hotel guests. When Martha R. Field, who wrote as Catherine Cole, the great travel writer of the south, visited Opelousas in the 1890s, she found delicious food at the Lacombe. In her book, *Louisiana Voyages: The Travel Writings of Catherine Cole, 1892–1894*, she wrote of her visit, "I must say there is a hotel in Opelousas where the cooking is as good as one might get in Paris." The old hotel stood in Opelousas for over a century until it was demolished around 1927.

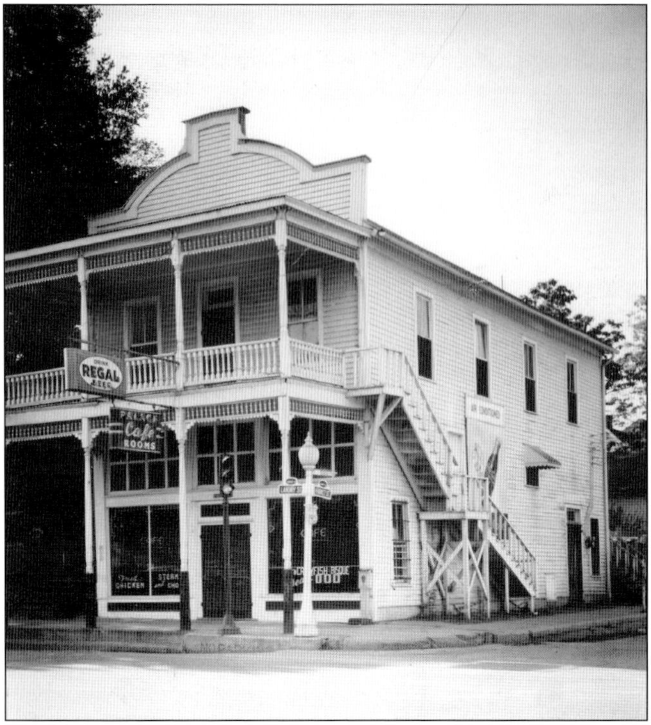

This photograph of the Palace Café on Landry Street shows the restaurant in its original historic building. That building was demolished and replaced with a brick structure in 1955. Established in the 1890s as the Palace Sandwich Shop, in 1927 it was renamed Palace Café by new owner George Doucas. Located on the southeast corner of Landry and Market Streets, this restaurant is the oldest eating establishment in Opelousas. Today, with new owners, it is called Chicory's at the Palace and is still in operation providing delicious meals to local citizens and visitors alike. The photograph below shows the interior of the Palace Café around 1928.

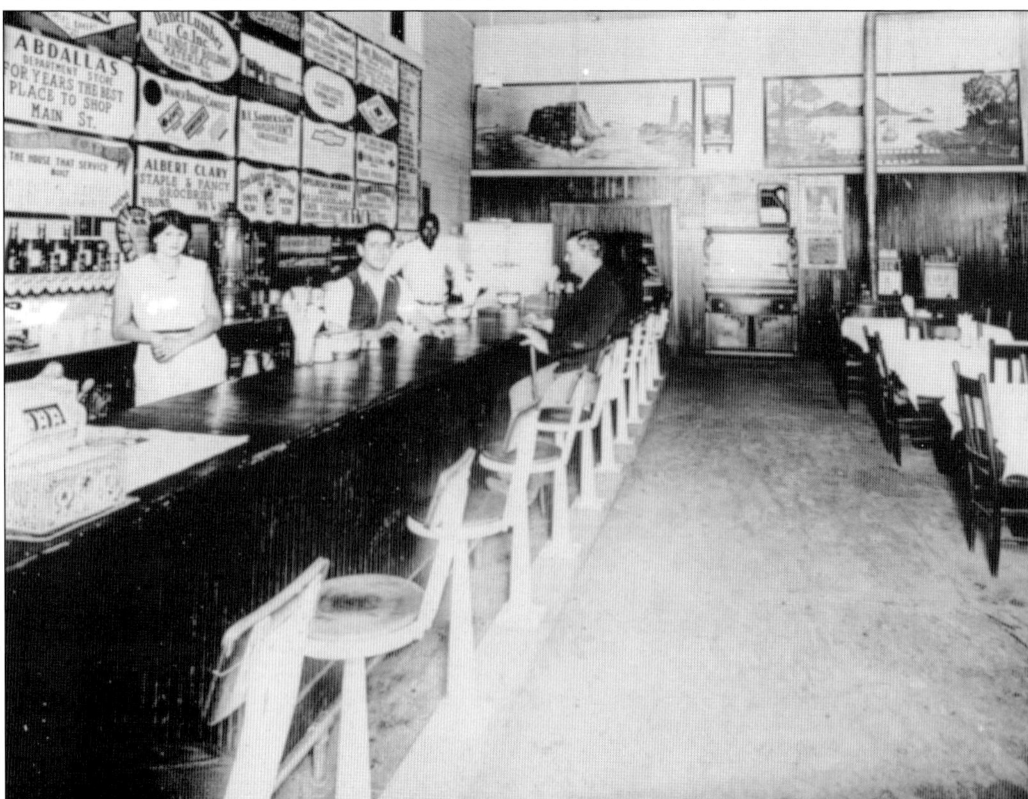

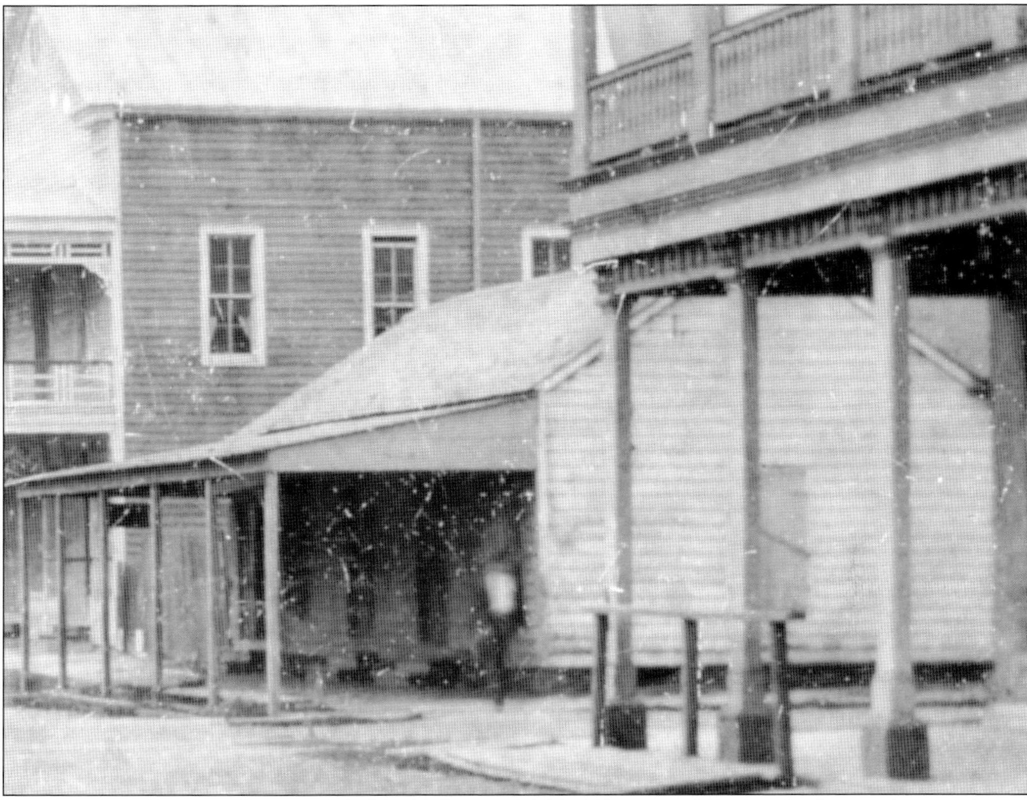

From its beginnings as a settlement, coffee was an important part of the culinary culture in Opelousas. Having a good cup of coffee is a tradition in Opelousas and south Louisiana. Many local folks drink coffee from the time they wake until they retire for the night. Some of the earliest eating establishments in town began as coffee shops, with many selling liquors as well. In 1892, the Bijoux Store and Coffee House, shown in this photograph, was located at the corner of Main and Bellevue Streets, next door to the Sandoz Opera House and across Bellevue Street from Joseph Bloch's store.

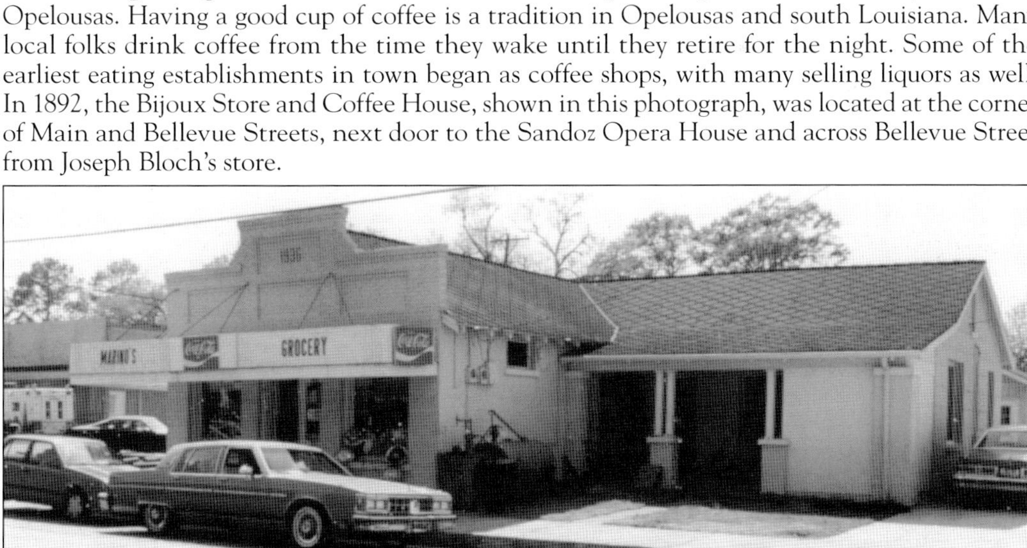

Mom-and-pop grocery stores dotted the Opelousas area in the early days of the community and into the 20th century. These stores sold food, meat, bread, and other staple items. Some of the family-owned stores that operated for decades were Lupo's Grocery located on East Grolee Street; Miller's Grocery located on West Grolee Street; and Marino's Grocery, pictured here, located on South Union St. in Opelousas.

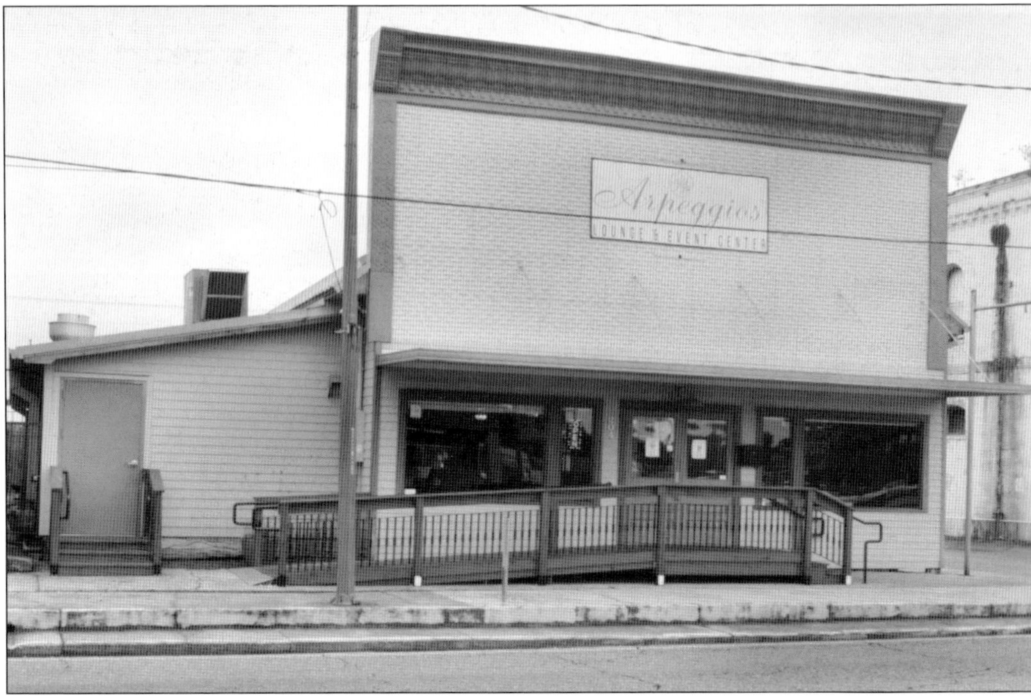

DelBuono's Place coffee house on the corner of Main and North Streets claimed to have the best coffee in Opelousas in an advertisement appearing in the *Clarion Progress* newspaper on February 3, 1928. Declaring it was always good, owner Anthony DelBuono said, "You will enjoy coffee at my shop." This recent photograph shows the building that housed DelBuono's Place a century ago. Later, the building was the Main Street Liquor Store for many years. Eventually, it became Le Zinc Main Street Bar and Restaurant and today is home to the Arpeggios Lounge and Event Center. (Photograph by Freddie Herpin.)

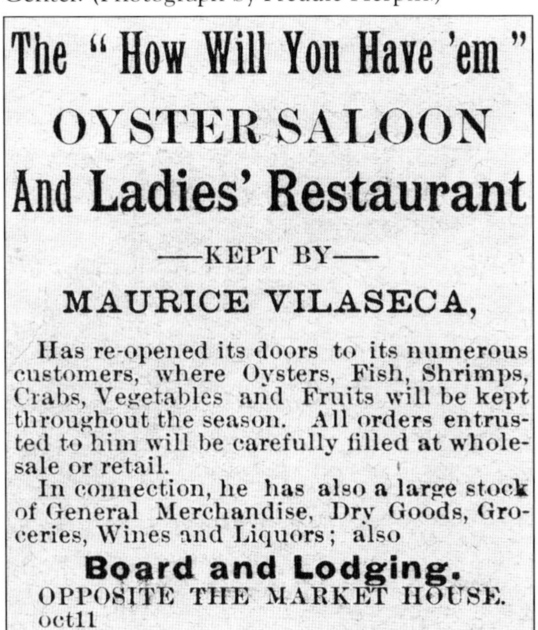

The "How Will You Have 'em"

OYSTER SALOON

And Ladies' Restaurant

—KEPT BY—

MAURICE VILASECA,

Has re-opened its doors to its numerous customers, where Oysters, Fish, Shrimps, Crabs, Vegetables and Fruits will be kept throughout the season. All orders entrusted to him will be carefully filled at wholesale or retail.

In connection, he has also a large stock of General Merchandise, Dry Goods, Groceries, Wines and Liquors; also

Board and Lodging.

OPPOSITE THE MARKET HOUSE.

oct11

A popular restaurant in Opelousas during the latter part of the 1800s was the "How Will You Have 'em" Oyster Saloon and Ladies Restaurant, owned by Maurice Vilaseca. It was located on the corner of Market and Bellevue Streets in Opelousas, opposite the Market House, which opened in 1870. The advertisement pictured here ran in the *Opelousas Courier* newspaper on October 11, 1890.

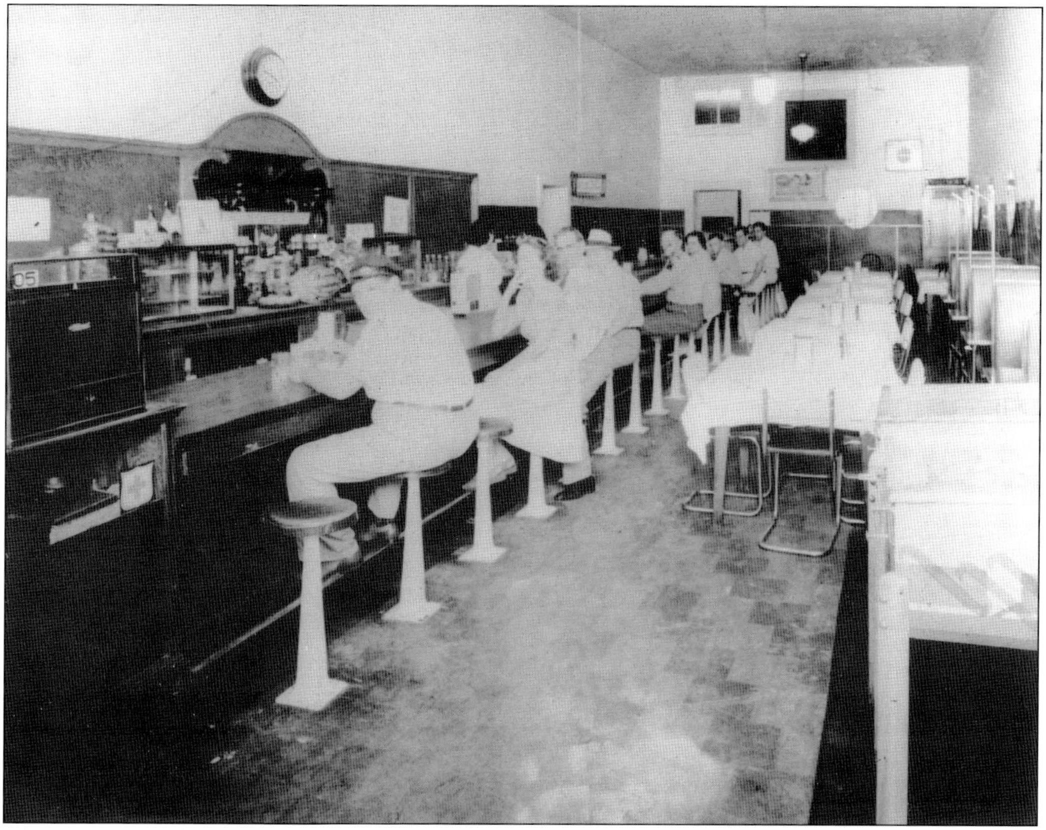

The DeLuxe Café, owned by the Etienne Daigle family, operated in downtown Opelousas during the 1930s and beyond. It was located on the north side of Landry Street between Union and Main Streets and at one time was on the Main and Landry Streets corner. Locals and visitors ordering breakfast at the DeLuxe Café enjoyed something special. The interior is shown in this 1940s photograph.

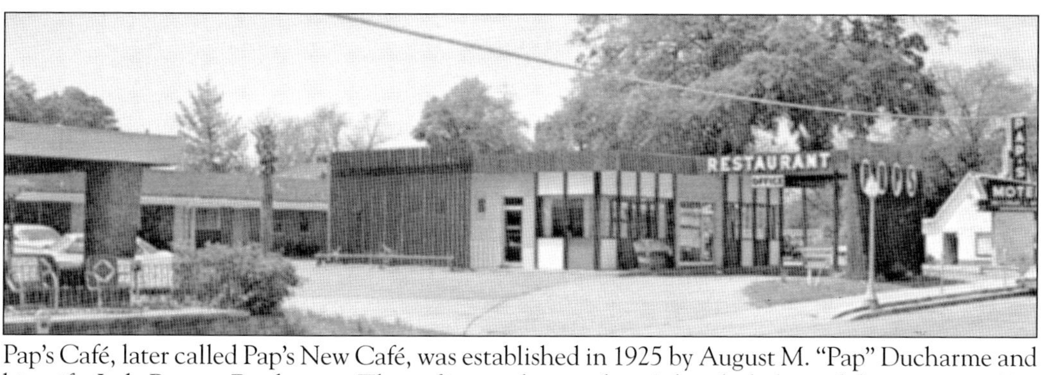

Pap's Café, later called Pap's New Café, was established in 1925 by August M. "Pap" Ducharme and his wife, Judy Breaux Ducharme. The café served a merchant's lunch daily, and dinners were 40¢. Other Pap specialties included his famous hot sandwiches, Creole chicken gumbo, and Mexican chili. When Pap's Café closed, the Ducharmes later opened Pap's Motel and Restaurant on West Landry Street in downtown Opelousas, shown in this 1950s photograph.

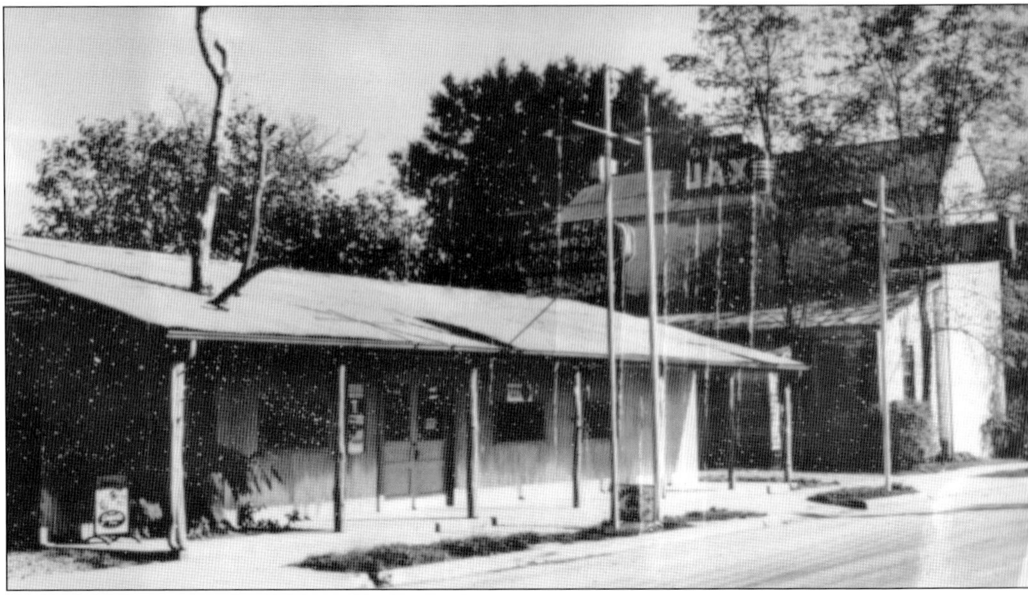

The Hut Drive Inn, located on North Union Street for several decades, was known for oysters on the half shell, plate lunch meals, and fresh fried oysters. Anthony "Tony" Graffagnino and staff really knew how to serve oysters. The back parking lot of the Hut was covered with all the shells left from "the oyster shukin'." Some of the award-winning oyster shuckers at the Hut included Dale Bodin, Jimmy Melancon, Tony Graffagnino (owner), and Tony Gene Graffagnino. (Courtesy of Robbie Sebastien.)

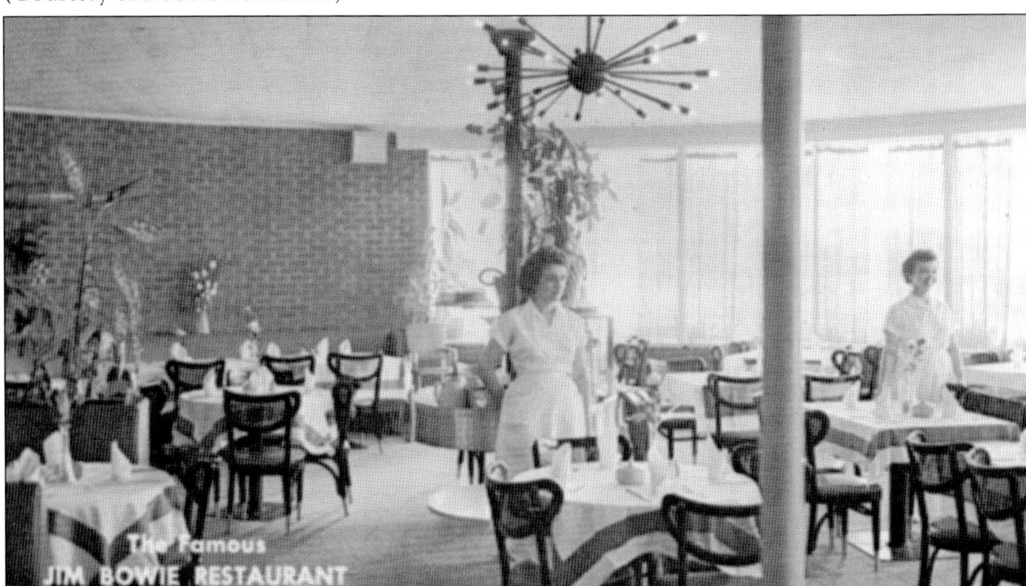

In the 1970s, the Cardinal Inn Motel had a great eatery called the Jim Bowie Restaurant, pictured here on a postcard from that decade. It was a favorite of Opelousas and St Landry Parish citizens. Many organizations and civic clubs held monthly meetings at this restaurant. During the 1970s, the Greater Opelousas Chamber of Commerce met there for the monthly board meetings. Advertisement for the restaurant in the early 1970s read "Enjoy Louisiana French Food at its Best, prepared by famous French Chef, E. D. Fuselier."

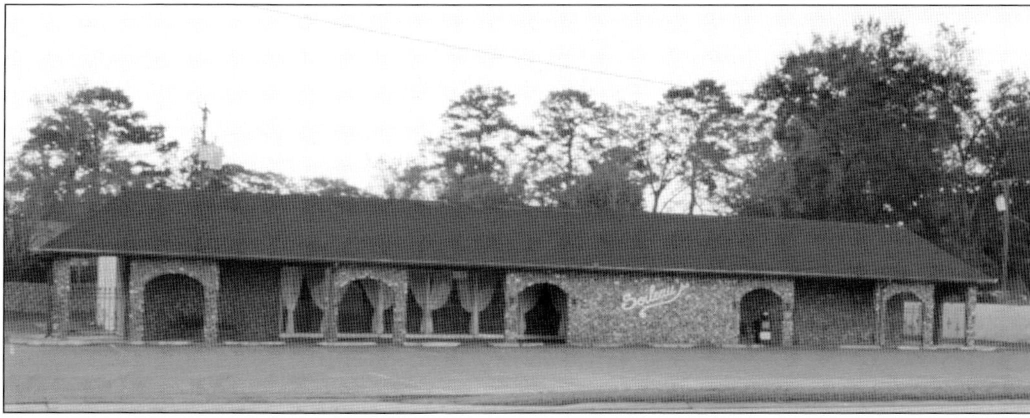

One of the oldest restaurants in Opelousas is the Soileau's Dinner Club on North Main Street. Started as a service station in the 1930s, it became one of the best-known eating establishments in south Louisiana after Clarence and Mable Soileau opened Soileau's Place in 1938. In 1947, Cliff Veillon joined Clarence in business and reopened the restaurant as Soileau's Dinner Club. Now owned by Scott and Beth Soileau and family, it remains in business today serving award-winning food. (Photograph by Sherri Landry.)

Tom and Eula Morris Savoie (1926–2010) opened Savoie's Grocery on the old Port Barre Road east of Opelousas in 1949. They purchased the store so Eula could work and still care for her growing family. In 1955, Savoie's began making sausage and other pork products. People loved Savoie's products, and as the company grew, new products were added, including real Cajun roux in the 1960s. Working hard, Eula grew the business to be one of the most successful in Louisiana. Today, Savoie's, run by Freddie Lafleur, sells its famous Cajun sausage, roux, and other products in Louisiana and across the United States. Eula is pictured here making Cajun sausage during the early years of the business. (Courtesy of Savoie's Sausage.)

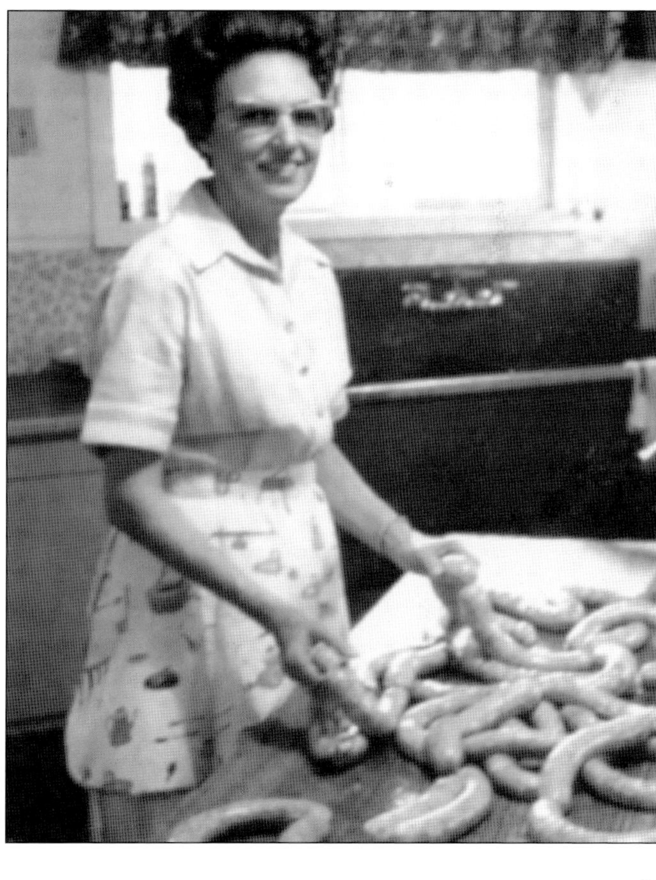

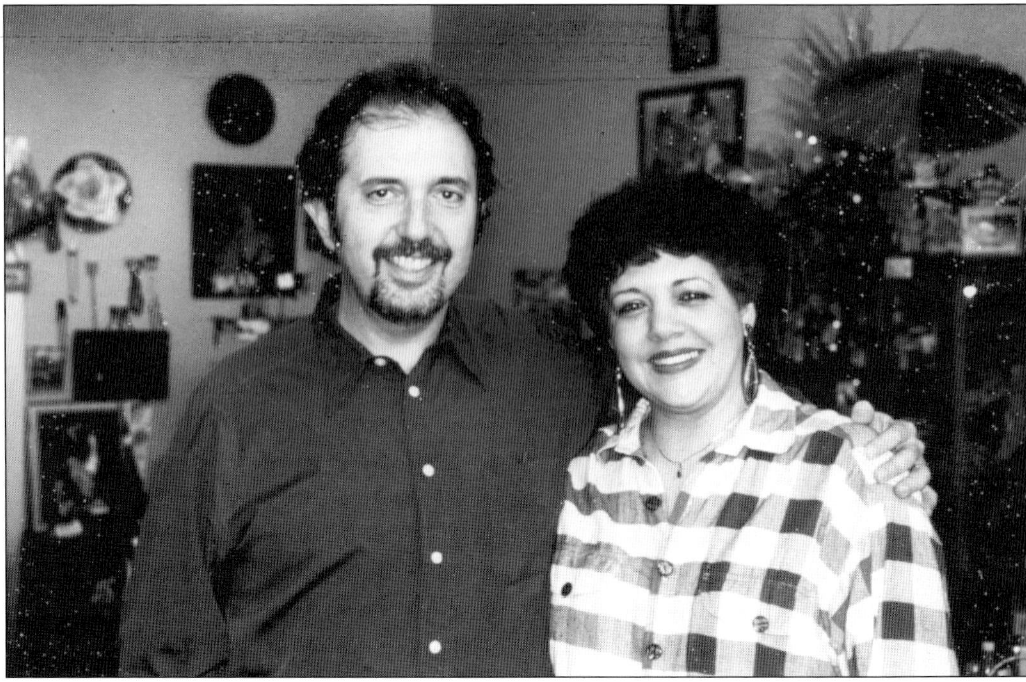

On May 3, 1993, Wanda Juneau's dream of owning her own restaurant became reality when she opened Back In Time on Landry Street in downtown Opelousas. After almost three decades, the restaurant continues to serve award-winning food to local citizens and visitors to the historic city. This photograph shows one of those visitors, Don Chaykin, with owner Wanda Juneau. Chaykin, a screenwriter from New York City, enjoyed a meal at Back In Time while touring Opelousas for a project with the Opelousas Film Commission in 1997. (Photograph by Phil Seifert.)

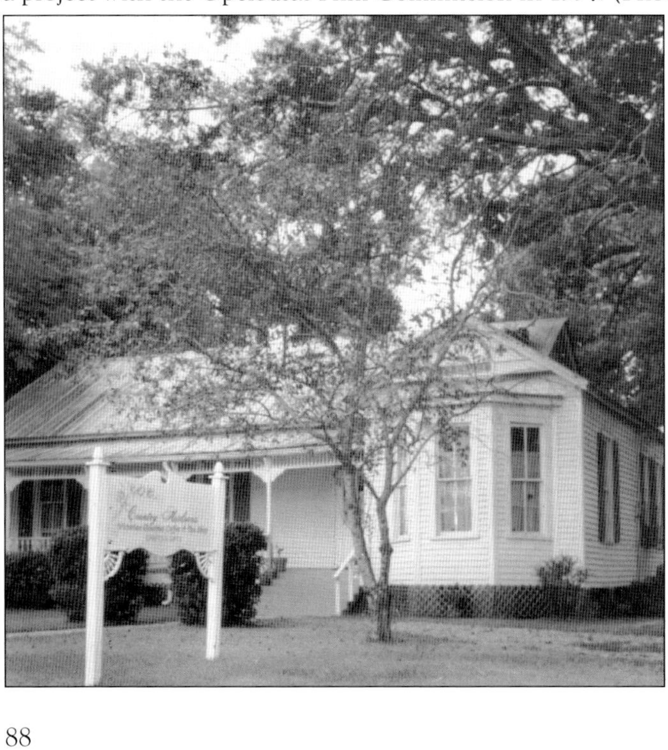

Seen in this 1993 photograph is the Country Heirlooms Victorian Gourmet Coffee and Tea Shop located in the historic Stubbs-Lastrapes home at 619 North Market Street in Opelousas. The business opened on October 5, 1991. Originally owned by Debbie Clavier, the business was later taken over by Terri Andrepont in 1993. This lovely shop was the place for tea parties, coffee, pastry, and lunch meetings for four years. The business operated until 1995.

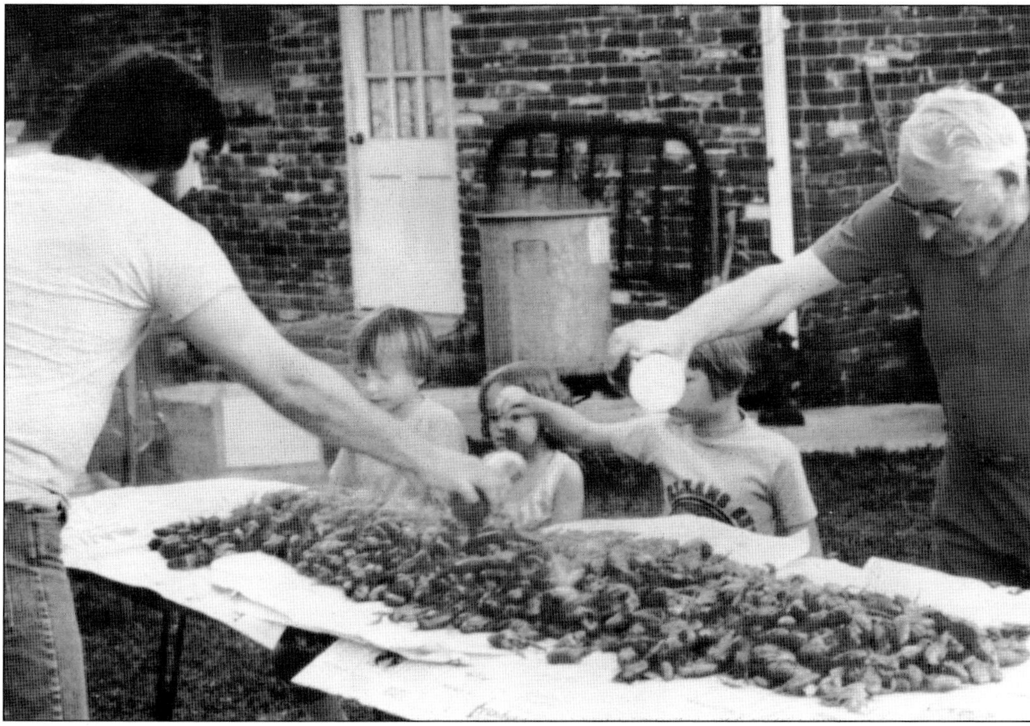

Crawfish is a staple food that is important to the culinary culture of Louisiana. During the season, citizens and visitors pack the local and area restaurants to enjoy special dishes like crawfish etouffee, crawfish bisque, boiled crawfish, and others made with the tasty freshwater crustaceans that resemble small lobsters. Special seasonal events are crawfish boils, like the one pictured here, held in backyards and venues in Opelousas and throughout Southwest Louisiana. Pictured around the table in this photograph are, from left to right, Kenneth Delcambre, Kiley Anderson, Mannie Anderson, Charles Lillie, and grandfather Charles Henry Lillie (1912–1993).

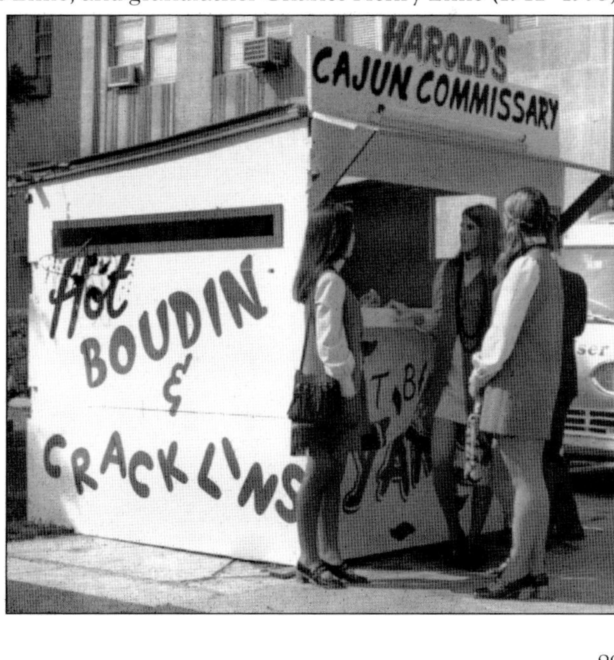

Boudin and cracklings are other staples of Cajun and Creole foods in south Louisiana. Boudin is a cooked sausage made from pork meat, rice, various vegetables, and seasonings, all stuffed in a casing. Cracklings are made from pork rinds, fried and seasoned to taste. Both products can be purchased from local shops and even gas stations across south Louisiana. When Opelousas celebrated its 250th anniversary in 1970, one of the food booths at the big event served boudin and cracklings prepared by Harold Fontenot, who owned a store in nearby Lewisburg. The girl standing second from left at the booth in this photograph is Kathy Mobley McBane.

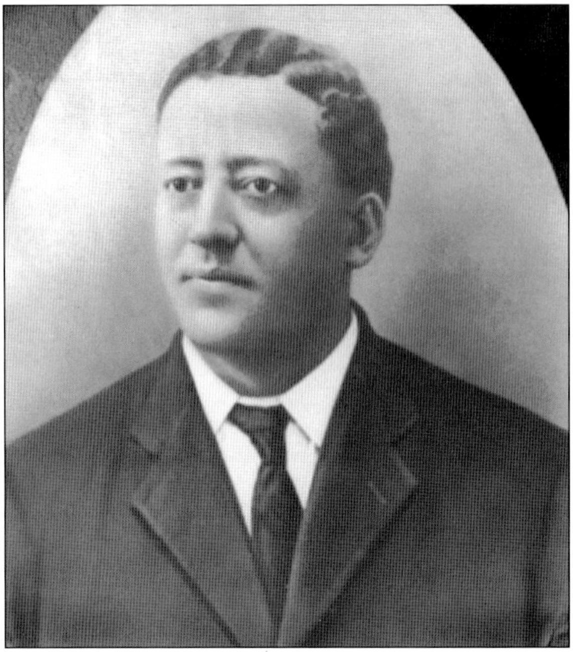

Celebrated Creole chef Charles "Didee" Lastrapes (1868–1947) operated the Elk Restaurant on Bellevue Street with his wife, Laura Guidry Lastrapes, from the early 1900s until 1919 when it was sold. When the Elk closed in 1920, Lastrapes and his second wife, Anna Alsandor, opened Didee's Restaurant on Market Street in 1921. It became a culinary treasure for Opelousas, known throughout the state and other areas for its delicious foods. Tourists; Louisiana governors; and celebrities like Marlon Brando, Lillian Hellman, Glen Campbell, and Ezzard Charles enjoyed Didee's Opelousas baked duck and other dishes he made special. Lastrapes died on April 22, 1947, in Opelousas. (Courtesy of Alex Da'Paul Lee.)

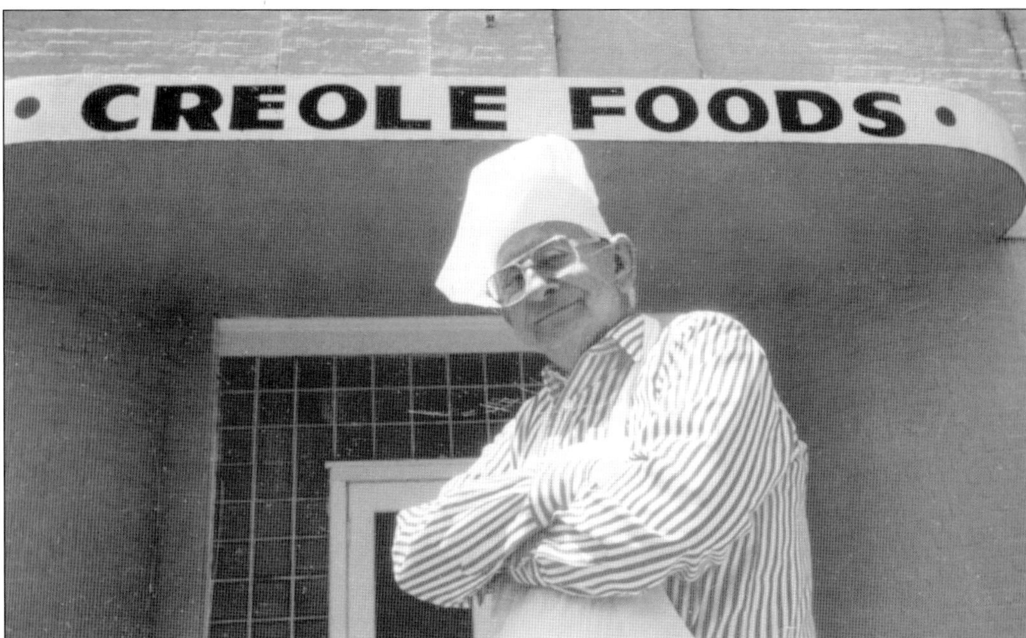

Anthony "Tony" Chachere (1905–1995), pharmacist, award-winning insurance salesman, business owner, and popular chef during his lifetime, opened Tony Chachere's Creole Foods in 1972 on North Lombard Street in Opelousas as a retirement hobby. The company produced Tony Chachere's Original Creole Seasoning. Later that year, Chachere, shown in this 1980s photograph, released his *Cajun Country Cookbook*, a bestseller. More cookbooks followed, with new products developed and produced by his company. Just one week prior to his death, Chachere was the first chef to be inducted into the Louisiana Chef's Hall of Fame. He died on March 19, 1995, leaving behind a culinary legacy that today is one of the leading businesses in St. Landry Parish and Louisiana.

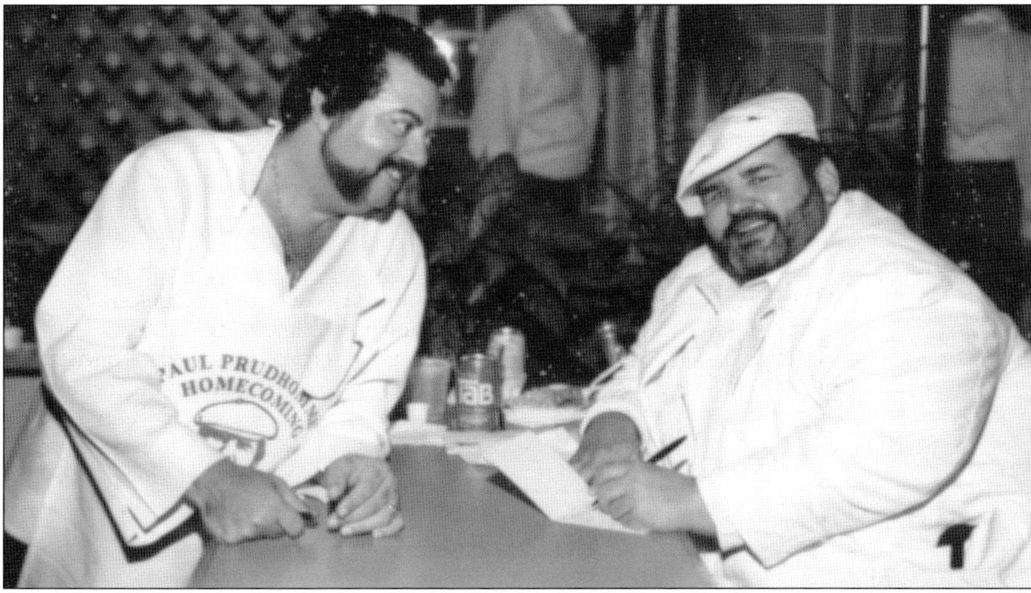

Internationally known Cajun chef Paul Prudhomme (1940–2015), at right, is shown with Opelousas chef Gene Paillet for the Paul Prudhomme Homecoming in Opelousas on March 7, 1988. An Opelousas native, Prudhomme was one of the most notable Louisiana chefs. He authored many bestselling cookbooks and owned K-Paul's Louisiana Kitchen Restaurant in New Orleans for years. Prudhomme developed his own seasonings, branded as Magic Seasoning Blends, and owned other businesses. He died on October 8, 2015. At left in the photograph is Gene "Daddy Pie" Paillet (1935–2019), also a native of Opelousas known for his culinary skills. He owned and operated Toby's Little Lodge for many years and worked in other restaurants. Paillet died on December 22, 2019. (Photograph by Sherri Landry.)

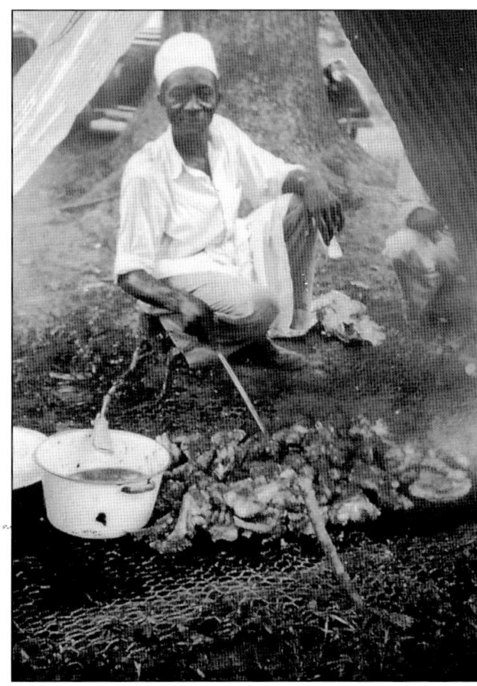

The famous barbecue prepared by Amos Daniels was a real treat in Opelousas for many years. Daniels, pictured here, had lines of cars waiting on Sunday mornings to pick up a plate of his food. As his customers said, "It was all about the sauce" that he used to baste his famous barbecue. Besides the barbecue, people raved about the rice dressing, baked beans, and potato salad he prepared as sides.

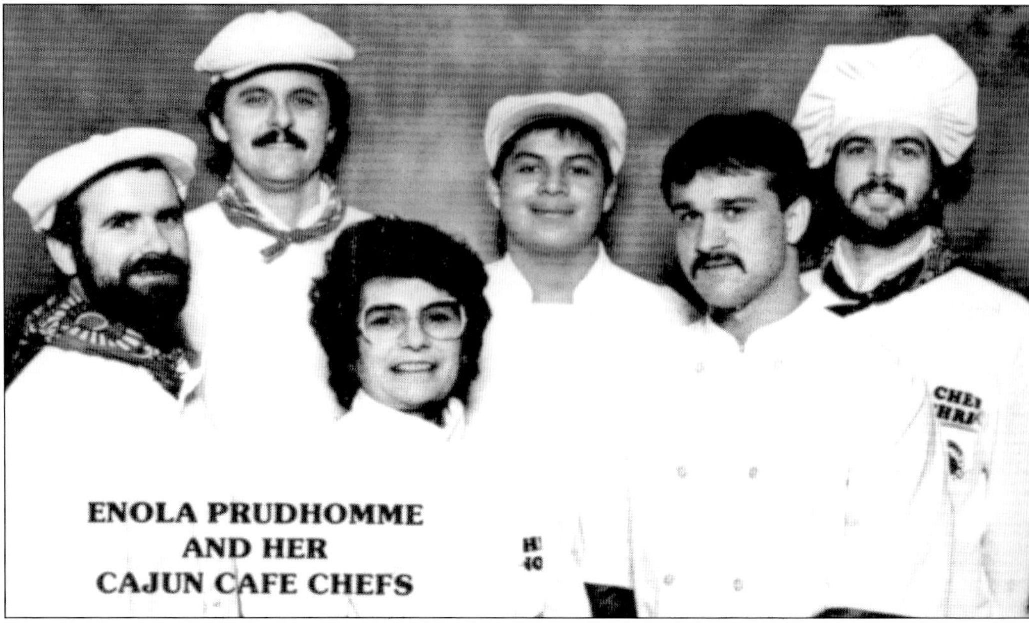

Chef Enola Prudhomme (1932–2012) is shown with other chefs at her restaurant in this postcard from the 1990s. Prudhomme, sister of Chef Paul Prudhomme and a native of Opelousas, was the owner of Prudhomme's Cajun Café in nearby Carencro, Louisiana, for many years. Voted Woman of the Year in Louisiana by Gov. Edwin Edwards, Enola authored three cookbooks and coauthored *The Prudhomme Family Cookbook*. She died on January 28, 2012, and is buried in Bellevue Memorial Park in Opelousas.

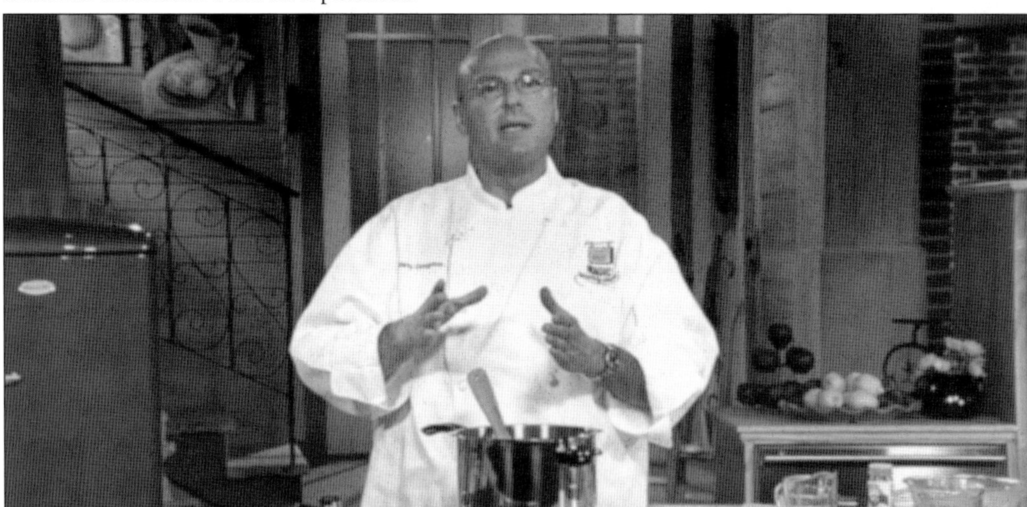

An Opelousas native, Chef Marty Cosgrove is leaving his mark on the culinary world. Early in life, Chef Cosgrove had a love for food preparation, and by age four, he could recite a soup recipe. A graduate of the Baltimore Culinary College and the renowned LaVarenne Ecole de Cuisine in Paris, he worked for K-Paul's Louisiana Kitchen in New Orleans, owned by celebrated Chef Paul Prudhomme, also an Opelousas native. Today, Cosgrove continues to work for the Prudhomme organization, serving as president of Chef Paul Prudhomme's Magic Seasoning Blends. (Courtesy of Marty Cosgrove.)

Seven

A Cultural Gumbo

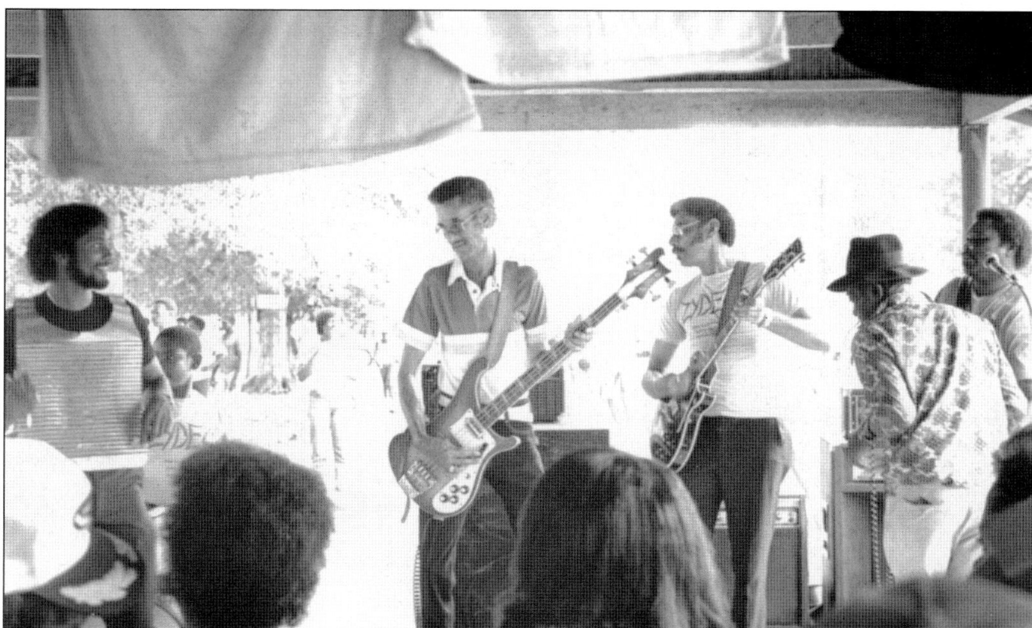

Opelousas, the "Zydeco Capital of the World," is also known for other varieties of music in its local culture. From its beginnings as a community, Opelousas has had a mixture of many different ethnic groups and cultures. From the native people who were first inhabitants to the French, Spanish, Africans, Acadians, Creoles, Germans, Italians, Irish, and others, all have contributed traditions to the mix that is today's Opelousas. It is often referred to as a cultural gumbo. (Courtesy of Wilbert Guillory.)

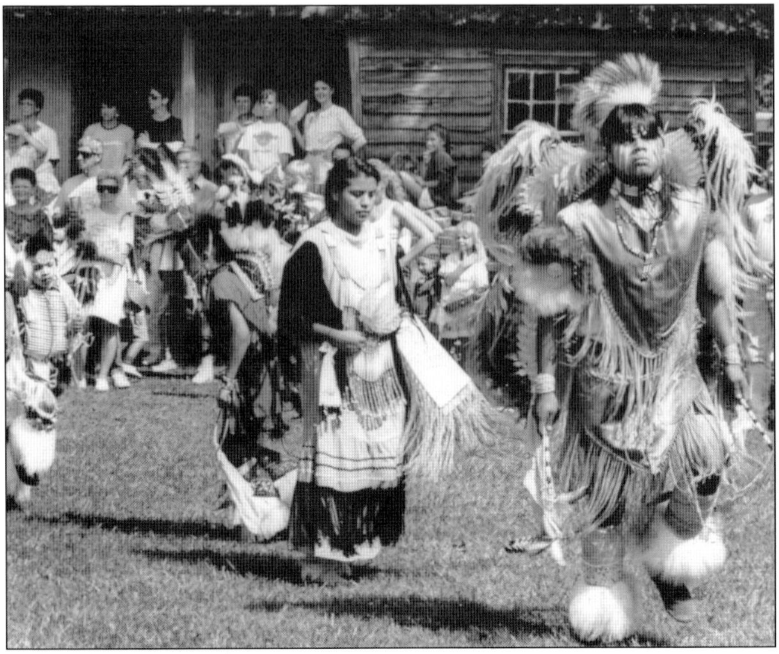

Kossati Dancers from the Coushatta tribe of Louisiana at Kinder perform for the Cultural-A-Fair at Le Vieux Village in 1992. The annual event, sponsored by the Opelousas Tourism and Activities Committee from 1992 to 1996, provided funding to help support the development of the historic village on Highway 190 at the east entrance to Opelousas. (Photograph by Freddie Herpin.)

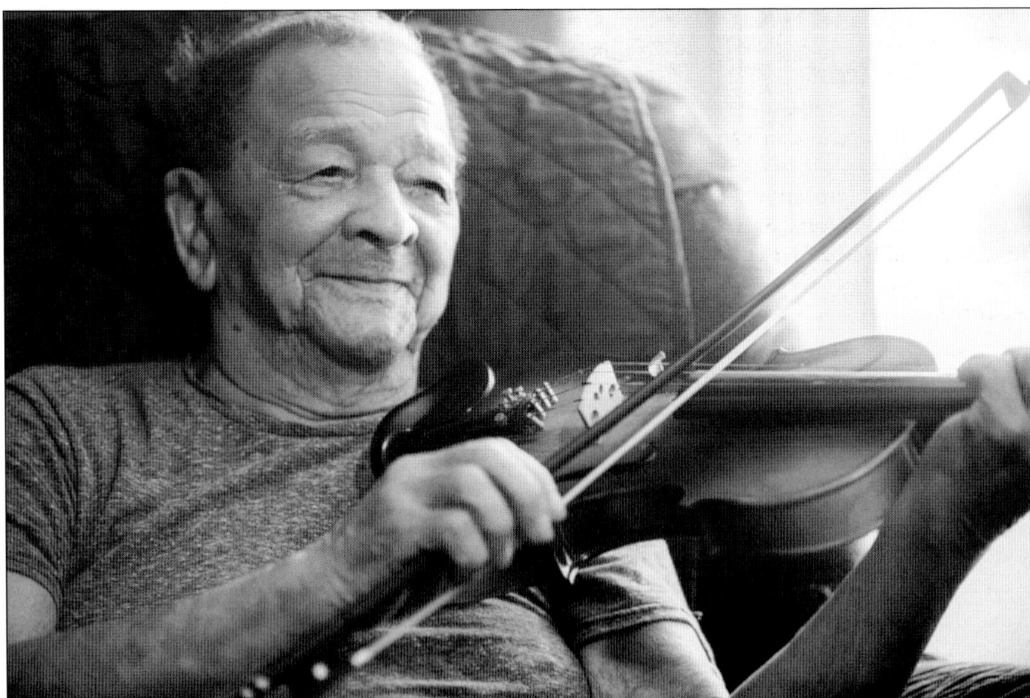

Creole fiddler Willie Durisseau played a style of music that went back to 17th-century Haiti. That Creole style helped to lay the foundation for the zydeco and Cajun music known today. Although he never made a record, he was famous for the house dances he played in St. Landry Parish during the days of the Great Depression in the 1930s. Durisseau, born in Mallett near Opelousas on February 20, 1918, lived a full life, dying at the age of 101 on December 17, 2019. (Courtesy of Angela Marie Roberson.)

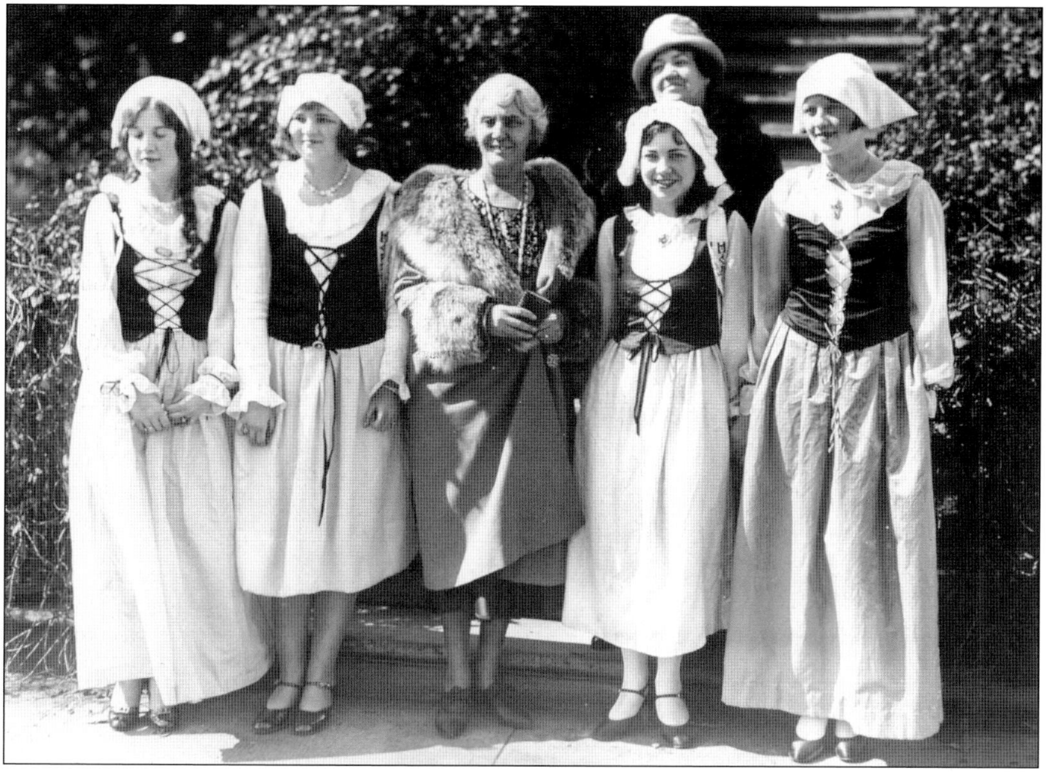

Taken in 1929 on the south steps of the White House in Washington, DC, this photograph shows Susan Walker Anding of Opelousas with the Evangeline Girls, a group of young ladies she formed in the 1920s to represent the Louisiana Acadians. The girls presented a bedspread, blanket, and rug, made by Acadians, as a gift to First Lady Lou Henry Hoover. Pictured from left to right are (first row) Mildred Shell of Bastrop, Lucille Newlin of New Orleans, First Lady Hoover, Monita Gary of St. Martinville, and Pearl Anding of Opelousas; (second row) Susan Anding. (Courtesy of Scott Longon.)

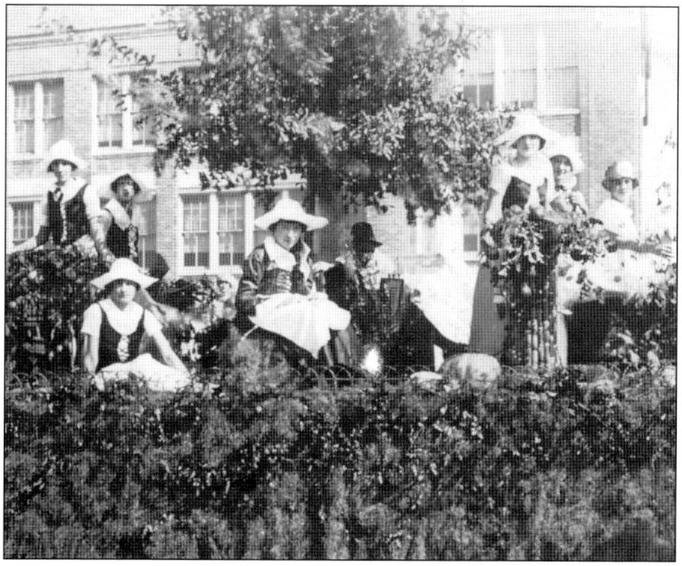

The Acadian float in the third annual Cotton Carnival Parade in Opelousas rolled through the streets on October 22, 1924. Susan Anding with the Opelousas Civic League was responsible for designing this float sponsored by the organization, and she chose an Evangeline theme. Float riders, dressed in early Acadian-style attire, represented Gabriel and Evangeline, and the court members were called Acadian Maids or Evangeline Girls. The building in the background is Opelousas High School, located on South Street at that time.

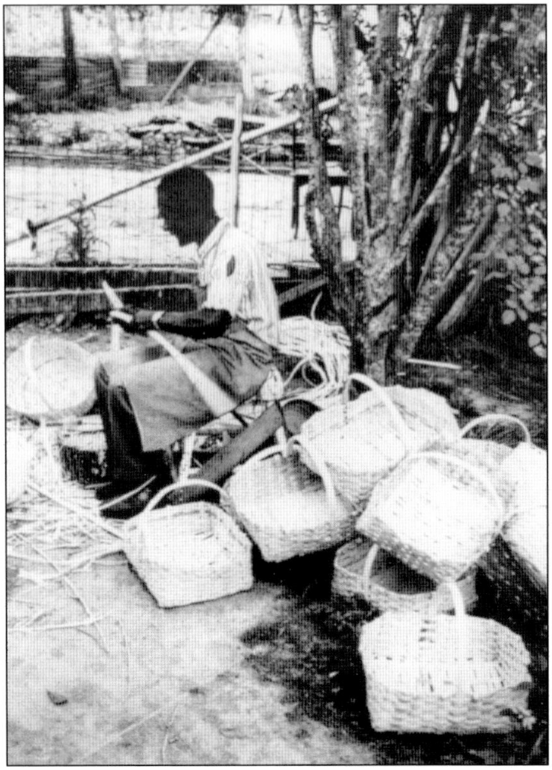

Thonis Robinson (b. 1911) is shown weaving one of his white oak baskets in this photograph taken in neighboring Washington, Louisiana. Robinson was known for this special art of weaving. Tourists would travel to St. Landry Parish to see him work and to purchase his baskets. In a 1972 interview, Robinson said his work starts with a white oak log, cut and made into strips. He explained, "It's hard to find the right wood. It must be just right so it can be made into strips for weaving. It has to be flexible." Many of his baskets are on display at art galleries and museums around the world, including the Smithsonian in Washington, DC.

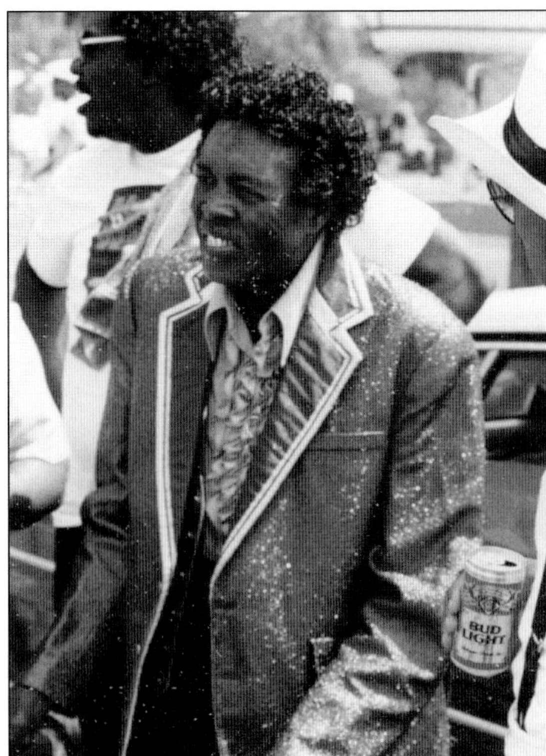

Grammy winner Clifton Chenier (1925–1987) is pictured at the Zydeco Music Festival in Plaisance on September 5, 1987. Chenier is internationally known for zydeco music, the unique Afro-American, Afro-French traditional music indigenous to Southwest Louisiana. The son of Olivia Kennerson Chenier and Joseph Chenier, he was born on June 21, 1925, in Leonville and reared in Opelousas. He devoted his life to spreading the sounds of zydeco music throughout the world. Because of his efforts, he was crowned the king of zydeco, and his hometown of Opelousas was proclaimed the "Zydeco Capital of the World." Chenier died on December 12, 1987. (Courtesy of Wilbert Guillory with Southern Development Foundation.)

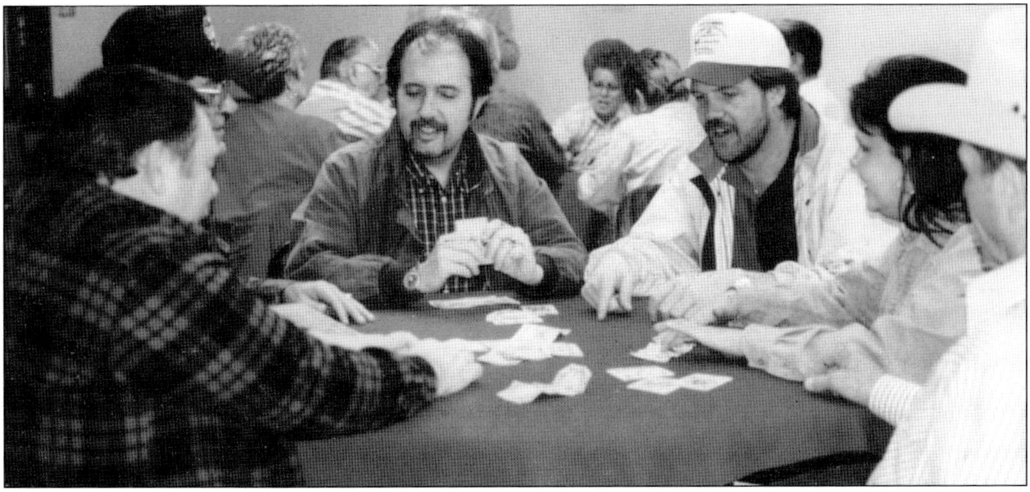

The Acadiana area of south Louisiana is known for its joie de vivre (the joy of living). Local culture is fostered by traditions brought to the area decades ago. Some of those include traditional music, dance, and games. For entertainment, locals like to play bourré, a trick-taking card game like spades played by two to seven players with a deck of 52 cards. Tournaments are often held on weekends at local bars in Opelousas. Shown at center playing bourré in a tournament at Frank's Bar in 1997 is Don Chaykin, a movie screen writer from New York who was visiting the area. Other players include Tim Hartley, Arleen Reviere, Carroll Vallien, Walter Hull, and Pappy Richard. (Photograph by Phil Seifert.)

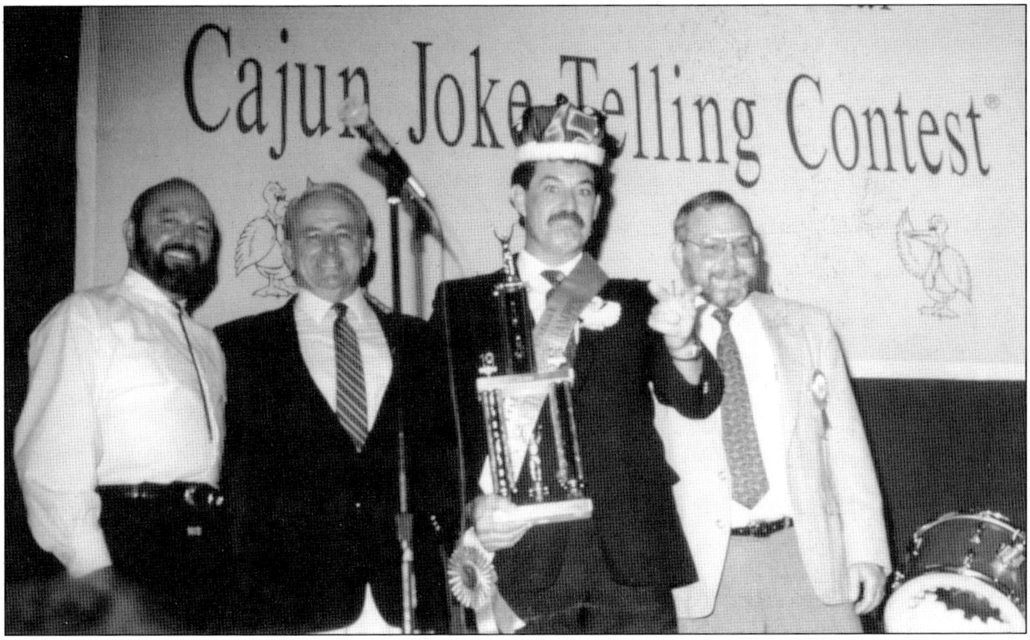

Humor is an important part of the Acadian (Cajun) culture in the Opelousas area. In 1988, the Opelousas Tourism and Activities Committee created the International Cajun Joke Telling Contest to help promote the humor of the area; it has been held each April in Opelousas for two decades. Shown in this 1991 photograph are the first four contest champions. From left to right are Ralph Begnaud, 1988 winner; Ed "the Guv" Pellissier, 1990 winner; A.J. Smith, 1991 winner; and Joe Lillie, 1989 winner. (Photograph by Sherri Landry.)

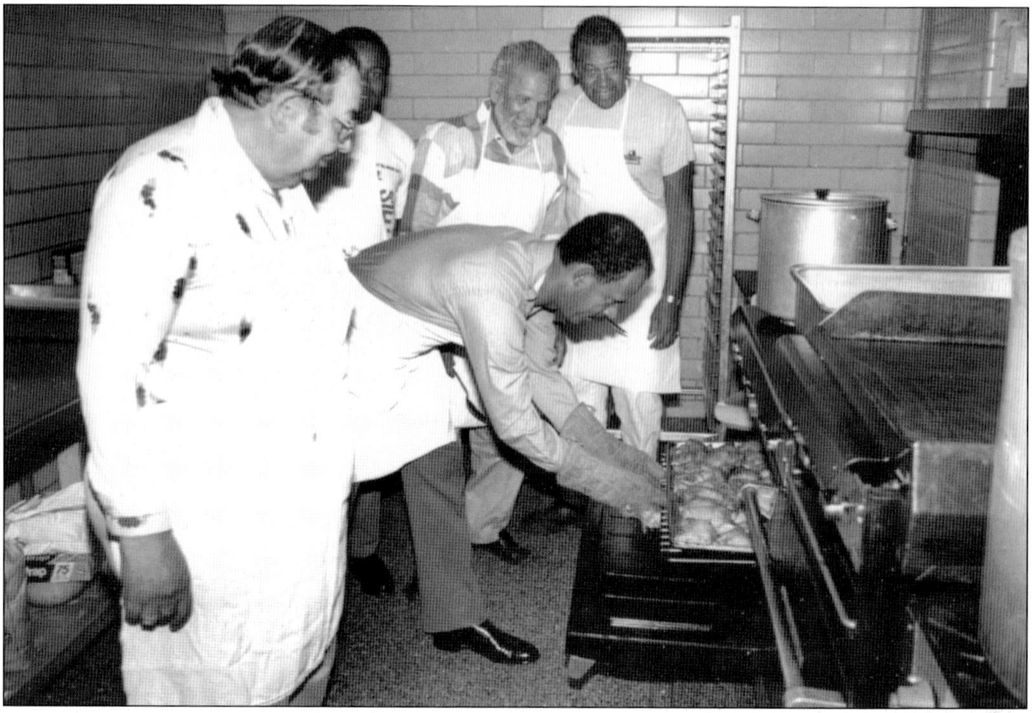

The annual Creole Festival is sponsored by the Holy Ghost Catholic Church in Opelousas. Originally in November, today it is held on the last weekend in October to benefit the church. The festival features food, music, games, and a street parade that rolls through Opelousas on its final day. Pictured here cooking for the first Creole Festival held November 3–4, 1990, are Warren Babineaux Jr., Wilbert Guillory, Charles Ray Tyler, Julius Guillory, and Larry Caillier.

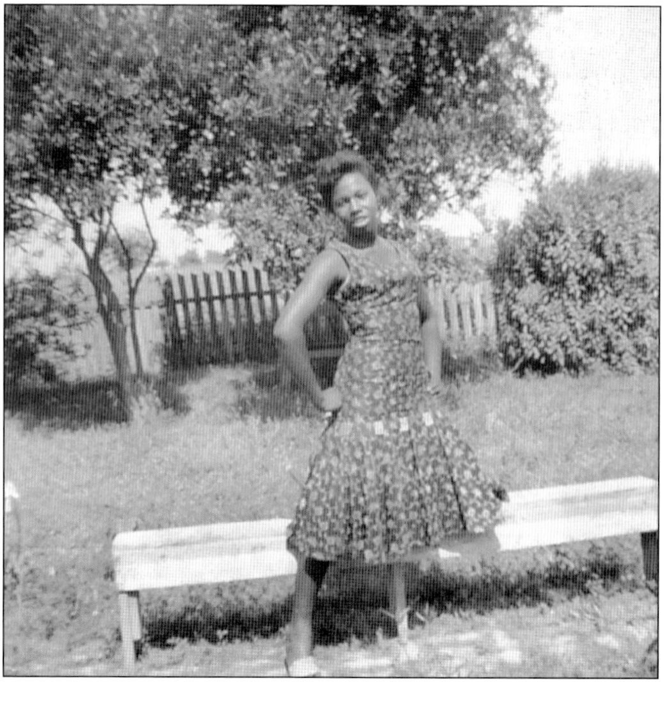

A native of St. Landry Parish, Creole folklorist Rebecca Henry has devoted her life to keeping the African American heritage of her ancestry alive by sharing it with others to ensure future generations know the importance of the culture. The daughter of a sharecropper born in the nearby town of Leonville, Henry is the founder of Creole Heritage Inc., Creole Heritage Folklife Center, the Juneteenth Folklife Celebration in Opelousas, and many other organizations that focus on her heritage. Henry is pictured in her earlier days in Bellevue, near Opelousas. (Courtesy of Nia Henry.)

During the 1780s, Joseph André Pont (Pons), son of Pierre Pons and Magdeleine Aymond, came from Marseilles, France, to settle in the Plaisance district in the Opelousas area. On May 11, 1789, he married Marie Therese Langlois, daughter of Felipe (Philip) Langlois and Maria Jeansonne (b. 1769). Eventually Joseph's middle name André and last name Pont were joined, and the family name became Andrepont. Many Andrepont descendants live in Opelousas and St. Landry Parish today. On Father's Day, June 7, 1978, a reunion of those descendants was held in Opelousas. Among the 650 plus in attendance were Chris Sebastien (left) and Billy Sebastien (right), seen in this photograph enjoying themselves in South City Park for that reunion.

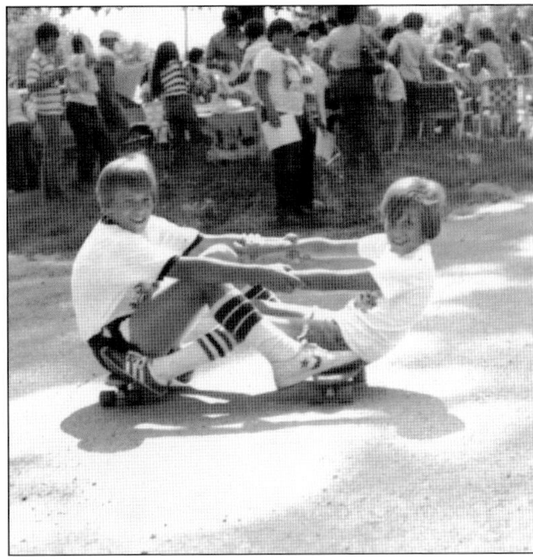

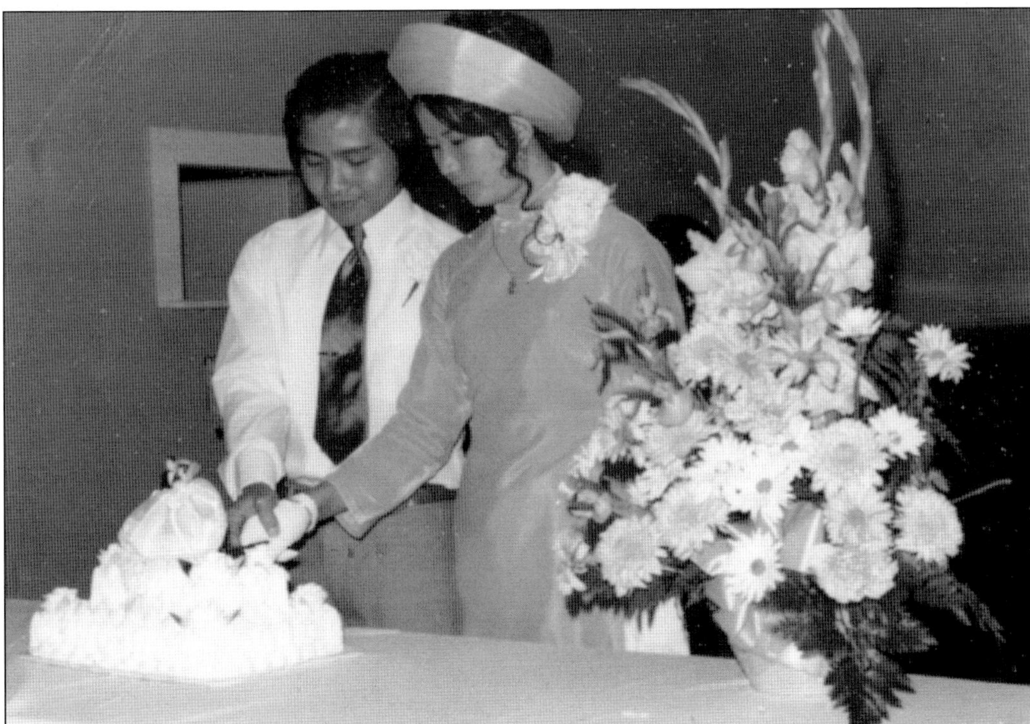

After the end of the Vietnam War in the mid-1970s, several refugees who fled that country settled in the United States. Some of the refugees came to live in Opelousas, sponsored by a local physician, Dr. Charles Bertrand. Several of the Vietnamese were employed by local businesses. At that time, Opelousas citizens learned firsthand some of the traditions from the Vietnamese culture. Many local folks were invited by Vietnam families to share in that culture and enjoy their food during the celebration of their New Year as well as traditional family parties. This photograph shows a Vietnamese couple, Mai and Tung, celebrating a customary Vietnam wedding in Opelousas in 1976.

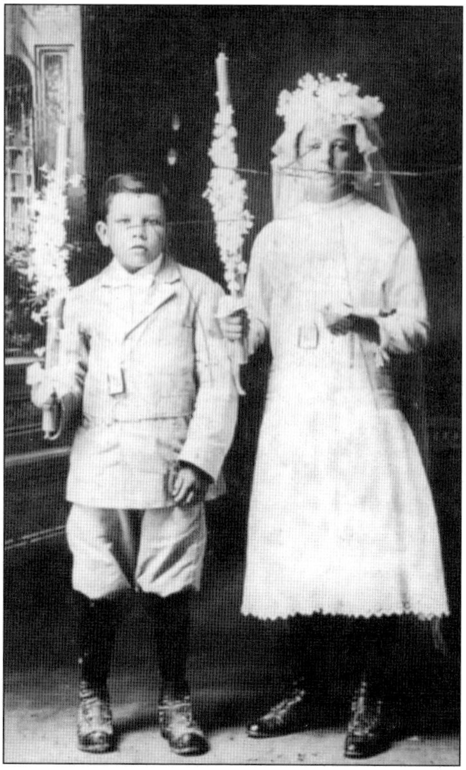

Some citizens of Opelousas today are descendants of New York orphans who came to Opelousas in the early 1900s. Known as the "Orphan Train Riders," the first children from New York arrived in Opelousas on April 5, 1907, and were adopted by area families. Stephen Sebastien (1901–1933) was one of the children on that first train, adopted by Josephine Emma and Aristide Sebastien. He is pictured here with his sister Agnes for their First Holy Communion.

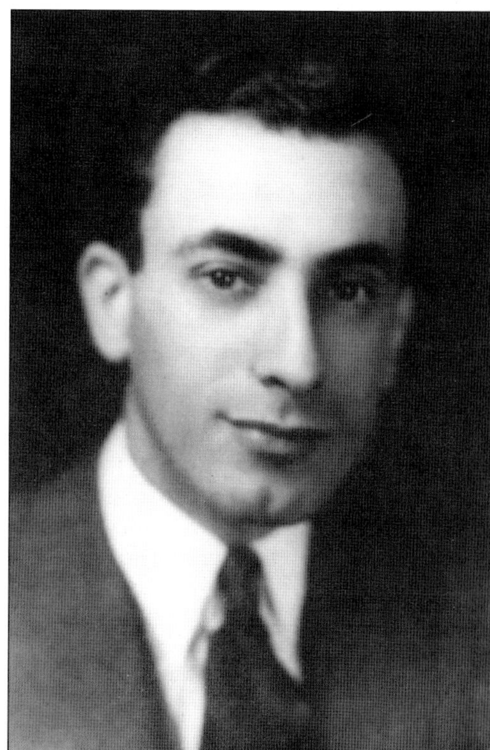

Many of the children who arrived in Louisiana on the orphan trains of the early 1900s lived in Opelousas and made great contributions to the community and the area. One of those was Martin A. Roy Sr., who was adopted by Arthur J. Roy and his wife, Eva Wyble Roy. Martin, shown in this photograph, grew to adulthood on a farm right outside of Opelousas. He attended the local high school, graduating in 1924. In 1927, he married 20-year-old Marie Holman, the daughter of Sylvester and Heloise Holman. The couple settled in Opelousas where Martin opened the Roy Motors car dealership in 1935. In 1942, he was elected mayor of Opelousas, serving until his tragic death in a boating accident on July 11, 1943. (Courtesy of the Roy family.)

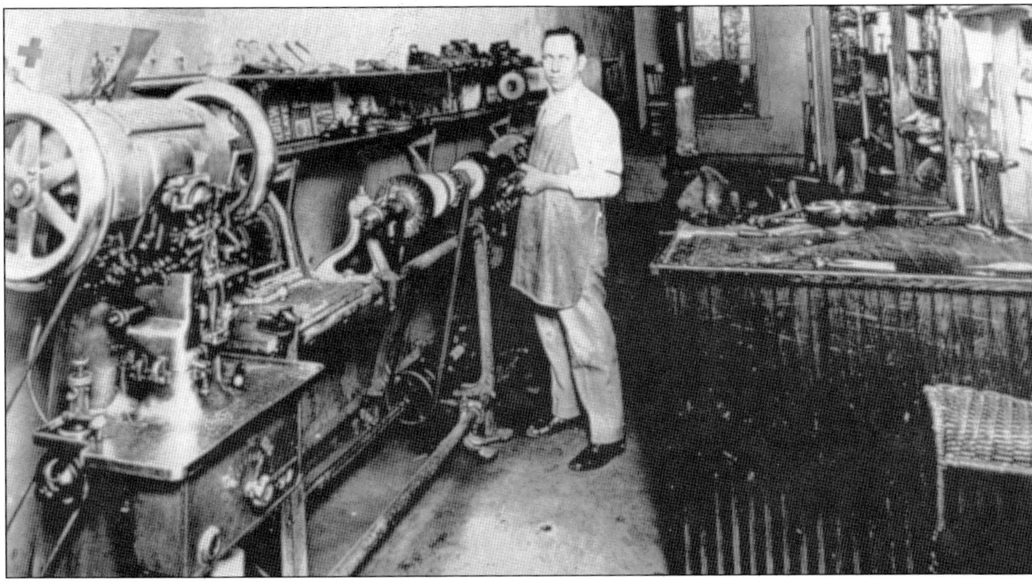

Some of the earliest Italians to settle in the Opelousas area prior to the Civil War were mostly professionals like doctors and lawyers. Following the war, many other immigrants arrived from Italy to help in the agriculture fields of the area. Some became farmers, while others became store merchants. In April 1921, Joe Greco Jr. opened his first-class Electric Shoe Shop next door to the Waldorf Restaurant on Landry Street. In 1925, he constructed a new brick building on the same block to house his growing business. Greco, pictured in his shoe shop during the early years, remained in business for over five decades. Today, the Greco store building houses the Back In Time Restaurant. (Courtesy of Wanda Juneau.)

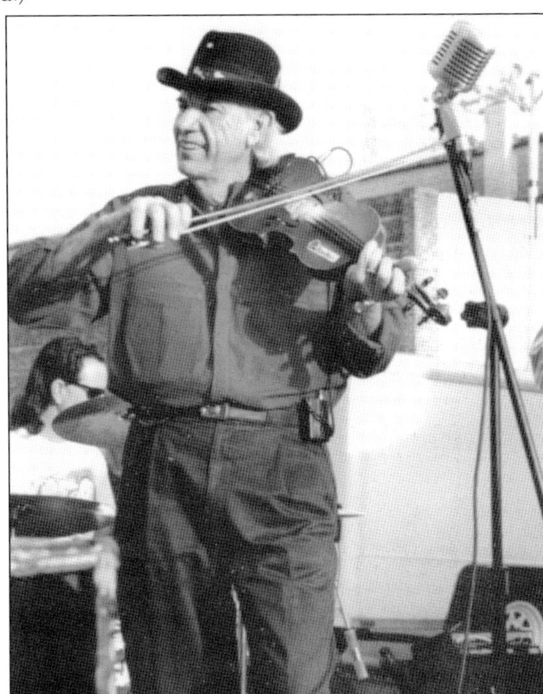

Cajun music fiddler Hadley J. Castille (1933–2012) called Opelousas his home. Castille was a true Opelousas treasure, known for his music and especially for his fiddle playing. He traveled the world promoting Cajun music, Opelousas, and Louisiana. Castille is pictured playing his fiddle for a Main Street Revived concert in downtown Opelousas in 1993. Although he is no longer living, his memory and the musical legacy he left behind is not forgotten.

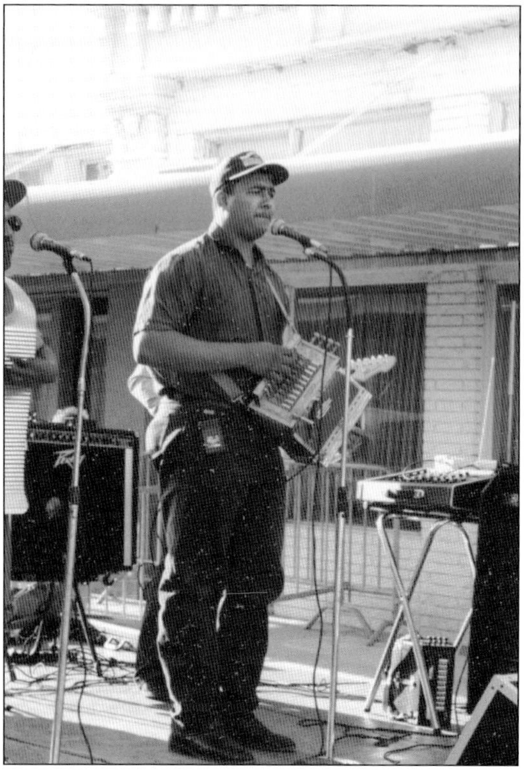

Main Street Revived concerts in downtown Opelousas on Fridays during the 1990s drew thousands of music lovers to the city. The concerts featured a different form of south Louisiana music each week. Concertgoers did more than just listen to the music; they were always ready to dance since that is part of the area culture. Famous zydeco musician Keith Frank is pictured at left performing at one of the concerts. The photograph below shows a couple dancing in the street while enjoying zydeco music in downtown Opelousas. (Both photographs by Sherri Landry.)

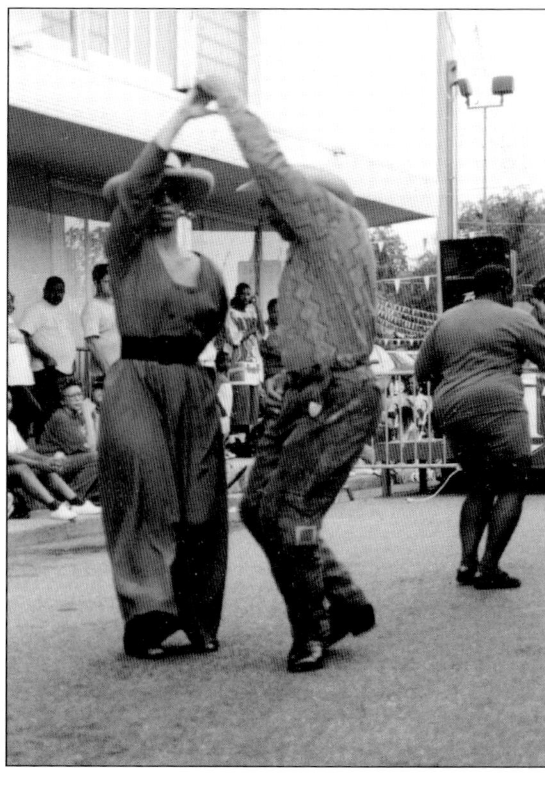

Eight

Historic District, Commerce, and Government

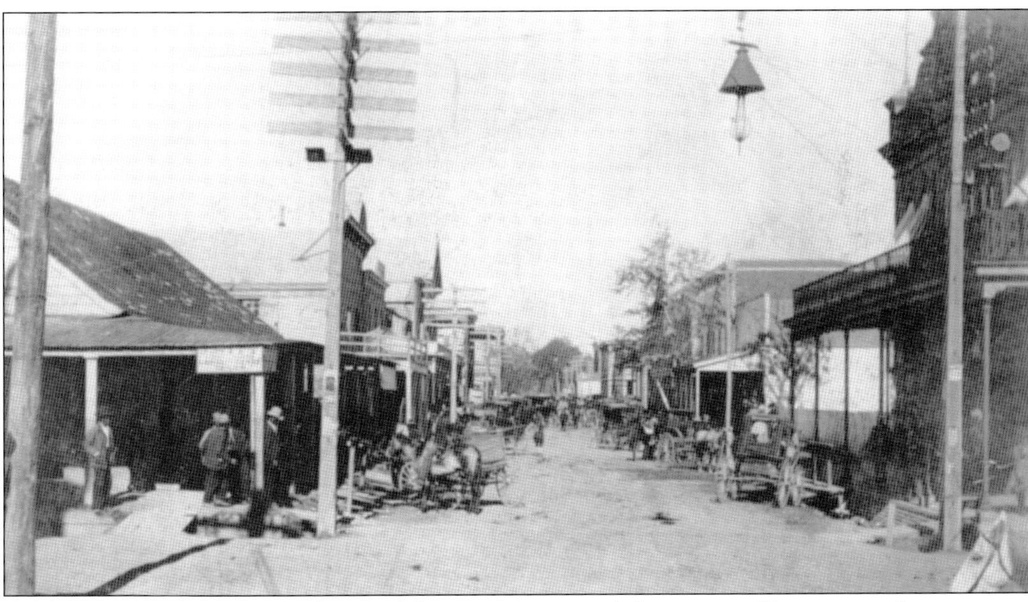

Downtown Opelousas is the heart of the community and the center of business and government for the parish. This photograph of Main Street in Opelousas in 1900 shows downtown as the primary commercial area of St. Landry Parish. Although it had ups and downs in the past, today the downtown is on its way back to again becoming an important part of the area's economy. On June 2, 1989, part of the commercial district was listed in the National Register of Historic Places as the Opelousas Historic District.

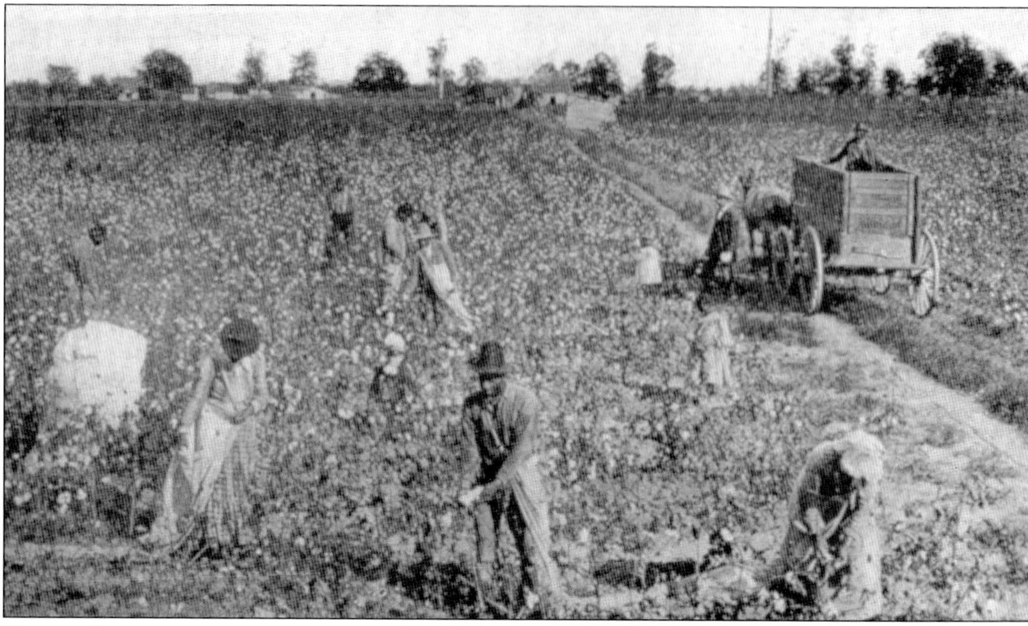

From its beginnings as a community, Opelousas was an agrarian society. Agriculture ran the local economy. Some of the major crops in St. Landry Parish for decades were cotton and sugar and later yams. This postcard produced by *Jacobs News Depot* shows a cotton field on the outskirts of Opelousas being picked by workers around 1888.

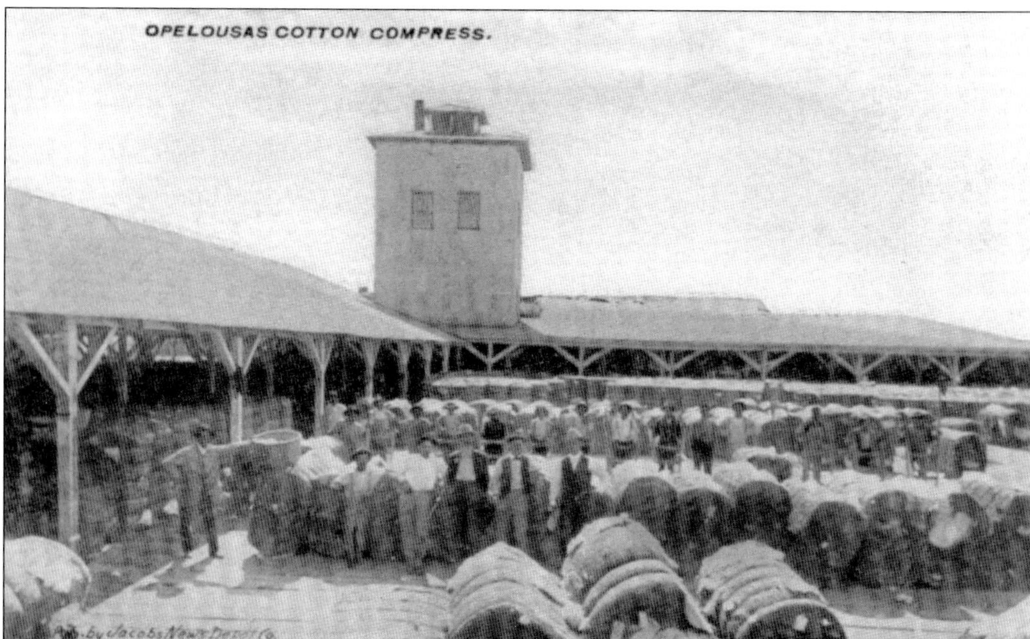

Cotton played a major role in the Opelousas economy for many years. Cotton gins and warehouses were prosperous businesses in the community. The Opelousas Cotton Compress Company was organized in 1892 by C.J. Thompson, who sold it a year later. Officers in the company in 1895 included Joseph Bloch, president; Isaac Roos, secretary; and C.J. Thompson, general manager. This postcard produced by *Jacobs News Depot* shows the Opelousas Compress Company around 1909.

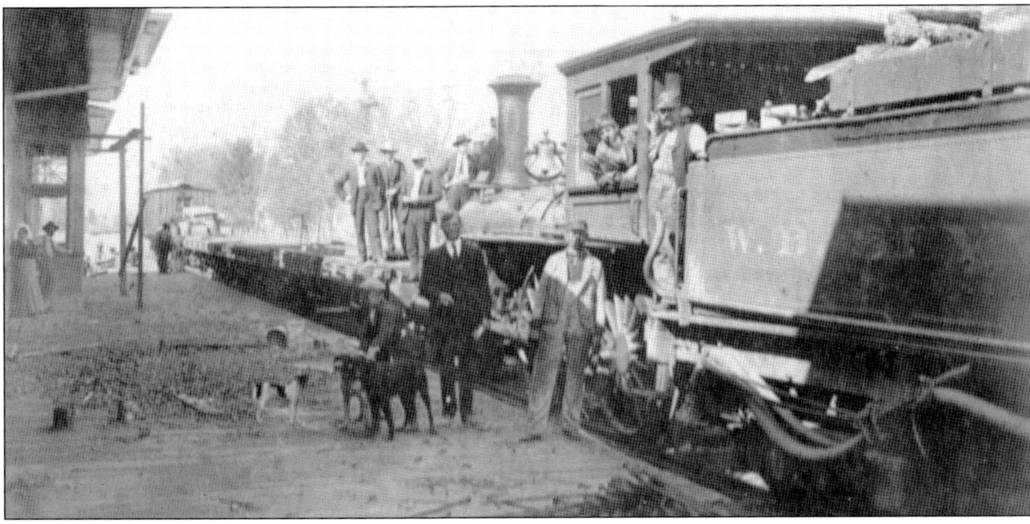

The coming of the railroad to Opelousas in the early 1880s had a positive effect on the local economy. Opelousas Gulf & Northeastern Railway Company, called the O'Gee Railroad, was a local company that connected Opelousas to Melville and Crowley and other towns along its route. It was established on June 20, 1904, with company stock sold to investors for $25 to $100 per share. Thomas H. Lewis (1836–1914), one of the founding fathers, served as its president. E.M. Boagni, E.P. Veazie, M. Halphen, M. Vilasico, J.J. Thompson, J.P. Saizan, Isaac Roos, J.B. Sandoz, F.J. Dietlein, H.E. Estorge, H.L. Garland, E.D. Estilette, Joseph M. Boagni, B.H. Pavy, O. Dardeau, and S.J. Dossman were members of the first board of directors. The company served the Opelousas area until 1915. This photograph shows the construction train for the O'Gee arriving in Opelousas on February 7, 1907.

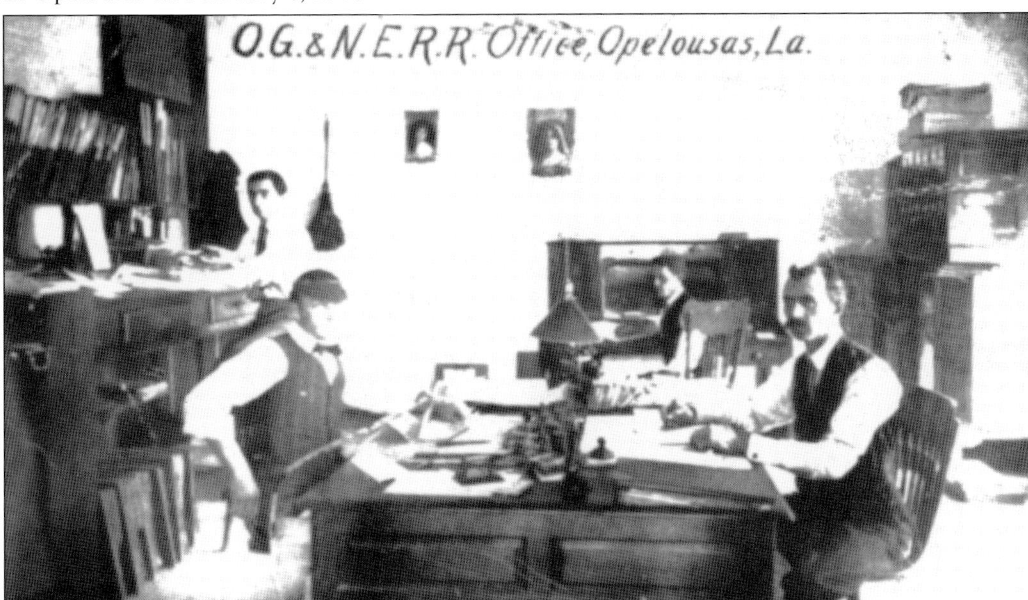

The office of the Opelousas Gulf & Northeastern Railroad Company, also known as the O'Gee Railroad and sometimes as the Opelousas Road, was in the Landau Building on West Landry Street in downtown Opelousas. The employees pictured in this c. 1908 photograph are, from left to right, (first row) J.A. Jung and Bert ?; (second row) Tommy Bowden and H. Bullard Anderson.

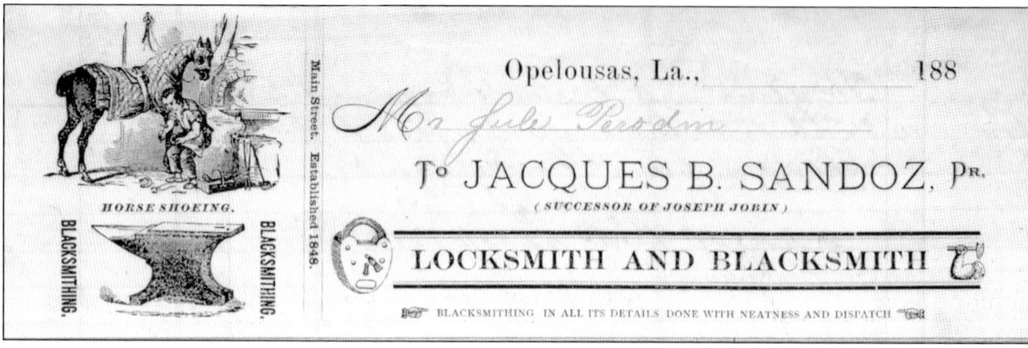

Opelousas, La., 188

To JACQUES B. SANDOZ, Dr.

(SUCCESSOR OF JOSEPH JOBIN)

LOCKSMITH AND BLACKSMITH

BLACKSMITHING IN ALL ITS DETAILS DONE WITH NEATNESS AND DISPATCH

HORSE SHOEING.

BLACKSMITHING.

BLACKSMITHING.

Main Street. Established 1848.

Local blacksmiths were necessary in the Opelousas community and contributed to the economy for many years. One of the early blacksmith shops was established by Joseph Jobin on Main Street in 1848. Following the death of Jobin in 1877, the business became J.B. Sandoz in 1878, owned and operated by Jobin's son-in-law Jacques B. Sandoz. J.B. Sandoz grew to be a hardware store that remained a family-owned business in the community for over a century. It was known as "the place you could find almost anything." It closed its doors in 2019. The above image is an invoice from Jacques B. Sandoz in the 1880s. The photograph below shows the company in the 1950s when the old wooden building was being replaced with a new modern structure.

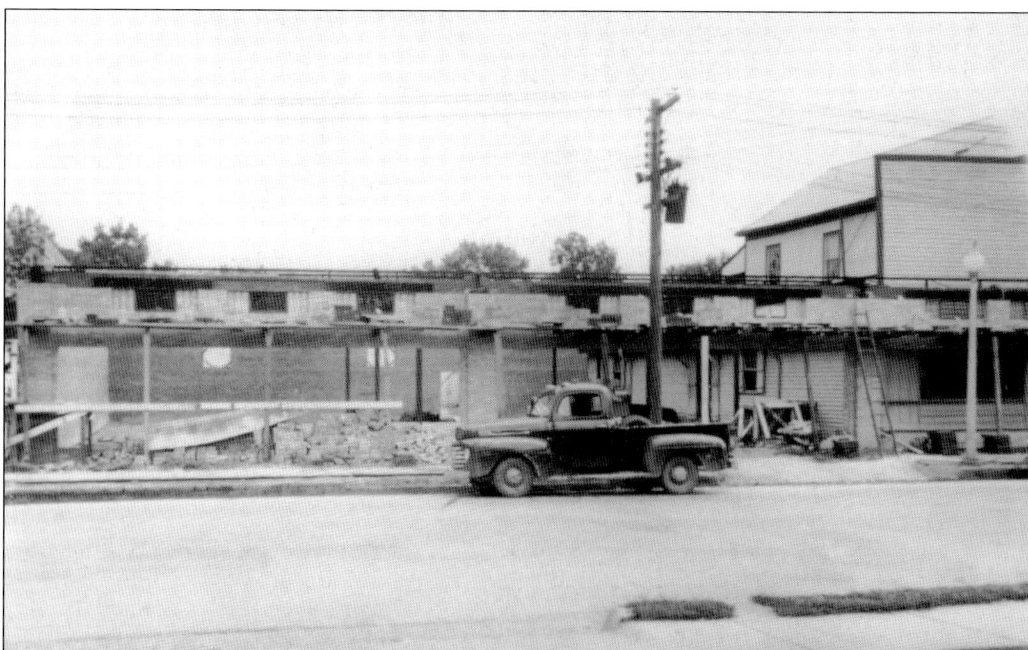

In 1906–1907, J.B. Sandoz had a new building constructed on the northwest corner of Main and Grolee Streets across from his hardware store. The building was used as the Fields-Larcade Furniture Store for many years and later used by Abdalla's Furniture Store for a while. Today, that building serves as the Opelousas City Court.

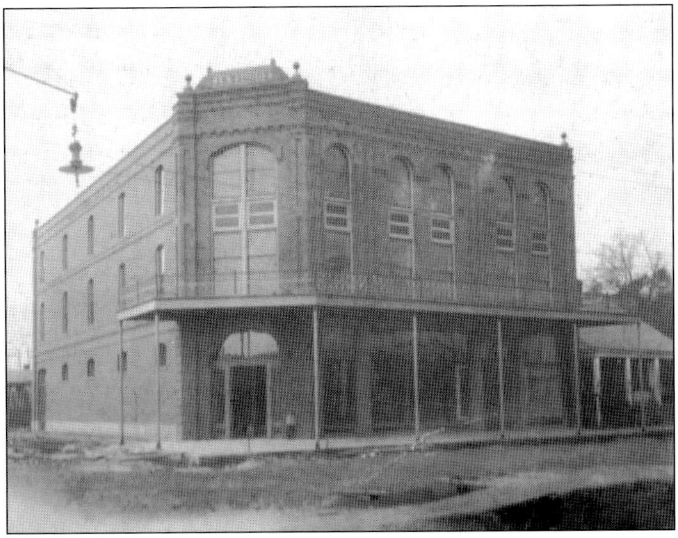

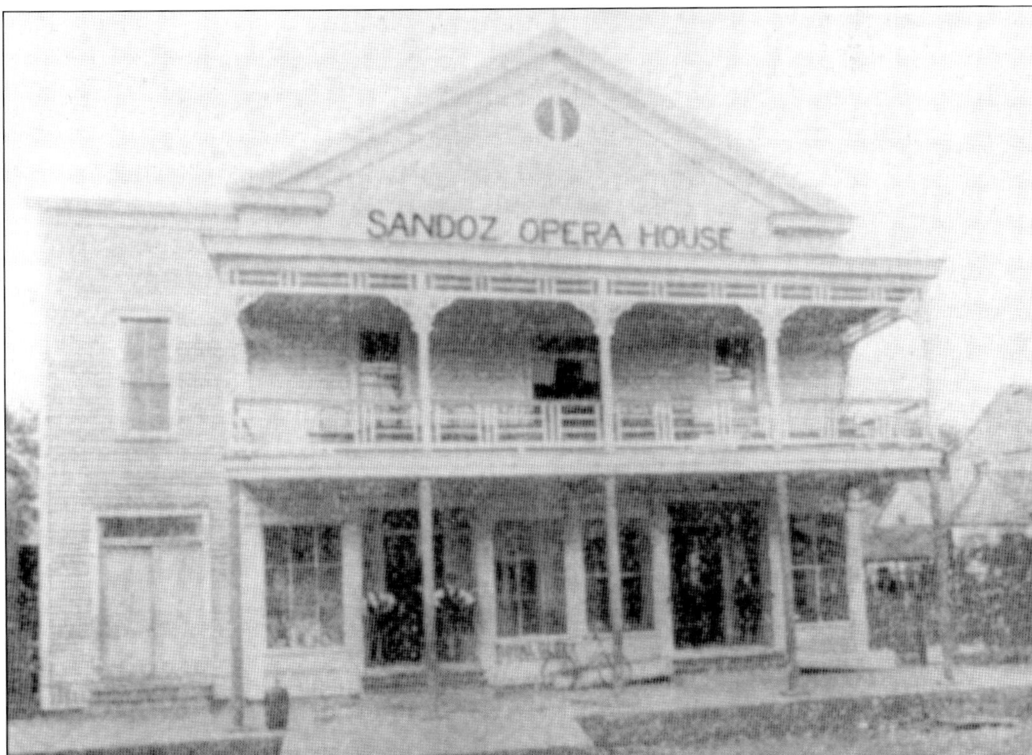

Sandoz Opera House on Main Street is pictured here in 1896. Built by Dr. Bob Littell as the Littell Opera House in 1892, it also housed the Littell Drug Co. and Mornhinveg & Son Jewelers on the first floor. It became the Sandoz Opera House after it was sold to Leonce Sandoz in 1896, and the first floor became home to the Opera House Drug Store, operated by A.S. Braud and Co. from 1899 to 1904. The Sandoz Opera House was in business until about 1916 when the building was remodeled to house the George Abdalla Bargain Store, which became Abdalla's Department Store. The old building was demolished in the mid-1920s, and a new brick Abdalla's store was constructed on the site.

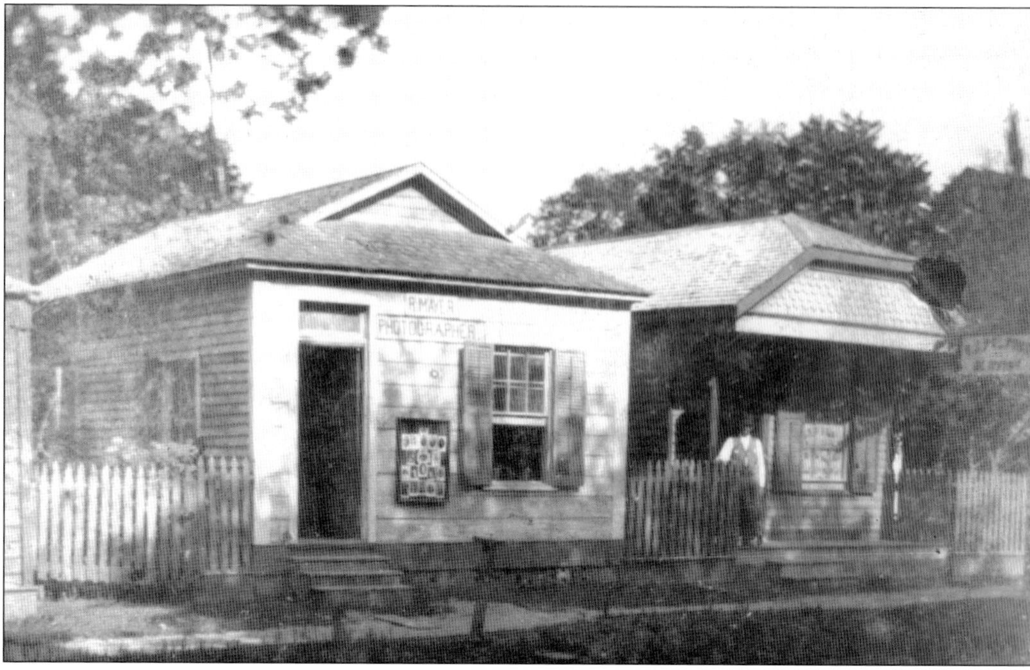

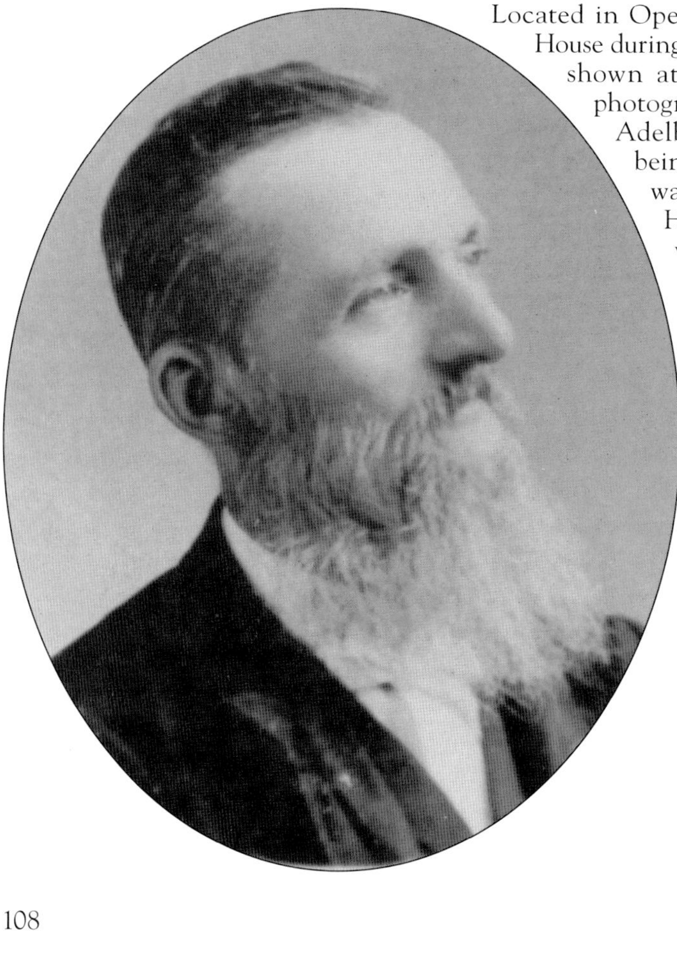

Located in Opelousas near the Sandoz Opera House during the late 1800s was the building, shown at left above, that housed the photography business of Prof. Rudolph Adelbert Sebastian Mayer. Besides being a photographer, the professor was known as a musical genius. He was the Opelousas music man who provided most of the musical entertainment for community events and for performances at the area opera houses during his lifetime. Also in this photograph to the right is the dental office of Dr. Pulford. Prof. Rudolph A. Mayer is shown at left in the latter part of the 1800s. (Both, courtesy of Robbie and Jonathan Sebastien.)

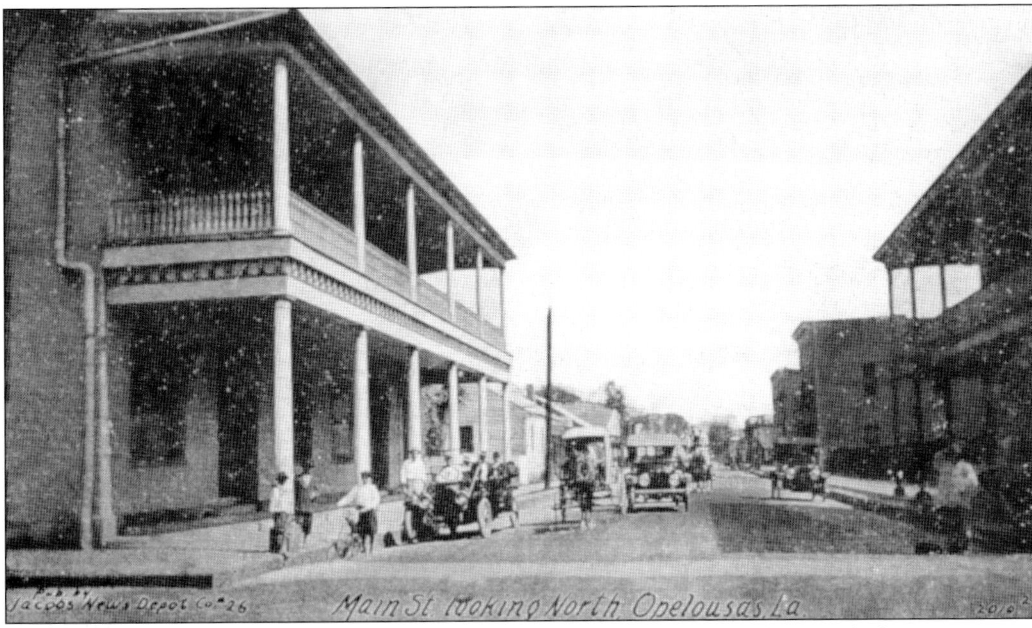

Downtown Opelousas was the major commercial district of St. Landry Parish for many years. This view, looking north, shows several people and busy traffic on Main Street around 1915. At left is the Elks Lodge located in the building that once housed the store of Joseph Bloch on the corner of Main and Bellevue Streets, known as the old Bloch Corner. At right across Main Street on Jacobs Corner is the store once owned by Solomon Jacobs.

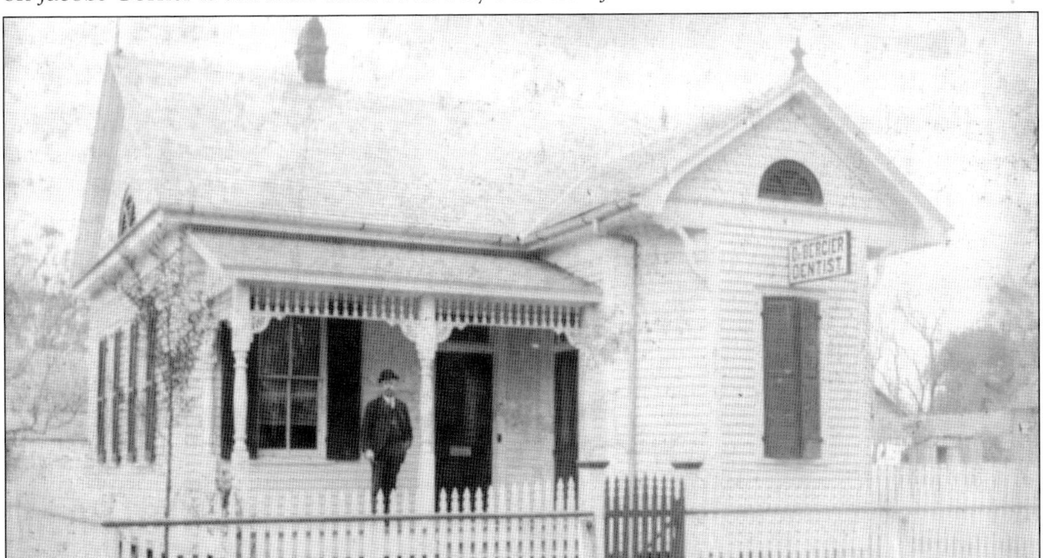

Dr. A.J. Bercier is pictured standing on the porch of his new dental office on the corner of Court and Vine Streets in downtown Opelousas soon after it was built in 1903. Dr. Bercier served the Opelousas area for over two decades as a professional and as a community leader. Besides his dental practice, he also raised a special breed of chickens that he entered in contests across the United States. Dr. Bercier's office building stands today on that corner in downtown Opelousas and is now owned by Vera Nagy, a local entrepreneur. (Courtesy of Emile Ventre IV, Chris Ventre, and Jonathan Sebastien.)

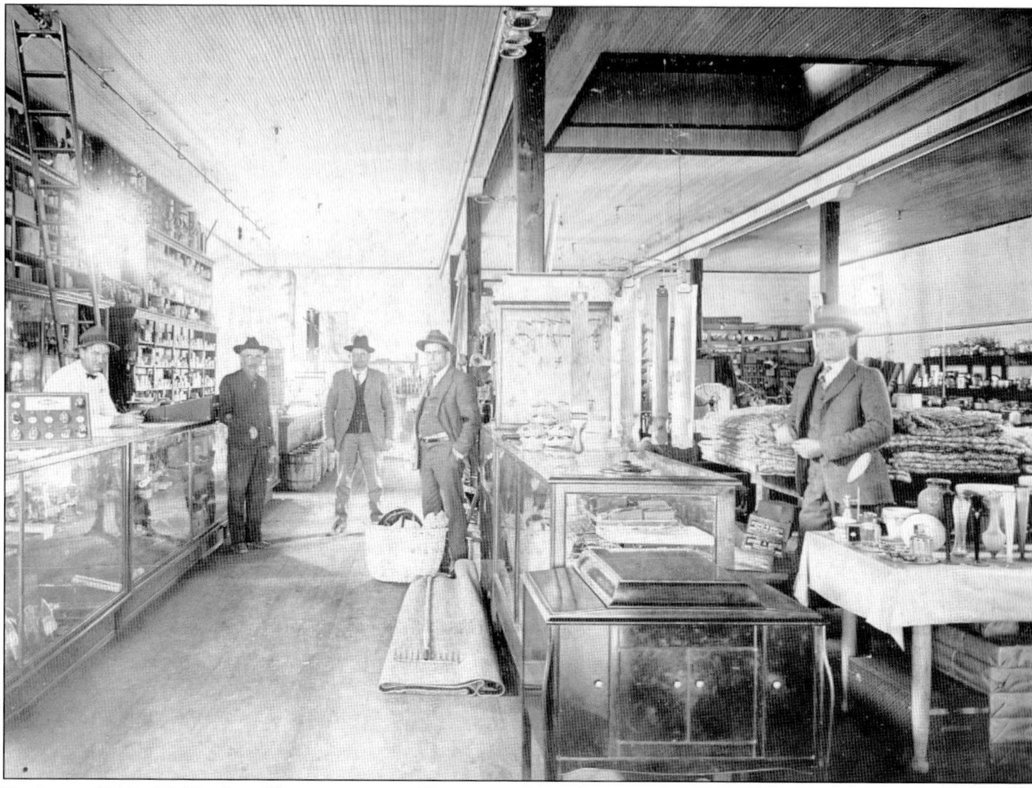

Built in 1919–1920, the Christman and Riseman Hardware Store on Market Street in Opelousas was owned by Ben Riseman and managed by his son-in-law Sam Kurtz. When the store closed, the building was sold in 1933 to Collins Conrad of Breaux Bridge, Louisiana, who converted it into the Conrad Movie Theater. In 1935, it became the Delta Theater, which operated until the 1980s. The building is used today as a venue for many community events and activities. The man standing behind the counter in this 1925 photograph is Sam Kurtz, and the man in front of the courter is his father-in-law, Ben Riseman.

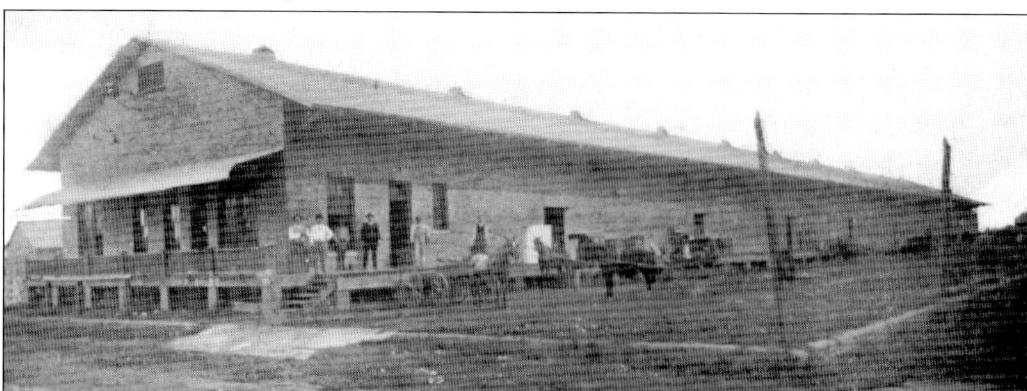

The Dietlein and Jacobs Warehouse is pictured on this c. 1909 postcard produced by *Jacobs News Depot*. The warehouse building was located on Railroad Avenue for many years. Later, the building was purchased by J.F. Dezauche & Son. From 1940 to 1943, Arthur G. Denes leased half of the building to house the American Paprika Pioneer Mills Inc., later called First American Paprika Mills. It was the first paprika production plant in the United States.

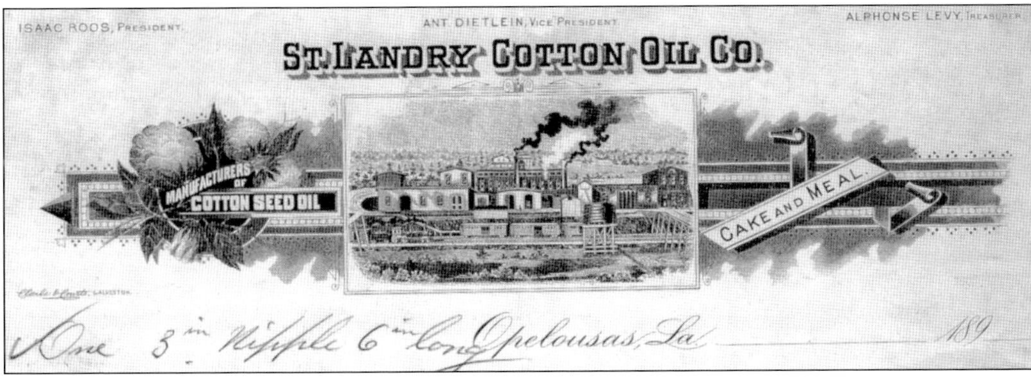

The St. Landry Cotton Oil Company opened for business in 1894 on Railroad Avenue on the property where the Franklin College of Opelousas was once located. It was eventually owned by the Barnette family, who sold it in the 1970s. At that time, it became Lou Ana Foods, which operated for over two decades. Lou Ana Foods was sold and today is known as Ventura Foods LLC, still producing Lou Ana products. An early invoice of the St. Landry Cotton Oil Company is shown above along with a photograph of some of the Lou Ana products produced in later years. The man at left in the photograph below is unidentified, and the man at right is William Fontenot, a Lou Ana Foods employee for 40 years.

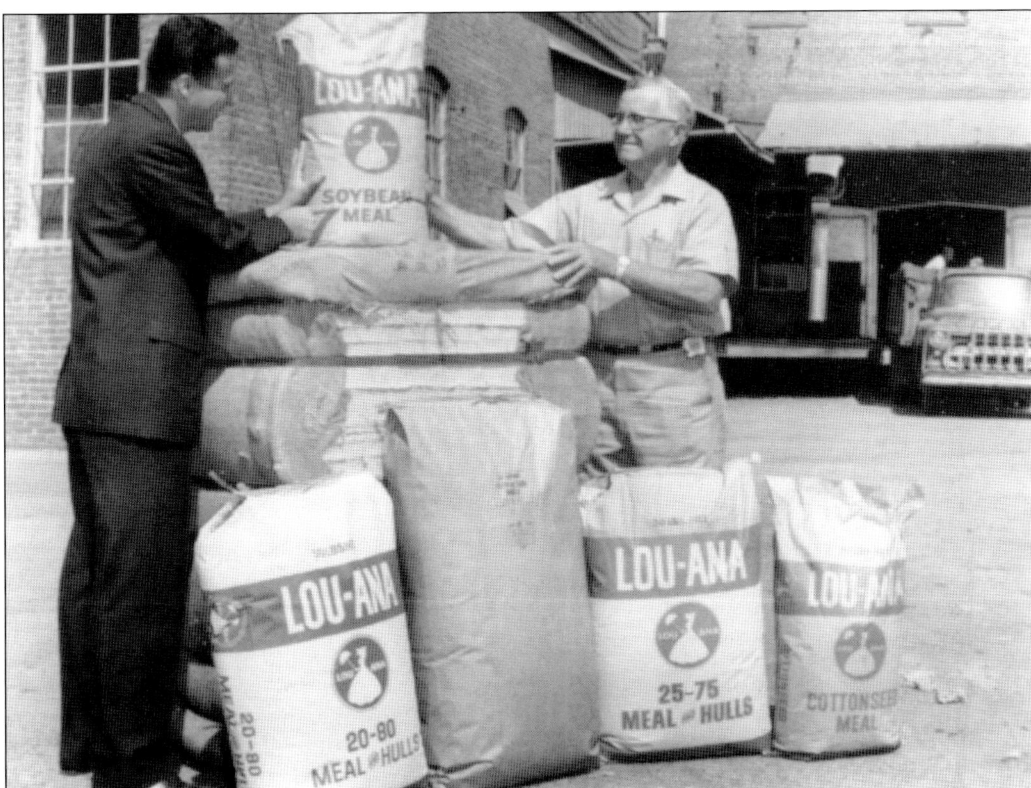

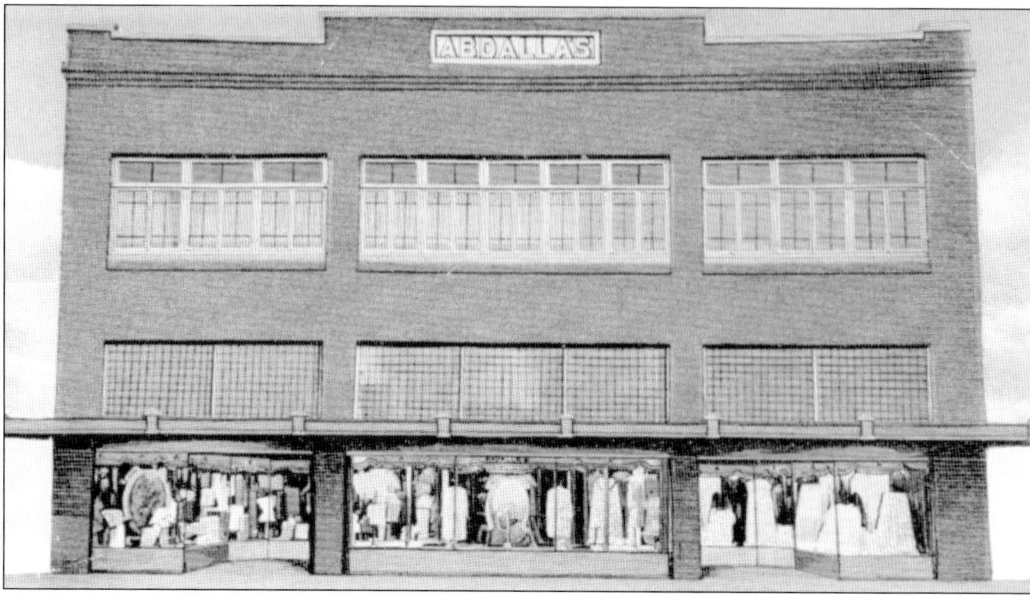

In 1895, George Abdalla (1865–1951) and his wife, Jasmine (1884–1976), left New Orleans and moved to St. Landry Parish. He started his business as a cart peddler in Washington, Louisiana, traveling around the area selling clothing and other merchandise. It was not long before he moved to Opelousas, where the railroad made the town a more desirable place to do business. He expanded his business to include stores in other area towns, and Abdalla's became one of the most successful department stores in Southwest Louisiana. This photograph shows Abdalla's in Opelousas in the 1930s.

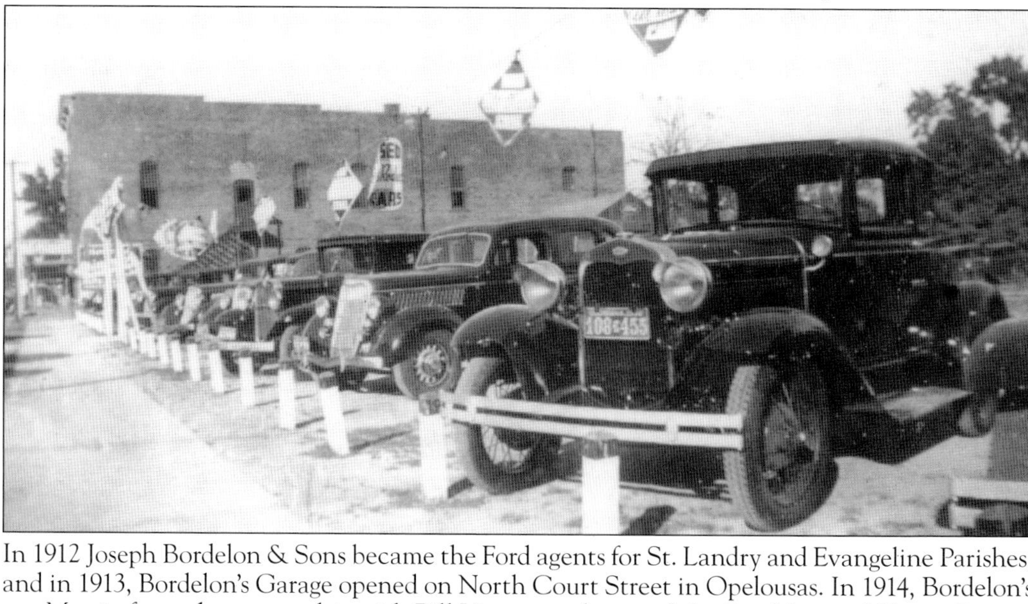

In 1912 Joseph Bordelon & Sons became the Ford agents for St. Landry and Evangeline Parishes, and in 1913, Bordelon's Garage opened on North Court Street in Opelousas. In 1914, Bordelon's son Martin formed a partnership with Bill Haynes and opened the Bordelon and Hayes Garage. The partnership was short lived, and by 1915, Martin Bordelon was the sole owner of the business. A year later he purchased the C. Dietlein Store on the corner of Main and North Streets, and Bordelon Motor Company was born. That company remained a family-owned business for almost 100 years before it closed in 2012. This photograph shows the used car lot of Bordelon Motor Company in the 1930s.

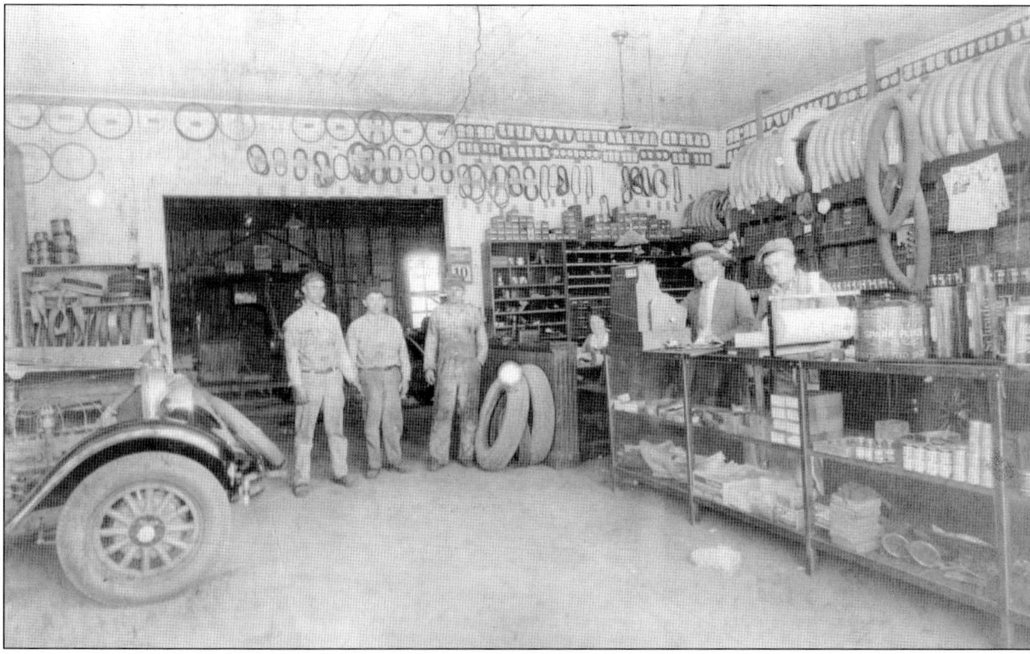

Daly Motor Company was opened in Opelousas in 1922 by Frank Truman Daly, the man behind the cash register in this photograph. Others in the photograph of the company interior include Edward Bertinot, Buddy Fontenot, Havard Burleigh, Naomi Burr Halphen, and Edward Hidalgo. The automobile shown is a 1928 Dodge Model DA standard six cylinder. The company remained in business on Union Street in downtown Opelousas until 1986. (Courtesy of Madeline R. and Thom Daly.)

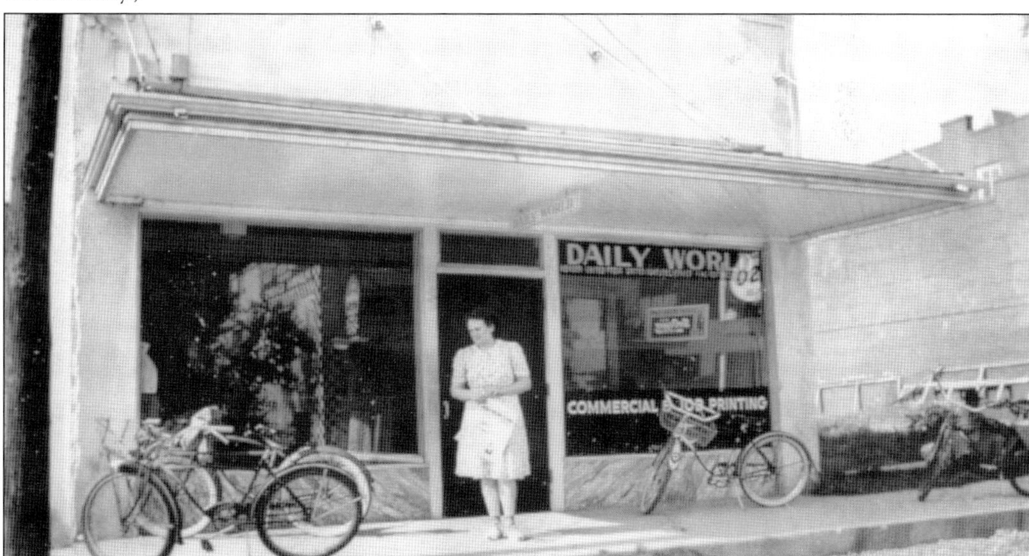

Journalism history was made in Opelousas in 1939 when John Thistlethwaite and Ducote Andrepont opened the *Daily World* newspaper. It was the first offset printed daily newspaper in the United States. Now owned by a national company, the paper is still published today. Dorothy Dunbar, an early *Daily World* employee, is shown here as she leaves the company office located in the old Pellerin Drug Store building on West Landry Street in downtown Opelousas during the early 1940s.

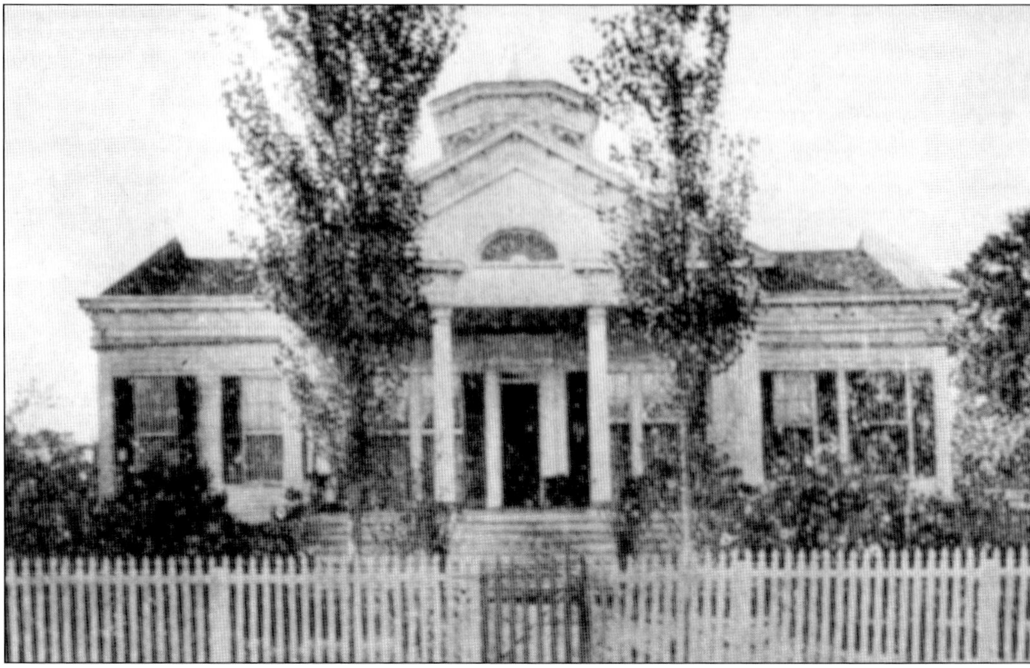

The Homer Mouton home stood on the corner of Liberty and Grolee Streets in Opelousas for over 150 years. During the Civil War, when Opelousas served as the capital of Louisiana in 1862, this house was used by Louisiana governor Thomas O. Moore. From that time on, it was known as the governor's mansion. The mansion, pictured in 1896, was destroyed in a fire set by an arsonist in 2016 while it was undergoing restoration.

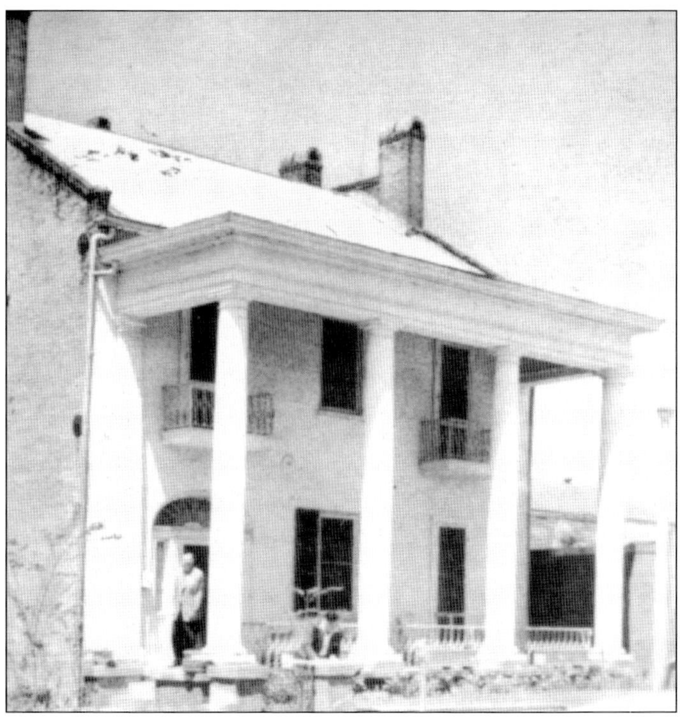

Frank "Frankie" J. Dietlein Jr. stands outside his home on Main Street in downtown Opelousas during the 1960s. The historic Dietlein Home was originally built for the family of Felix King, who owned a business during the mid- to late 1800s on the corner of Landry and Main Streets, known as King's Corner. The King family sold the home to Leonce Sandoz, the owner of the *Opelousas Courier* newspaper. In 1919, Frank J. Dietlein Sr. purchased the home from Helen Sandoz for $6,000. The Dietlein family owned that home until it was sold to St. Landry Bank in the early 1970s. It was demolished in 1974 so that a parking lot could be constructed on the property.

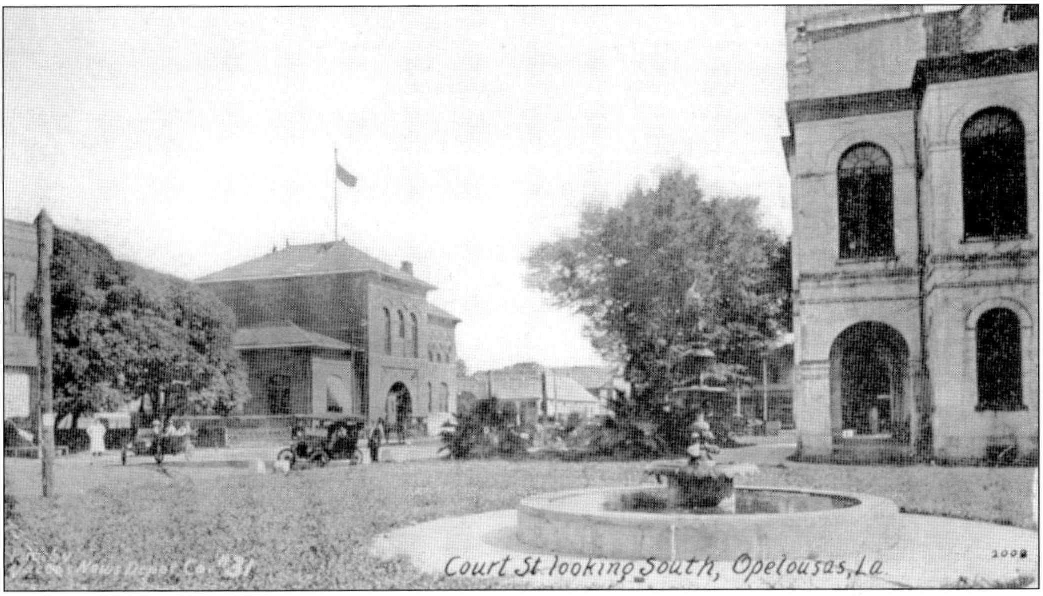

The Opelousas Post Office and Federal Building is seen at far left in this postcard produced by *Jacobs News Depot* around 1909. Pictured to the right is one of two fountains located on the grounds of the St. Landry Parish Courthouse Square from 1903 to 1939. The courthouse building, constructed in 1886, is shown at right. In 1939, the old courthouse was demolished, and a new building was constructed that is still in use today on the square.

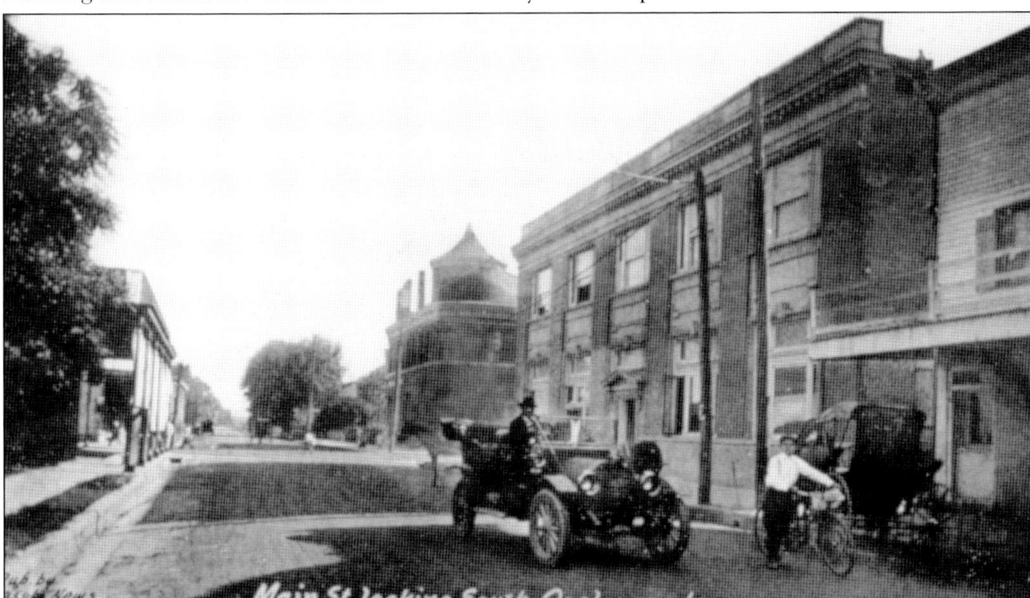

This view of Main Street in Opelousas is looking south. The postcard was produced by *Jacobs News Depot* in Opelousas. The large building at right on the northwest corner of Main and Landry Streets is the Opelousas National Bank, which opened in 1907. Across Landry Street on the southwest corner is the St. Landry State Bank. These two banks eventually merged to become the St. Landry Bank. At one point, Opelousas had so many banks operating at the same time it was known as the "City of Banks."

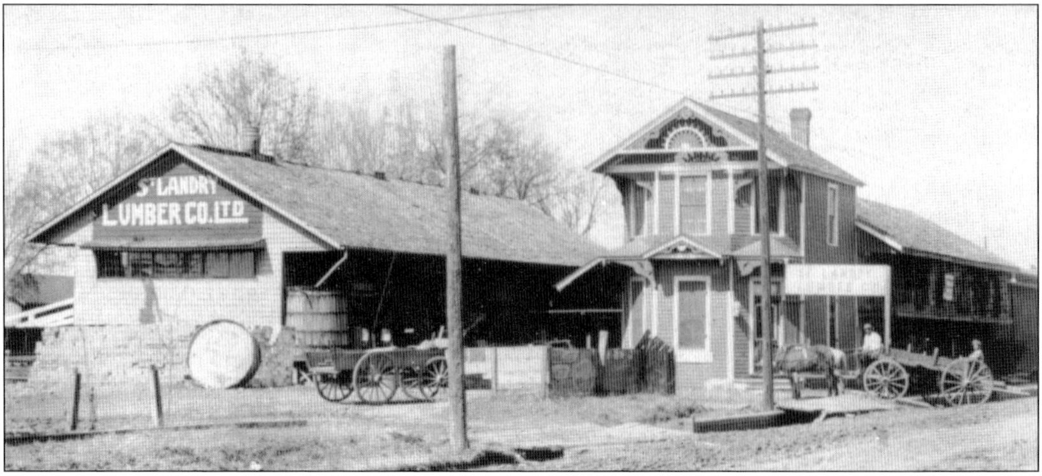

The St. Landry Lumber Company is one of the oldest businesses still operating in Opelousas today. Opened over a century ago, the building that housed it for all those years is listed in the National Register of Historic Places, entered on August 7, 1989. This photograph shows the St. Landry Lumber Company on Railroad Avenue during the 1920s.

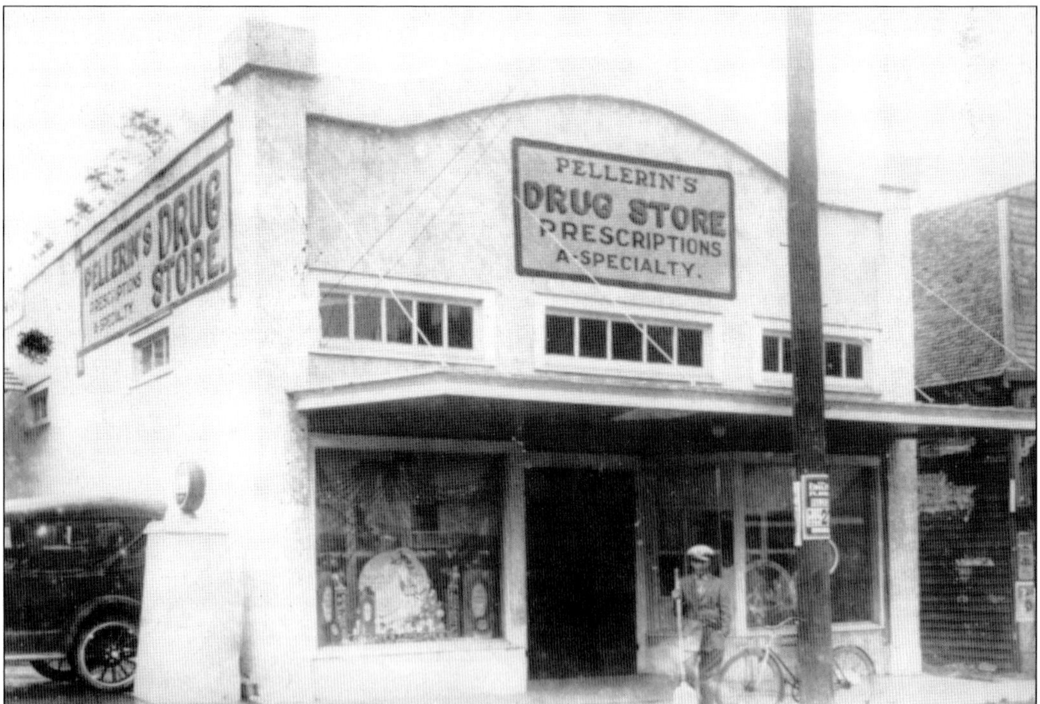

Pellerin's Drug Store was a thriving business in Opelousas for about two decades. During the 1920–1930 years, Donel Mitchel "D.M." Pellerin and his family played an important role in the Opelousas business community. Pellerin, born on February 10, 1892, came to Opelousas in 1921 to open his drugstore business. The building in this photograph was constructed on West Landry Street in 1924. After the drugstore closed, the *Daily World* newspaper opened its first office in the building in 1939. The building has survived on that site for almost a century and remains a viable part of the community today.

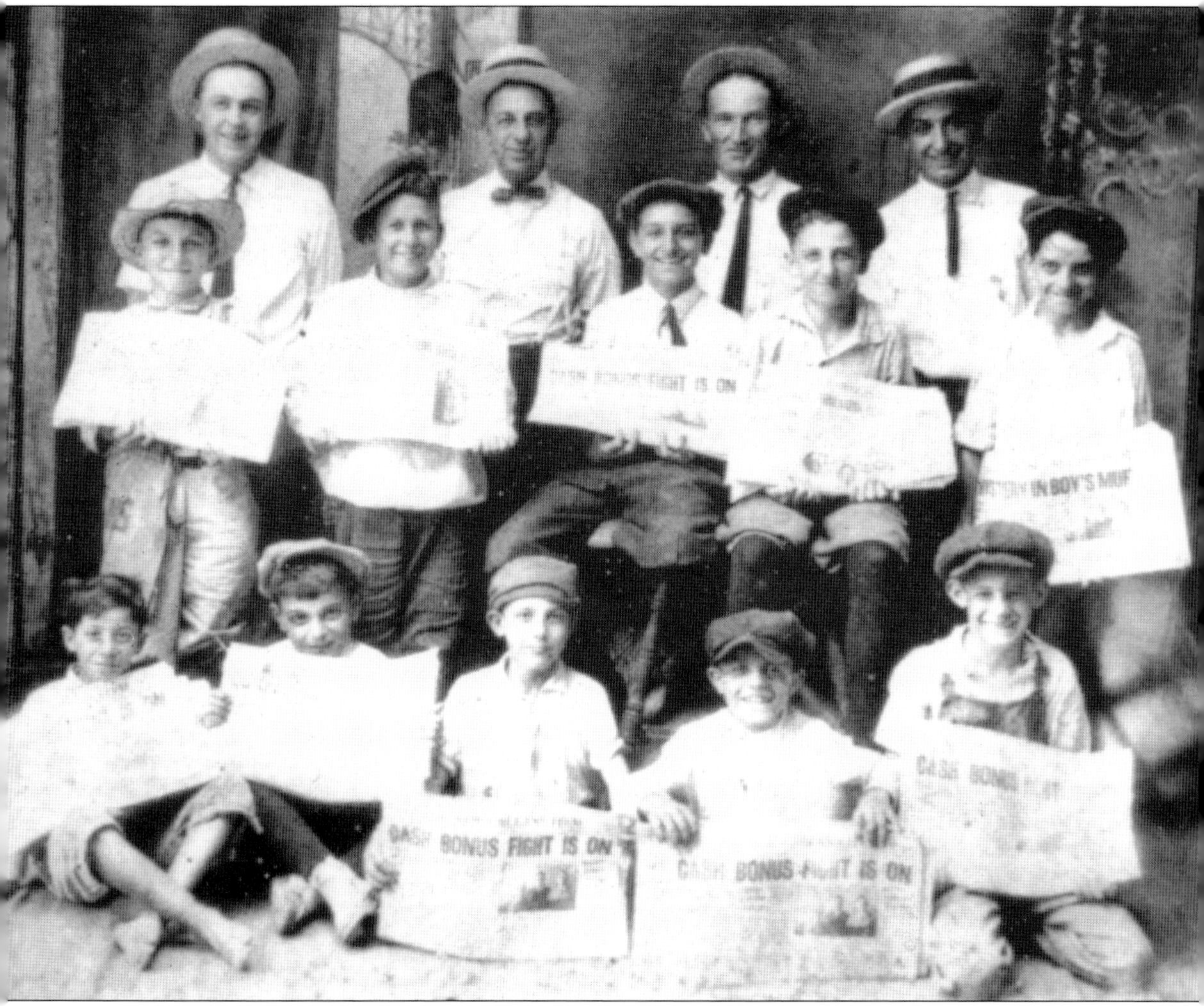

As in other towns, newspapers were an important part of life and the economy in the early days of Opelousas. Besides local newspapers, those from other towns were sold by local stores, including *Jacobs News Depot*, owned by Aaron Jacobs. Many of the newspapers Jacobs sold were delivered or sold on downtown streets by newsboys, sometimes called "newsies." This photograph shows a group of the boys employed by *Jacobs News Depot* along with the men who supervised them in the early 1900. Pictured from left to right are (first row) Joe Terracina, Dommick Romero, Joe Graffagnino, Levy Richard, and Russell Burke; (second row) Lear Titard, Ogden Mistric, John Ruffino, J.O. "Gabe" Hargroder, and Louis Ruffino; (third row) Percy Devalcourt, Aaron Jacobs, Gary Tatman, and Charles Ruffino.

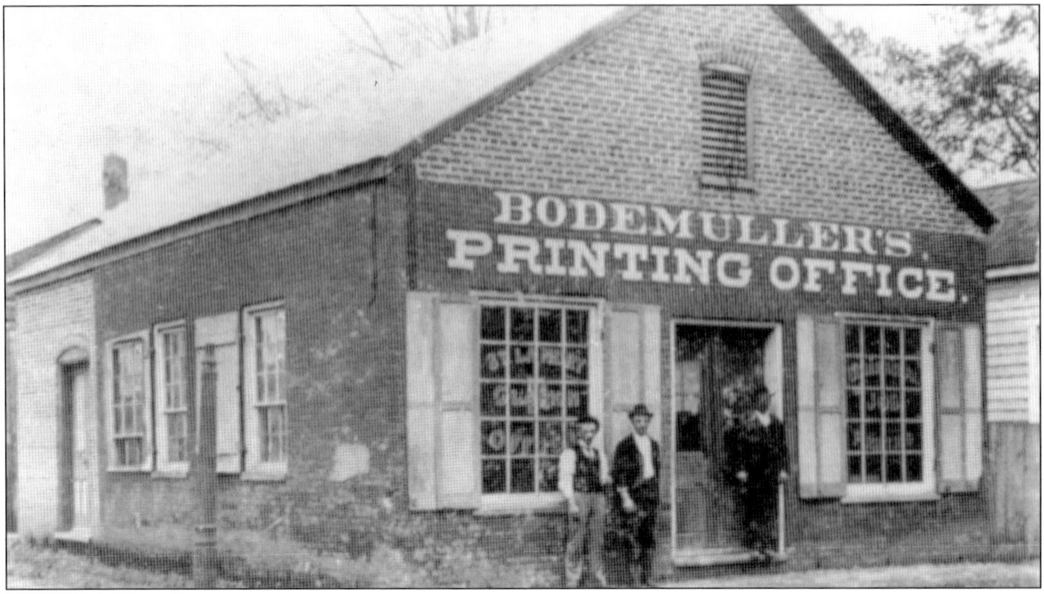

The history of printing in Opelousas goes back as far as the 1820s when the *Opelousas Gazette* newspaper opened for business. That paper and the many that followed provided not just newspapers to the community, but job printing as well. The first commercial printing business in Opelousas was opened in 1891 by Herman Bodemuller. This photograph shows Bodemuller the Printer in the building on the corner of Court and Bellevue Streets during the 1890s. Also in the building is the office of the *St. Landry Clarion* newspaper. Later, Bodemuller moved across Bellevue Street where it remained for five decades until it moved to its present location on Main Street. Bodemuller is one of the longest-running businesses in Opelousas. (Courtesy of Bodemuller the Printer Inc.)

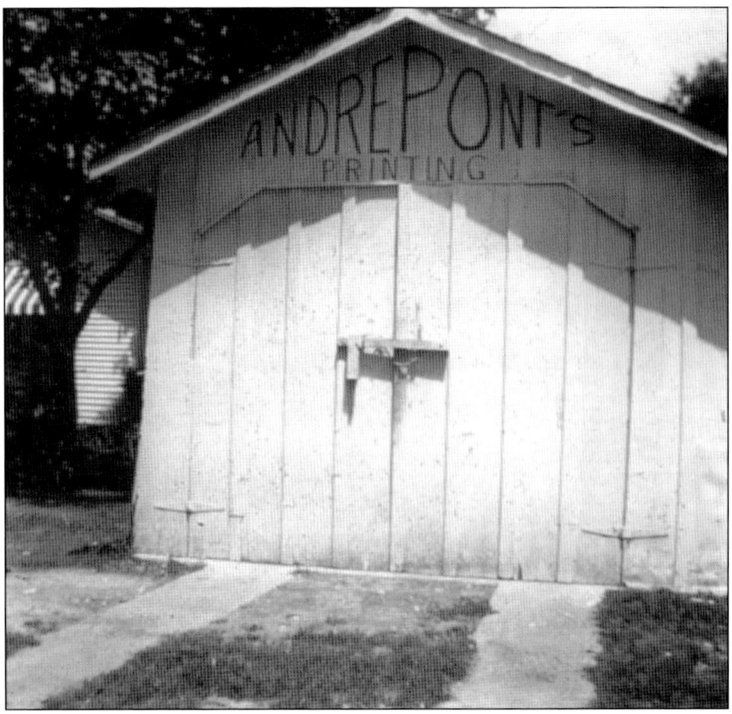

During the 1950s, Opelousas had another printing shop when Lawrence Andrepont started a printing business in his garage on the corner of East Grolee and Cane Streets, pictured here. He later moved Andrepont Printing to North Main Street where it remained until 1991 when it moved to its new location on Interstate 149 south of Opelousas. (Courtesy of André Andrepont.)

Pharmacist Malcolm Miller opened Service Drugs on Market Street in Opelousas during the 1950s. Prior to that he worked as a druggist at the Opelousas Drug Store on the corner of Landry and Main Streets. The photograph at right shows Miller at work at his drugstore on Market Street in 1957. The photograph below shows the outside of the Service Drugs store during that same decade. Later, Miller's son Tim purchased the drugstore from his father and reopened it as Miller Pharmacy in the north side of the building. Malcolm continued to work for the business until 1999 when he fully retired. Miller Pharmacy remains on North Market Street today. (Both, courtesy of Malcolm Miller family.)

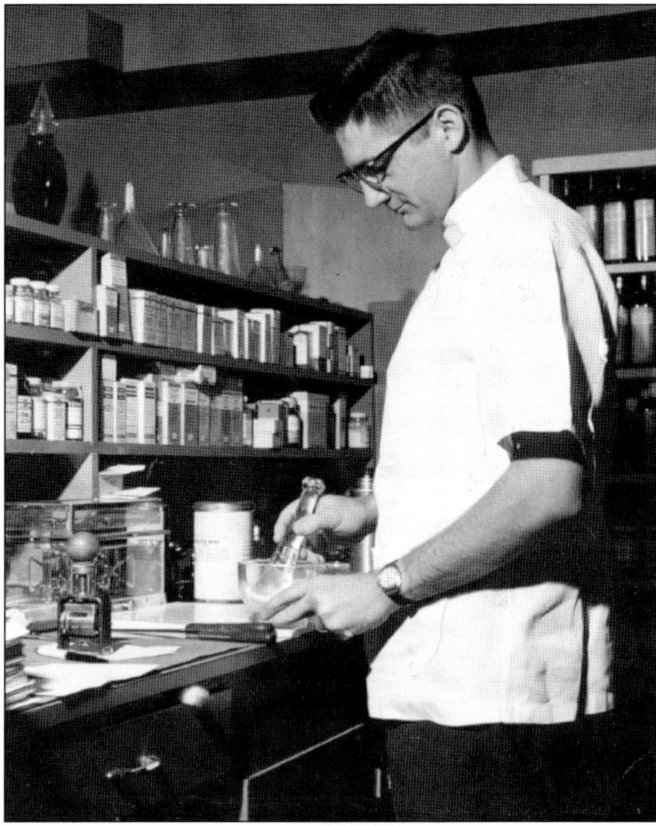

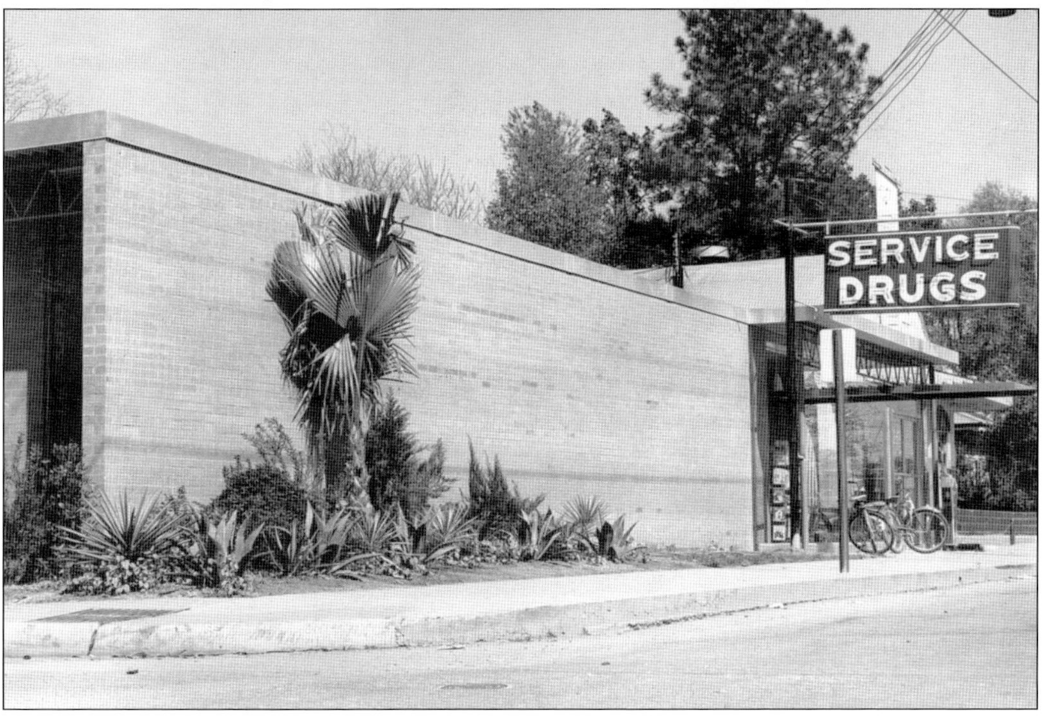

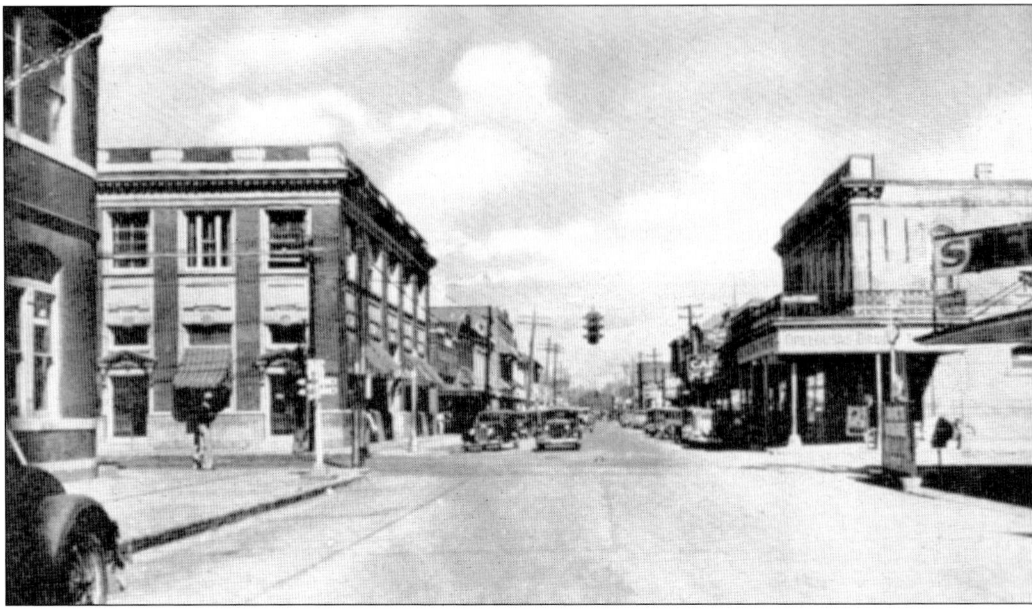

The view of Main Street is looking north at the corner of Landry Street in the 1930s and shows downtown Opelousas during that decade. Businesses in the photograph that operated during that time included the St. Landry Bank, the Opelousas Drug Store, and the DeLuxe Café. The Barnette Building that housed Winsberg's Department Store, with the telephone company and a dentist office on the second floor, can be partially seen at left in this postcard produced by the New Drug Store.

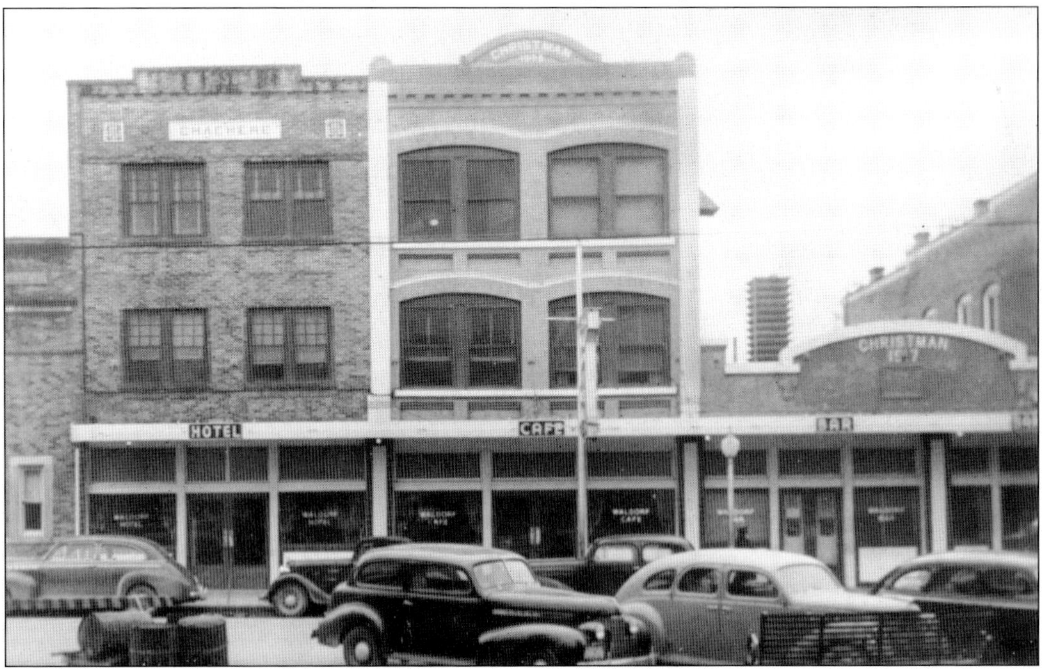

A view of Landry Street from Court to Market Streets in downtown during the 1940s illustrates life as it was at that time. Downtown Opelousas was a booming place with the Waldorf Hotel, Café, and Bar located directly across from the St. Landry Parish Courthouse. That block also had Greco's Shoe Repair Shop, Harry Tankle's store, the Palace Café, and several law offices.

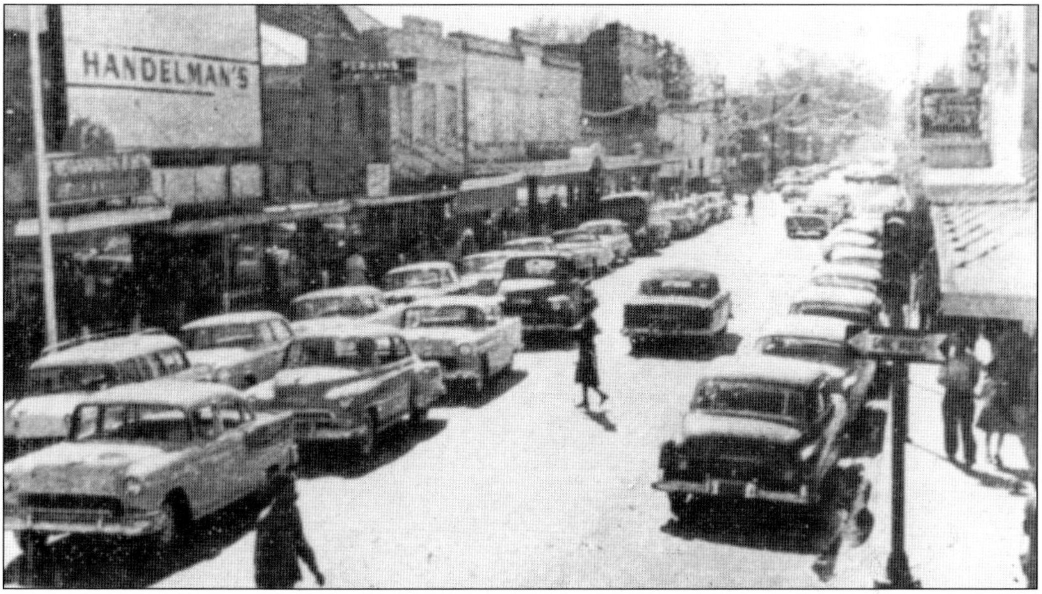

Traffic and shoppers crowded Landry Street in downtown Opelousas in the 1950s, as shown in this photograph taken during the holiday season. Businesses like Mornhinveg & Son Jewelers, Handelman's Department Store, Perkins Jewelry Store, FaKouri's Store, Heyman's Department Store, and the Opelousas Drug Store were popular stops for shoppers at that time. Although all these businesses have closed or moved to other locations, some of the buildings remain and house different types of businesses today. (Photograph by J.A. Bourdier.)

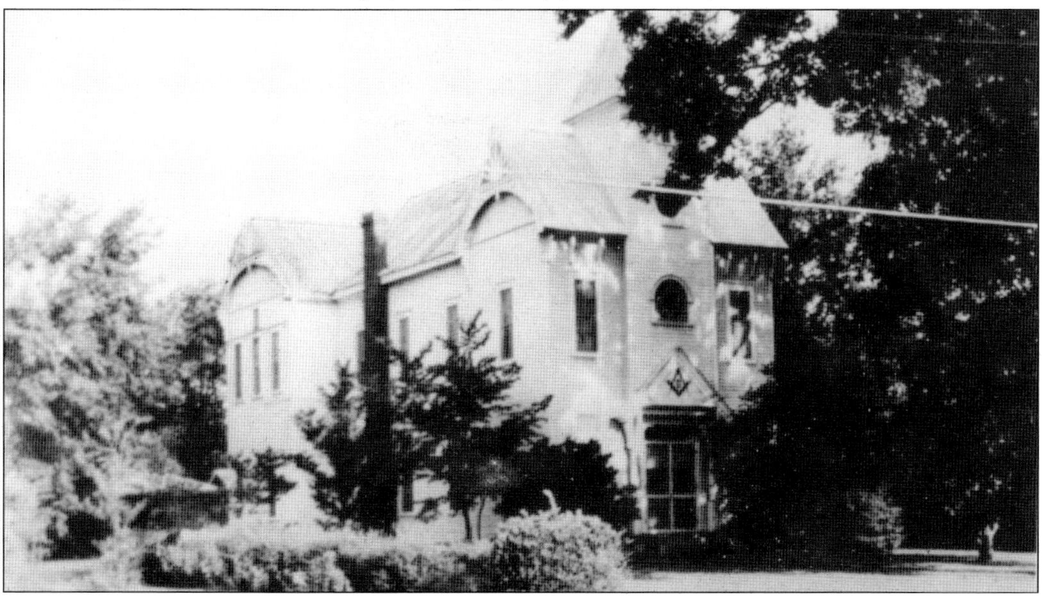

The first Masonic Lodge outside of New Orleans in Louisiana was established in Opelousas in 1820 as the Humble Cottage Lodge No. 19, F & AM. It was formally consecrated and dedicated under the distinctive title and number of Loge L'Humble Chaumiere No. 19 on September 23, 1820. The first officers were Celestin Lavergne, Auguste Larochette, and Theodore Moynier. This photograph shows the 1907 lodge building on South Main Street shortly before it was demolished in 1955.

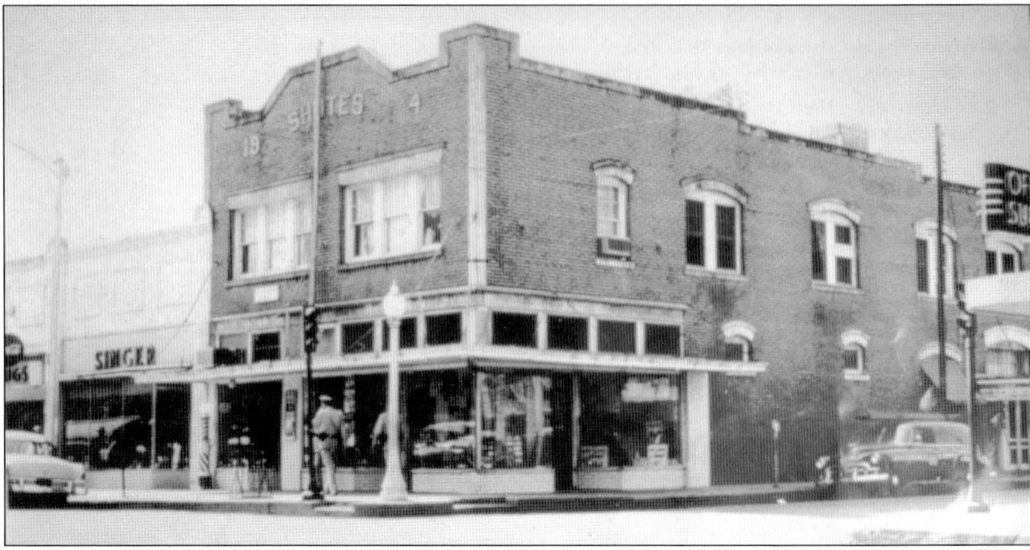

Shute's Drug Store, pictured here in the 1950s, is located on the southwest corner of Court and Landry Streets in a building constructed in 1924. The drugstore remained in this building for decades until the business was sold and moved to a different location. Also located in the Shute's Building from 1926 until 1989 was the Star Barber Shop.

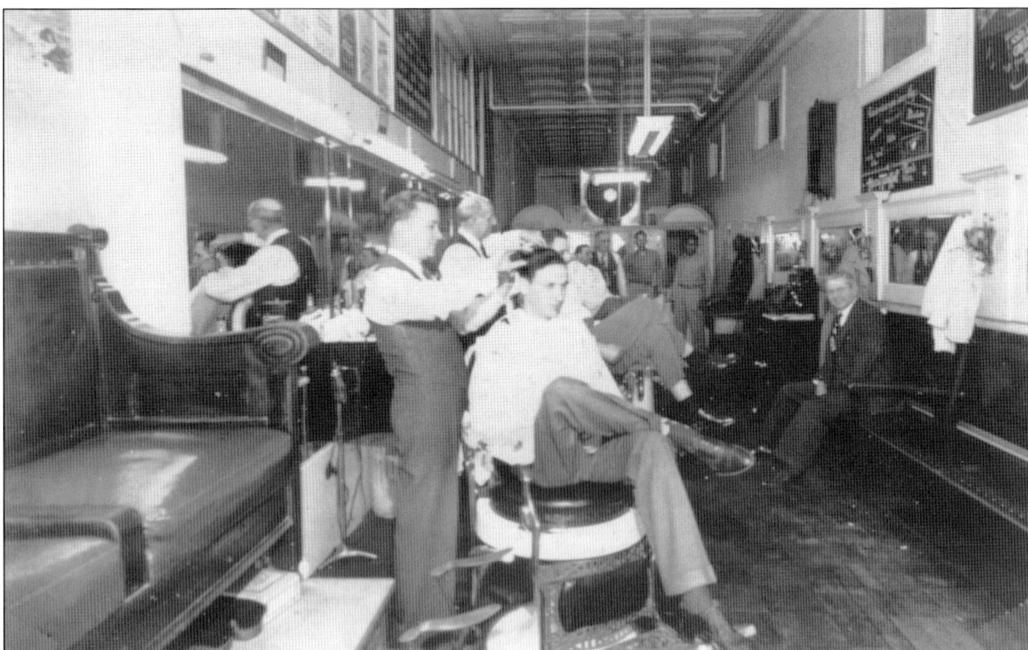

Otis Welch opened the Star Barber Shop in the Shute's Building in 1926. Welch retired in 1975, and the business closed its doors in 1989. And through all those years, over half a century of haircuts and shaves, many a tale was swapped between the barber and his clients in the old barbershop, but none was as intriguing as the story of the day Bonnie and Clyde came to Opelousas. Throughout his lifetime, Welch shared the story of the day he gave the outlaw a shave in 1934, not long before the couple was killed near Arcadia in north Louisiana. Otis Welch is pictured inside his barbershop giving an unidentified man a haircut in 1943.

This full-service gas station opened on the southwest corner of Court and Bellevue Streets during the 1920s. In 1928, it was the Louisiana Oil Refining Corporation, known as Loreco Filling Station, managed by Raymond McBride. In July of that year, McBride left that job and went to work for Bordelon Motors. During the 1930s, when this photograph was taken, it was still the Loreco Filling Station. Later, the station was owned and operated by Frank and Viola Graffagnino for several years before it was demolished so the new St. Landry Parish jail could be located on that corner.

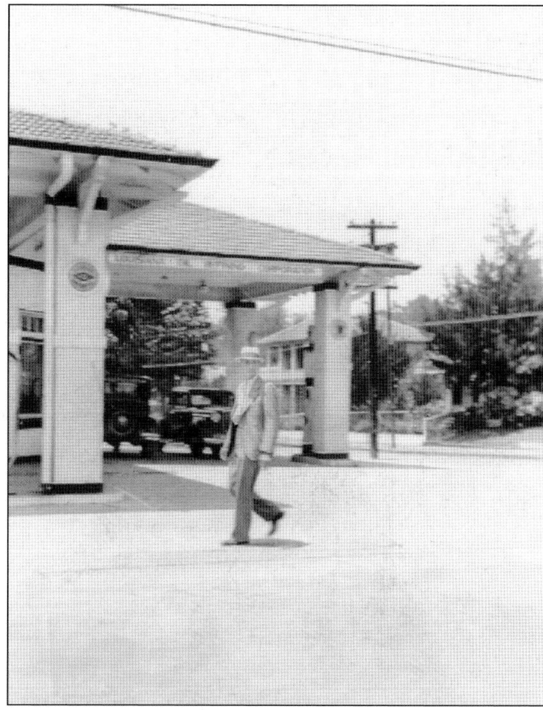

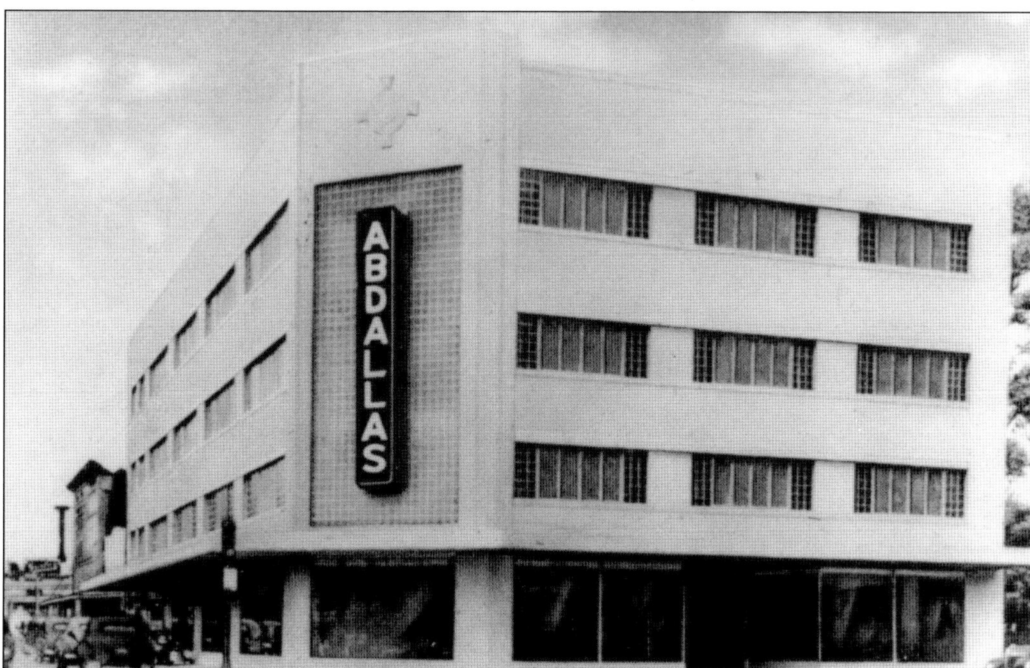

Jake Abdalla opened Abdalla's Furniture Store on the corner of Main and Bloch Streets, known as Bloch Corner, in 1948. In the 1960s, Vernon Schiff moved Schiff's Furniture Store to the building, where it remained opened for several years. Later, Dwayne Hargroder with Hargroder Insurance Company operated from this building. Today, the building houses the Opelousas City Hall and the office of the mayor.

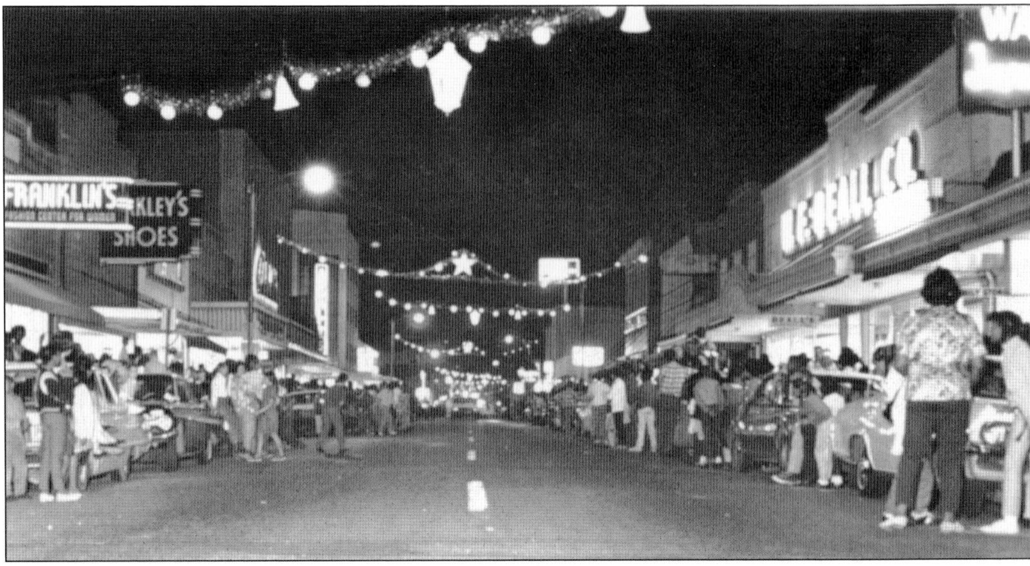

Hundreds of people lined Main Street in downtown Opelousas on Monday evening, November 27, 1972, anticipating the arrival of the Opelousas Jaycees Children's Christmas Parade, produced by the Opelousas Retail Merchants Association. Although Opelousas had many Christmas parades roll through town in prior years, this one was said to be one of the best of its kind with local and area news media reporting on the event. Beside Santa, who arrived from the North Pole, other special guests who rode in that parade included Buckskin Bill, Polycarp, and Mike Wade, with others dressed as Big Bird and Cookie Monster from *Sesame Street*. Television personalities from Lafayette, Alexandria, and Baton Rouge judged the floats constructed by local clubs, organizations, and schools, with East Junior High School winning the grand prize.

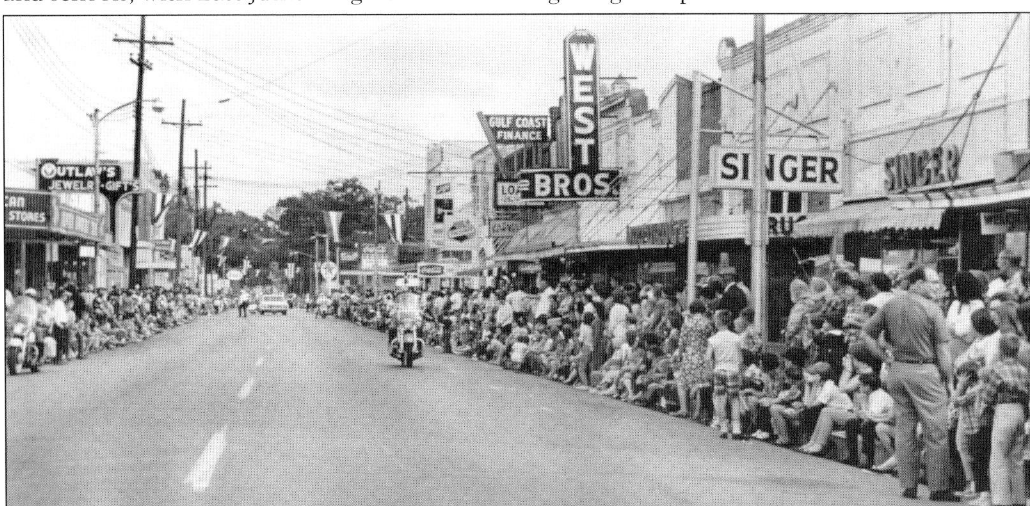

Parade-goers line Landry Street in downtown Opelousas patiently awaiting the start of the big parade celebrating the 250th anniversary of Opelousas on June 7, 1970. Landry Street was the heart of the commercial district in Opelousas for many decades. The 1960s and 1970s saw the beginning of the end to that commercial district as it was at that time. Soon after this celebration, many of the stores seen in this photograph began moving to new strip malls on the outskirts of town or just closed their doors for good.

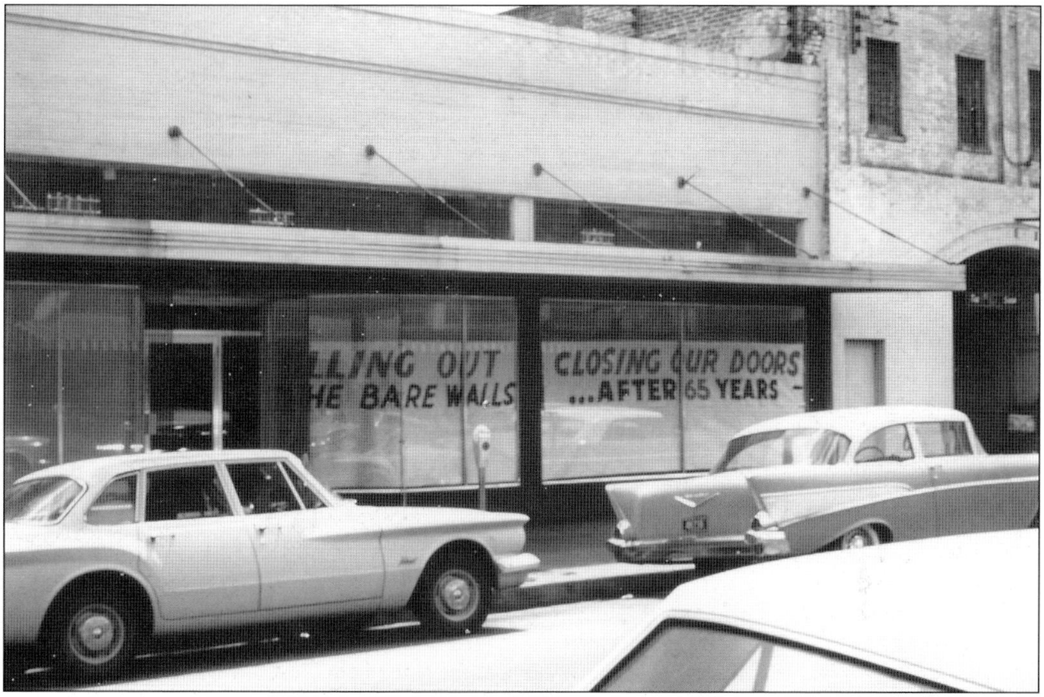

As in most small towns across America, Opelousas experienced hard times in its historic downtown commercial district from the 1960s through the 1980s. At that time, many of the long-operating businesses closed their doors or moved out of downtown to shopping malls on the outskirts of town. One of those businesses was Winsberg's Department Store, which opened on Landry Street in 1901. It is pictured here at its going-out-of-business sale in 1964. The building at right is the old Rex Theater, which served Opelousas for over three decades.

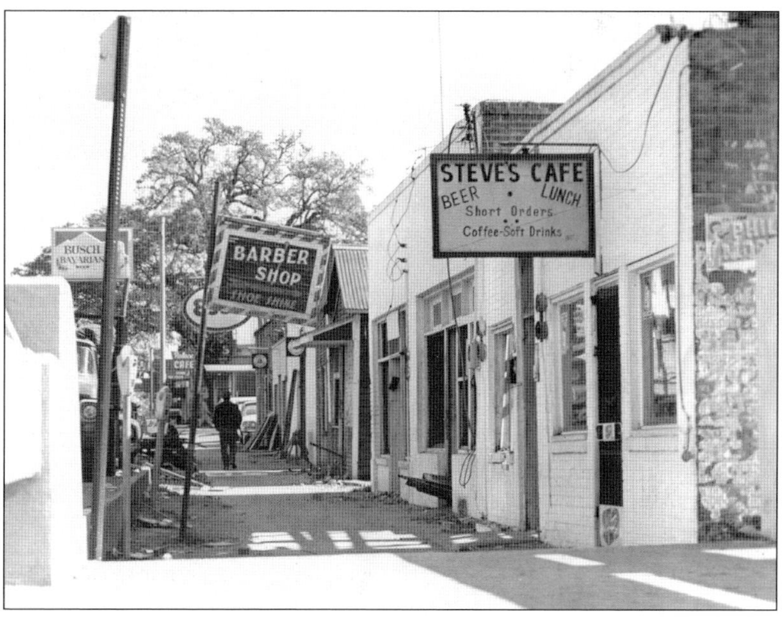

The area in downtown Opelousas called The Bottom is pictured in the 1970s. The buildings pictured housed successful businesses at one time. This photograph was taken not long before all the businesses were closed and the buildings were demolished.

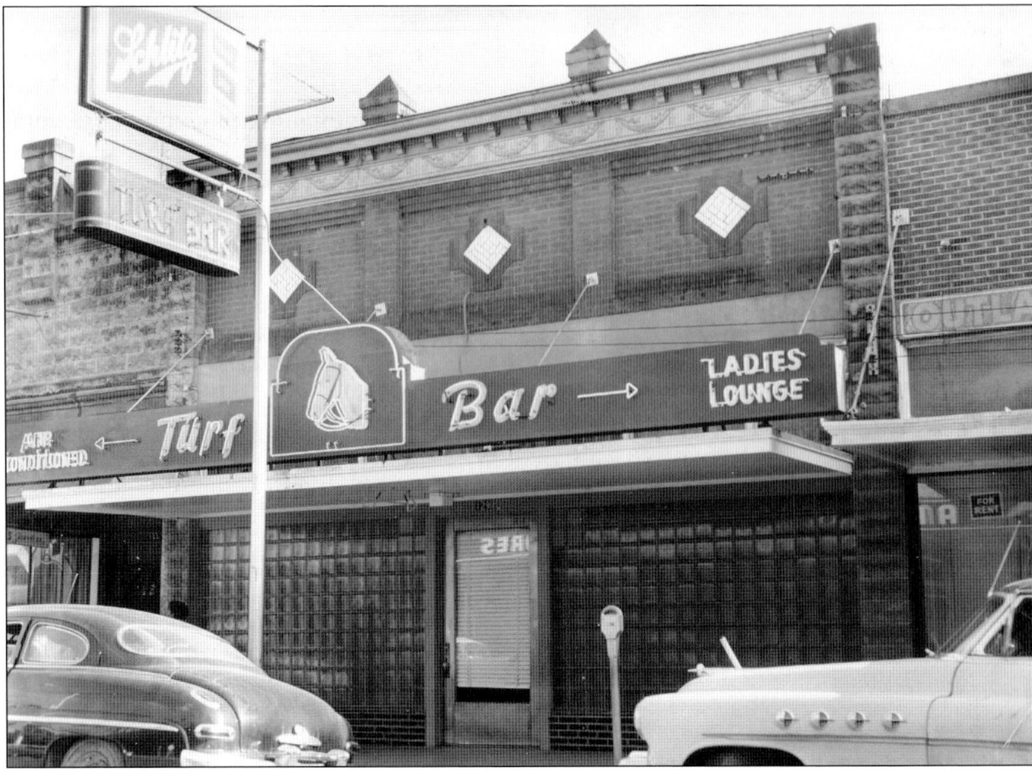

The Turf Bar on Landry Street in downtown Opelousas is pictured above in September 1956 when it was being investigated for having illegal gambling. Stories about gambling in St. Landry Parish were printed in New Orleans and other newspapers across the state. Articles claimed gambling activities in St. Landry Parish were going on at the Turf Lounge, the Southern Club, and the Tampico Motel. This prompted St. Landry Parish sheriff D.J. "Cat" Doucet to state in a newspaper article, "I know every man in the parish. I know those who gamble and where they gamble. We don't have any outsiders muscling in on these family affair games. If a gambler entered St. Landry with some of his big-town shenanigans we'd throw him out." He added, "It's a family affair when a few friends gather to play. Any outsider would be out of luck playing 'bouree' because the conversation is in the kind of French we speak here. . . . After the cotton crop gets in every year there's a little gambling going on. It's in the open among St. Landry citizens; we don't have to hide it here," he declared. The photograph below shows the Tampico Motel and Bar located on the west end of town that was also being investigated that year.

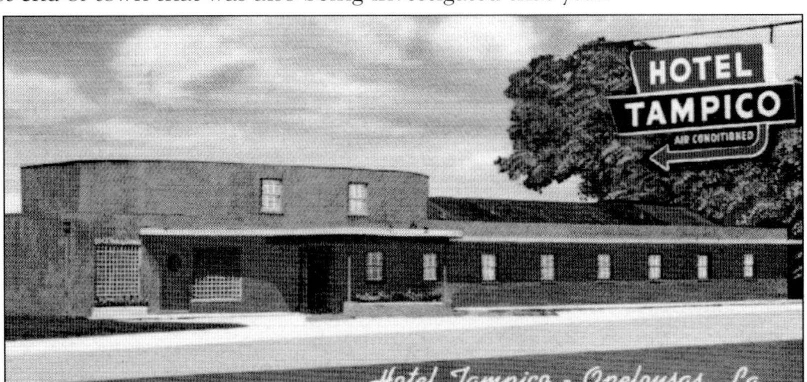

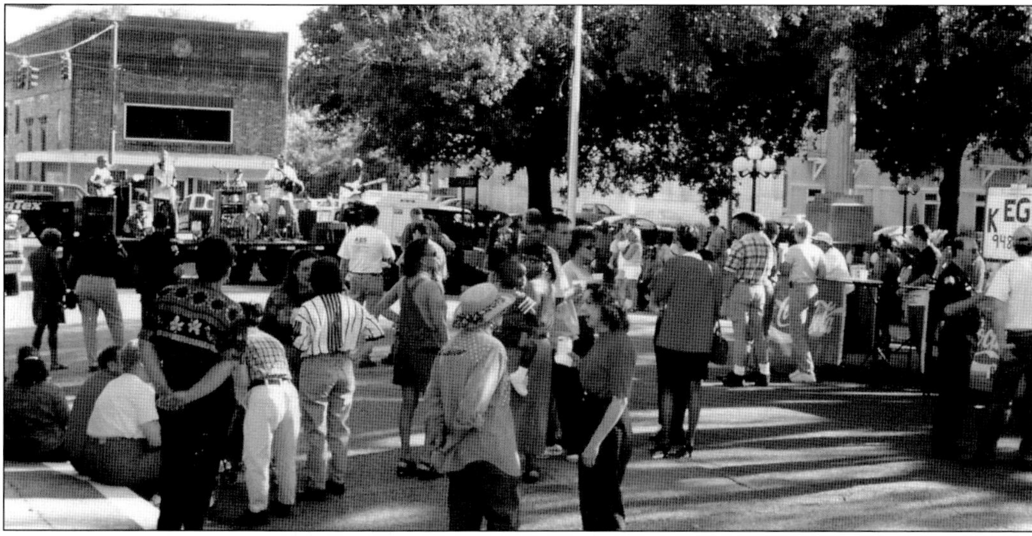

Crowds gather on Court Street in downtown Opelousas at different times for activities, concerts, and festivals. Many of these events are sponsored by the Opelousas Main Street Program. The town was certified as a Main Street Program through the Louisiana Office of Historic Preservation and the National Main Street Center in Washington, DC, in 1993. Since that time, the community is making a difference in the revitalization of the historic downtown commercial and historic district. The organization had several different directors over the years, and today is directed by Melanie Lee Lebouef.

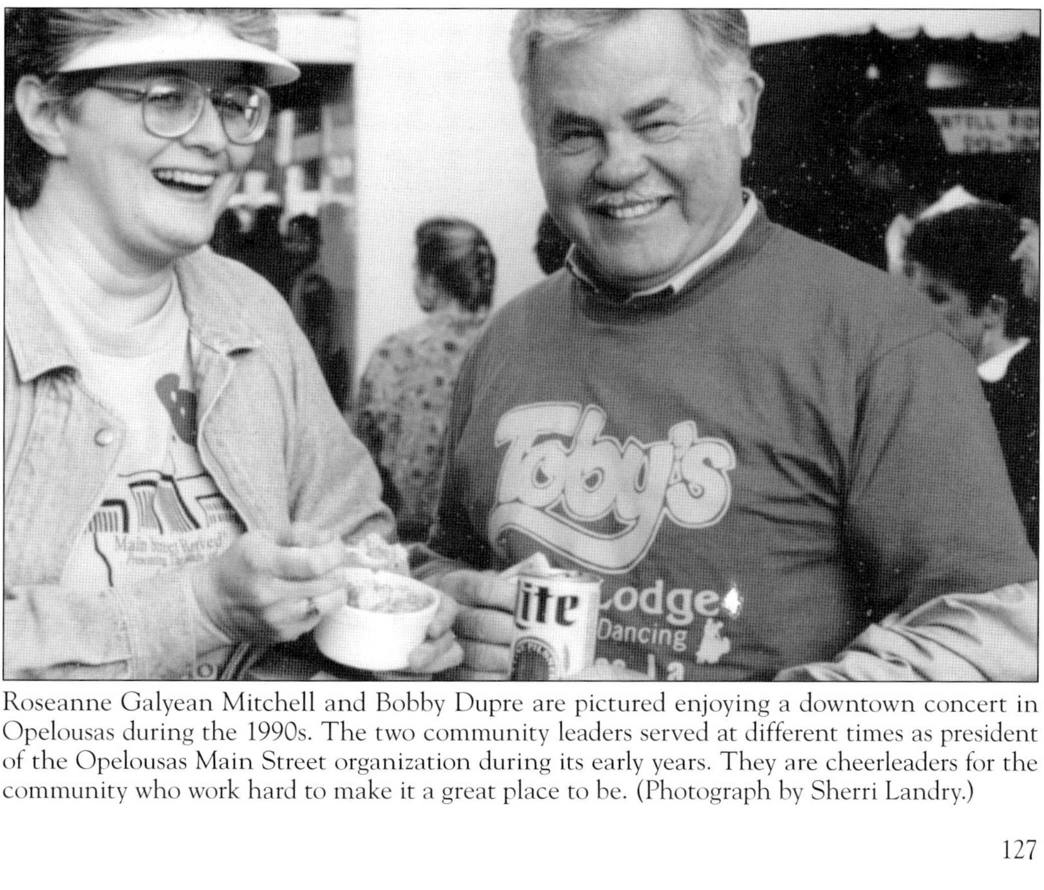

Roseanne Galyean Mitchell and Bobby Dupre are pictured enjoying a downtown concert in Opelousas during the 1990s. The two community leaders served at different times as president of the Opelousas Main Street organization during its early years. They are cheerleaders for the community who work hard to make it a great place to be. (Photograph by Sherri Landry.)

Consistent with our mission to preserve history on a local level, this book was printed in South Carolina on American-made paper and manufactured entirely in the United States. Products carrying the accredited Forest Stewardship Council (FSC) label are printed on 100 percent FSC-certified paper.

MADE IN THE USA